THE GENESIS OF FICTION

The Genesis of Fiction
Modern Novelists as Biblical Interpreters

TERRY R. WRIGHT
Newcastle University, UK

ASHGATE

© Terry R. Wright 2007

All rights reserved. No part of this publication may be reproduced, stored in a retrieval system or transmitted in any form or by any means, electronic, mechanical, photocopying, recording or otherwise without the prior permission of the publisher.

Terry R. Wright has asserted his moral right under the Copyright, Designs and Patents Act, 1988, to be identified as the author of this work.

Published by
Ashgate Publishing Limited
Gower House
Croft Road
Aldershot
Hampshire GU11 3HR
England

Ashgate Publishing Company
Suite 420
101 Cherry Street
Burlington, VT 05401-4405
USA

Ashgate website: http://www.ashgate.com

British Library Cataloguing in Publication Data

Wright, T. R. (Terence R.), 1951-
   The Genesis of fiction : modern novelists as biblical interpreters
   1.Bible. O.T. Genesis – In literature 2.American fiction – 20th century – History and criticism 3.English fiction – 20th century – History and criticism
   I.Title
   823.9'14093822211

Library of Congress Cataloging-in-Publication Data

Wright, Terry R.
The Genesis of fiction : modern novelists as biblical interpreters / Terry R. Wright.
       p. cm.
   Includes bibliographical references and index.
   ISBN-13: 978-0-7546-1668-9 (hardcover : alk. paper)
  1. Bible. O.T. Genesis – In literature. 2. American fiction – 20th century – History and criticism. 3. English fiction – 20th century – History and criticism. 4. Religion in literature. 5. Religion and literature – History. 6. Twain, Mark, 1835-1910 – Religion. 7. Steinbeck, John, 1902-1968 – Religion 8. Mann, Thomas, 1875-1955 – Religion. I. Title.

PS374.R47W75 2007
809.3'9382–dc22

2006018127

ISBN 978-0-7546-1668-9

Printed and bound in Great Britain by Antony Rowe Ltd, Chippenham, Wiltshire.

Contents

Acknowledgements	vii
Preface	ix

1	**Introduction: Wrestling with the Book of Genesis**	**1**
	The Stories of Genesis: Literary and Biblical Criticism	1
	Generating New Stories: Midrash and Intertextuality	10
2	**Adam, Eve and the Serpent: Mark Twain**	**27**
	Twain against God: Refiguring the Fall	27
	The Diaries of Adam and Eve and *Letters from the Earth*	39
3	**Cain and Abel: John Steinbeck**	**51**
	The Growth of a Novel: Ginzberg, Campbell and Fromm	51
	East of Eden: The Choice between Good and Evil	61
4	**From the Flood to Babel: Jeanette Winterson**	**69**
	Bloom, Frye and Biblical Revision: *Boating for Beginners* and *Lighthousekeeping*	69
5	**The Sacrifice of Isaac: Jenny Diski**	**85**
	Diski's Journeys: Rediscovering Jewish Roots	85
	Midrashic Intertexts: Ginzberg, Spiegel, Zornberg, Alter	91
	'The Residue of the Akedah': *Only Human* and *After These Things*	102
6	**Rachel and Her Sisters: Anita Diamant**	**113**
	The Red Tent: A Publishing Phenomenon and its Liberal Jewish Context	113
	Kushner, Midrash and Feminism: *In the Wake of the Goddesses*	118
	The Red Tent: Recovering a Sacred Space for Women	127
7	***Joseph and His Brothers*: Thomas Mann**	**133**
	Mann's Spiritual Journey: From the Bourgeois to the Fully Human	133
	Philosophical Intertexts: Schopenhauer, Nietzsche, Freud	140
	Midrashic Sources: bin Gorion's 'Joseph-Novel' and *Die Sagen Der Juden*	146
	Mann's Part in the Tradition: Exploring 'the Depths Beneath'	163

Conclusion	169
Select Bibliography	173
Index	183

Acknowledgements

For the completion of this book I am indebted to a sabbatical year, half of which was paid for by the University of Newcastle and the other half (September 2005 to January 2006) by the Research Leave scheme of the Arts and Humanities Research Council. Some of the material in the book appeared in a different form in earlier publications: 'Midrash and Intertextuality: Ancient Rabbinic Exegesis and Postmodern Reading of the Bible', in John Hawley, ed., *Divine Aporia: Postmodern Conversations about the Other* (Lewisburg, Bucknell University Press, 2000) pp.97-119 and '*East of Eden* as Western Midrash: Steinbeck's Re-Marking of Cain', in *Religion and the Arts* 2 (1998) pp.488-518.

I should also thank Tate Enterprises Ltd for permission to publish a photograph of Epstein's sculpture, "Jacob and the Angel", on the cover of the book, Anita Diamant for allowing me to quote passages from her novel *The Red Tent* in chapter 6 (and for answering my emails) and Daisy Malaktos of the permissions section of Time Warner Books, the publishers of Jenny Diski's work, for permission to quote from her novels in chapter 5.

My heartfelt gratitude for help in writing this book goes to Rabbi Dr. Robert Ash, who allowed me to follow his Hebrew classes in Religious Studies at the University of Newcastle, explaining in the process a great deal about Judaism and midrash. He also checked early drafts of some of my chapters, eliminating a number of mistakes. Any remaining errors, of course, are my own responsibility.

Finally, as ever, I would like to thank my wife Gabriele not only for her general support and encouragement but for helping me with the German of Thomas Mann. For the most part I worked with English translations (checking the German for key passages) but bin Gorion's anthologies of midrash exist only in German. For these therefore I relied entirely on Gabriele to help me with the translation. I should also thank my children, Catherine and Andrew, for putting up with my long-term obsessions, not to mention Minnie (my dog) for whose reassuring company through the final stages of the project I am also very grateful.

Preface

I should at the outset explain the title of this book, one of those self-consciously 'clever' titles which work on several levels. It refers most obviously to novels which take stories from the Book of Genesis as their starting point, attempting to make sense of them in the twentieth century. Secondly, the book explores the ways in which fiction is generated, how one story prompts the telling of another, a process which can be traced back to the Bible itself (stories from Genesis themselves reworking earlier Babylonian and Sumerian accounts of creation and the flood). Rabbinic midrash, to be discussed along with modern theories of intertextuality in the opening chapter, also found it useful when interpreting biblical narrative to do so creatively, producing additional stories to explain details which were unclear or only implicit in the original. There are additional intertextual allusions in my own title, firstly to Nietzsche, whose books on *The Birth of Tragedy* and *The Genealogy of Morals* lurk in the background of this study. Some of the authors considered in this book, most notably Thomas Mann, were familiar with Nietzsche's strong misreading of the Book of Genesis, his admiration for the power of the original stories being tempered by a dislike of the way in which they had been maimed firstly in the process of redaction (by the Priestly Writer) and then by generations of weak institutional appropriation (the churches instructing their emasculated members how to read them). Finally, to pull the last allusion out of my title, there is a tribute here to Frank Kermode, whose study of *The Genesis of Secrecy* provided me with a model of the way a literary critic could bring narrative theory to bear upon the Bible.

Kermode puzzled over the significance of 'the boy in the shirt' who flees from the Garden of Gethsemane in Mark 14:51-2, whether he is a secret lover, an authorial signature representing Mark himself, or simply what Roland Barthes called a 'catalyser', a piece of insignificant detail giving an air of realism to the scene.[1] Gabriel Josipovici asked similar questions of 'the man in the field' who directs Joseph towards his brothers in Genesis 37:15-17, a mysterious figure whose role in the story seems altogether unnecessary but is made highly significant both by the midrash and by Thomas Mann, who identify him as an angel.[2] For the midrash the angel is protective, a messenger of God sent to accomplish his providential plan (that Joseph should be sold to the Midianites and taken into Egypt, where he would be joined by the rest of his family). For Mann, as we shall see, the angel is much more ambiguous, a literary device to emphasise the moral freedom and resultant complexity of human beings.

These details are illustrative of the difficulties of reading an ancient text in the modern period, the inevitability of our bringing very different expectations and

---

1 Frank Kermode, *The Genesis of Secrecy* (Cambridge, Mass.: Harvard University Press, 1979), p.53.
2 Gabriel Josipovici, *The Book of God* (New Haven: Yale University Press, 1988), pp.276ff.

questions to the text from those brought (and anticipated by the authors) at the time of writing. The rewriting of biblical stories by modern novelists nearly always brings changes; the novelists inevitably bring to the original stories horizons of understanding vastly different from those pertaining when the stories were first told. I have to use the plural for these horizons both because of the plurality of worldviews circulating in the modern world and because of the very different times at which the biblical stories were first told.

The Book of Genesis, of course, is a collection of stories from vastly different times and cultures brought together and to some extent harmonised by later editors. The details of this process, the whole, now less confidently-held, documentary hypothesis will be discussed in more detail in chapter one. These stories, of course, were never supposed to be taken literally though they nevertheless contain important 'truths' about the purpose of creation, the moral responsibility of human beings and the mixed, not always pleasant, nature of their existence. Although in some ways 'primitive', lacking the sophistication and complexity of the modern novel (they are certainly much shorter), these stories remain powerful and provocative, which is why they have stimulated so many modern writers to emulate them, to produce their own versions of the stories, attempting to tease out their mysteries and ambiguities, to make sense of them, for our own time.

I have chosen to focus upon six such novelists, each of whom engages deeply with one of the key stories in Genesis. My choice reflects my own preferences, though I hope that others will share my view that the questions these writers pose, along with some of the answers they propose, are worth careful consideration. I have limited myself to only one novelist per story because in each case I want to explore the whole intertextual process, not only the central encounter between biblical text and novel but the role of other intervening intertexts, in particular of books that feed into the readings the novelists produce. I want, in other words, to consider in each case where the novelists come from as well as the texts at which they finally arrive, the creative process as well as the product.

Another factor in my choice is the extent to which these authors were aware of, and in some cases modelled their work on, rabbinic midrash, which I will discuss in more detail in the opening chapter. It is enough for now to say that all the novelists considered in this book were aware of rabbinic midrash, some rather more than others. Twain's own publishing firm, for example, published an anthology of rabbinic midrash while Steinbeck had his own editor consult Louis Ginzberg, author of *The Legends of the Jews,* about the translation of a key Hebrew word in Genesis chapter 4. Winterson's knowledge of midrash, as far as I have been able to discover, is indirect (through her reading and reviewing of Harold Bloom) but both Jenny Diski and Anita Diamant have acknowledged serious study of midrash. Thomas Mann, as I will demonstrate in the final chapter, incorporates into *Joseph and His Brothers* whole passages from two German anthologies of midrash. This awareness of the midrashic tradition, as I will argue in chapter one, on the part of all these novelists reinforces the plausibility of the seemingly extravagant claims made by Geoffrey Hartman, Harold Fisch and others in *Midrash and Literature* that there is some historical and intertextual continuity between the rabbinic retelling of biblical narrative and the way in which a number of modern novelists attempt to make sense of these stories.[3]

The novelists are considered in the order in which the stories which they retell appear in the Book of Genesis. This almost (but not quite) coincides with the chronological order in which the novels were written (Diski's novels appeared just after Diamant's while *Joseph and His Brothers* is the most obvious exception, chronologically prior to all but Twain). I begin in chapter two with Mark Twain agonising over the story of Adam and Eve at the turn of the twentieth century; he started writing about the subject in the 1890s, in fact, but his obsession continued until his death in 1910. I could, of course, have selected D.H. Lawrence for this opening chapter, since he too was fascinated by Adam and Eve, as by the Flood, but I have written of his rewriting of the Bible elsewhere.[4] John Steinbeck, the subject of chapter three, is one of a number of modern novelists to retell the story of Cain,[5] but his, I would argue, is by far the most sustained interrogation and supplementation of that tale. Jeanette Winterson, as I acknowledge at the beginning of chapter four, is only one of a number of recent novelists who have retold the story of the Flood (I give the details) but her engagement with this particular story is both more prolonged (over time) and incisive (with an awareness of what is at stake for readers of the Bible). She may play with the biblical narrative but she does so in a manner which contributes to our understanding of the difficulties in the original text.

It is in the work of the last three writers studied in this book that the engagement not only with the biblical stories but with their midrashic interpretations becomes the most sustained. This is partly, of course, because both Jenny Diski and Anita Diamant, the subjects of chapters five and six, are Jewish. Having returned at a relatively late and self-conscious stage of their lives to their religious roots, they have been delighted to discover their rabbinic precursors. In the case of Thomas Mann, for whose four-volume novel written over sixteen years the word sustained is less than adequate, there were other historical forces at work in Germany from the late 1920s which made a return to the Jewish roots of western culture compelling. Seeking a counterbalance to Nazi propaganda, Mann discovered in the religion he had previously scorned the values necessary to withstand the threat of fascism.

None of these writers, it should be recognised, subscribe to any form of 'orthodoxy', though all at some stage of their lives have belonged to communities of faith. It is partly the tension between their own personal response to the biblical stories and that of the communities to which they once adhered, it could be argued, which forced them away from 'orthodoxy'. All, however, can be called 'religious' in the broadest etymological sense of that term, driven by temperament and inclination to seek meaning and purpose in life, to bind their lives into some kind of unity. This is why they continue to read the Bible in this attempt to find significance, even if the

---

3   Geoffrey Hartman and Sanford Budick, eds, *Midrash and Literature* (New Haven: Yale University Press, 1986).

4   T.R.Wright, *D.H.Lawrence and the Bible* (Cambridge: Cambridge University Press, 2000).

5   See Ricardo Quinones, *The Changes of Cain* (Princeton: Princeton University Press, 1991).

meanings they eventually find there are at odds with orthodoxy. Mark Twain's rage and indignation at the doctrine of the Fall as a harmful misreading of the opening chapters of Genesis is perhaps the most extreme example of this although Winterson's subversive account of the Flood and Diski's revulsion at the traditional readings of the Akedah follow close behind. All three find the 'God' of the original narrative either incomprehensible or reprehensible. Of the other novelists considered, neither Steinbeck nor Diamant give much credence to God; only Mann makes a sustained attempt to provide an alternative theological understanding of the leading character in the original Book of Genesis.

That in itself is significant: modern writers, it appears, have difficulty in giving imaginative substance to the concept of God. Nor is He the only character with whom they have difficulties: the patriarchs too come out of the re-writing process in a fairly poor light, not least for their treatment of their wives and daughters. This emerges most clearly in the work of Diamant and Diski, who offer contrastingly optimistic and pessimistic accounts of the effect of patriarchy and the possibility of overturning it. Diamant finds enough encouragement in the presentation of women in the Book of Genesis to build a more positive role for them within Judaism. For Diski, in contrast, the damage inflicted by the father (Abraham) both upon his wife and his son cannot be undone.

The fact that all of these writers return to the Book of Genesis, however, reflects not only the power of the original stories but a belief that the Bible still remains worth reading, still retains a value in the modern world. For Mann, as we shall see, it was the foundation for the only effective values with which to resist the ideology of the Nazi period. Like all stories, biblical narratives are not in the end reducible to abstract doctrines, even though any believing community will feel a need to define the limits of acceptable interpretation. What I hope will emerge from a study of all the novelists considered in this book is that each has made a significant contribution to the understanding of the Book of Genesis, from which everyone can benefit. At the very least they illustrate the difficulties involved in making sense of some aspects of these stories. At best, like the rabbis responsible for midrash, these novelists succeed in opening up the biblical texts creatively, posing new and different questions of the text which may point towards new answers to the 'big' questions of our lives. As Hermann Hesse told Thomas Mann after reading his expansion of the story of Tamar from a few verses in Genesis to several chapters of *Joseph and His Brothers,* this book may serve to demonstrate that even in questions of biblical criticism, 'poets are not altogether superfluous'.[6]

---

[6] Donald Prater, *Thomas Mann: A Life* (Oxford: Oxford University Press, 1995), p.348.

Chapter 1

Introduction: Wrestling with the Book of Genesis

The Stories of Genesis: Literary and Biblical Criticism

'In Jerusalem, nearly three thousand years ago, an unknown author composed a work that has formed the spiritual consciousness of much of the world ever since.'[1] These are the opening words of Harold Bloom's introduction to *The Book of J*, a new translation and 'interpretation' of the oldest strand of the Pentateuch, including much of the Book of Genesis. Bloom, of course, is a strong believer in the originality and power of individual authors of great genius. He therefore plays down the extent to which the Yahwist (distinguished from the Elohist by his name for God, which begins with a J in German) would himself have drawn on earlier oral traditions from his own and other ancient near-east cultures. Unlike another Jewish literary critic who has produced his own translation of the Book of Genesis, Robert Alter,[2] he also plays down the role of R, the redactor responsible for the final form of the text, who wove together not only J and E but those other hypothetical personages invented by Higher Criticism, P, the Priestly Writer, and D, the Deuteronomist. Bloom is not very keen on the whole documentary hypothesis, which he sees as the product of overconfident German biblical critics, Hegelians to a man, who 'saw Israelite faith as a primitive preparation for the sublimities of the true religion, high-minded Christianity, a properly Germanic belief purged of gross Jewish vulgarities and superstitions'.[3] He is also dismissive of the 'long, sad enterprise of revising, censoring and mutilating J' within normative Judaism, beginning with the Priestly Writer and continuing with orthodox rabbis of the present.[4] This process, by which 'an essentially literary work becomes a sacred text' and its reading 'numbed by taboo and inhibition', Bloom argues, blinds us to the power of the original text.[5] Like an art historian, Bloom seeks to scrub away the layers of varnish with which J has been encrusted to reveal the ancient narrative in all its original glory.

Bloom suffered much ridicule from reviewers for speculating, on the grounds of the narrative's sympathy towards women, that J might have been a woman, possibly the wife or daughter of a member of King Solomon's court. The misogyny often

---

1 Harold Bloom, *The Book of J*, trans. David Rosenberg (London: Faber and Faber, 1991), p.9.
2 Robert Alter, *Genesis: Translation and Commentary* (New York: Norton, 1996).
3 Bloom, *The Book of J*, p.19.
4 *Ibid.*, p.21.
5 *Ibid.*, p.33.

associated with the Book of Genesis he attributes to 'a long and dismal history of weak misreadings of the comic J', who devotes six times the space to Eve's creation than to Adam's.[6] She has Rebecca totally efface Isaac, 'the first of the mama's boys', producing in Tamar 'the most remarkable character in the book' and in the attempted seduction of Joseph by Potiphar's wife one of her 'most delicious episodes'.[7] 'The only grown-ups in J', according to Bloom, are the women, Sarai, Rebecca, Rachel, Tamar, whose sheer *gevurah* (toughness) he clearly admires.[8]

J, for Bloom, is not really 'a religious writer', certainly 'no theologian'.[9] Her central character Yahweh has fierce qualities which make him threaten to murder both Moses and Isaac. Later revisionists would be embarrassed by his sheer 'impishness', replacing him with a less obviously anthropomorphic, more abstract figure.[10] It is difficult, Bloom recognises, to classify J's work generically. But she tells stories, some of them claiming to be partly historical, and she also creates personalities, so the nearest modern equivalent would be a novelist, though not one in the classic realist tradition: 'There is always the other side of J: uncanny, tricky, sublime, ironic', which makes her 'the direct ancestor of Kafka'. It is this 'antithetical element', Bloom claims, 'that all normative traditions— Judaic, Christian, Islamic, secular— have been unable to assimilate, and so have ignored, or repressed, or evaded'.[11] She is, above all, a powerful *creative* writer and this means (for Bloom) that the most appropriate response is further creative writing.

The following section of this chapter will develop the argument (also to some extent indebted to Harold Bloom) that in rabbinic midrash and modern intertextual fiction we have precisely such an imaginative response. For the moment, however, I want to focus on the Book of Genesis in its final form as a collection of the most powerful and influential fiction in world literature. This is not, of course, to deny that it contains elements of other genres, including myth, saga, history, folklore, poetry, genealogy, and even theology, but to recognise with Robert Alter that 'prose fiction is the best general rubric for describing biblical narrative'.[12] There may be significant differences between the Bible and other ancient forms of narrative. Erich Auerbach's pioneering study of *Mimesis: The Representation of Reality in Western Literature* analysed some of these differences between the Bible's mysterious secrets, for example, and Homeric epic, in which 'a clear and equal light floods the persons and things with which he deals'.[13] In the biblical narrative of the sacrifice of Isaac, as Auerbach demonstrates, we are given very few details about the main characters and events, 'only so much of the phenomena as is necessary for the purpose of the narrative':

---

6   *Ibid.*, pp.146-7 and 175.
7   *Ibid.*, pp. 183 and 192.
8   *Ibid.*, p.194.
9   *Ibid.*, pp.243 and 12.
10 *Ibid.*, p.23.
11 *Ibid.*, p.13.
12 Robert Alter, *The Art of Biblical Narrative* (London: Allen and Unwin, 1981), pp.23-4.
13 Erich Auerbach, *Mimesis: The Representation of Reality in Western Literature*, trans. Willard Trask (Garden City, N.Y.: Doubleday Anchor, 1957), p.23.

Time and place are undefined and call for interpretation; thoughts and feelings remain unexpressed, are only suggested by the silence and the fragmentary speeches; the whole, permeated with the most unrelieved suspense and directed toward a single goal...remains mysterious and 'fraught with background'.[14]

This, according to Auerbach, forces readers to engage with this mystery, to penetrate the surface of the text and thus to supply the 'secret' meaning of a God 'hidden' in history: 'Far from seeking, like Homer, merely to make us forget our own reality for a few hours, it seeks to overcome our reality: we are to fit our own life into its world'.[15] If it is fiction, then, it is fiction of a very special kind. 'What we witness in Genesis and elsewhere' in the Bible, Meir Sternberg argues, 'is the birth of a new kind of historicized fiction' whose 'very raggedness and incoherence forces the reader into an extra effort of imagination'.[16] It is certainly not easy reading.

It is possible perhaps to make too much of the *art* of biblical narrative. Robert Alter, in his influential book of that title, constantly compares the effects of biblical story-telling with that of the great novelists. As in Flaubert, he argues, there is minimal narrative intrusion; literary effects are achieved through dialogue and unspoken contrasts of character.[17] Elsewhere, for example in the focus on 'blessing' and 'birthright' in the Jacob tales or on 'master' and 'slave' in the Joseph stories, a word or word-root 'recurs significantly in a text', along similar lines to Fielding's playing with the word 'prudence' in *Tom Jones* or Joyce's repetition of the word 'yes' in Molly Bloom's monologue in the final part of *Ulysses*.[18] Such subtle effects are clearly suggestive of a designed artfulness in these stories. But Alter recognises that it is sometimes the very terseness of biblical narrative that requires readers to supply details: 'we are compelled to get at character and motive, as in Conrad...through a process of inference from fragmentary data'. Key information is 'strategically withheld', forcing us to read psychological complexity into surprising changes of character.[19] In Genesis 42, for example, Joseph recognises his brothers without in turn being recognised by them; in 'a rare moment of access to a character's inward experience', he recalls his earlier dreams before accusing them of being spies. 'No causal connection is specified....The narrator presumably knows the connection or connections but prefers to leave us guessing'.[20] Here, as in some of Alter's examples of sophisticated techniques of 'montage', where the redactor of Genesis is attributed with extraordinary subtlety in weaving together the separate documents at his disposal, I would be less confident than Alter how much is produced by the art of the narrator and how much by the subtlety of the reader, trained to pick up the nuances of later and more sophisticated narratives. It is clear nevertheless that biblical narrative

---

14 *Ibid.*, p.9.

15 *Ibid.*, p.12.

16 Meir Sternberg, *The Poetics of Biblical Narrative* (Bloomington: Indiana University Press, 1987), p.24. He cites Herbert N.Schneidau, *Sacred Discontent: The Bible and Western Tradition* (Berkeley: University of California Press, 1977), p.215.

17 Alter, *Biblical Narrative*, p.86.

18 *Ibid.*, pp.93-4.

19 *Ibid.*, p.126.

20 *Ibid.*, p.163.

in general and the Book of Genesis in particular display 'a surprising subtlety and inventiveness of detail', a delight in 'imaginative play...deeply interfused with a sense of great spiritual urgency'. By learning to enjoy the biblical stories as stories, as Alter argues, we can 'come to see more clearly what they mean to tell us about God, man, and the perilously momentous realm of history'.[21]

Biblical critics themselves, at least in recent years, have also come to recognise the power of these stories as they stand (rather than seeking behind the text for their original life-contexts or place in ancient cult). For Wellhausen and Graf, originators of the documentary hypothesis in the late nineteenth century, the main interest was historical. The point of Wellhausen's *Geschichte Israels* was 'to understand, evaluate and use the sources available in order to present a picture of Israel's history in the Old Testament period'. To that end he used criteria of vocabulary, style, theology and local colouring to identify the sources.[22] Even for Hermann Gunkel, sensitive as he was to the generic qualities of oral and written story-telling, the goal of *Gattungsgeschichte* (form or type criticism) was primarily historical: 'to uncover from the Old Testament writings a picture of the spiritual life and ideals of early Israel'.[23]

Gunkel's analysis of *The Stories of Genesis*, however, along with the other powerful German commentaries on the Book of Genesis by Gerhard von Rad and Claus Westermann, are worth close attention for their recognition of the nature and power of the stories to be found in this opening book of the Bible. For Gunkel they were *Sagen,* 'popular, poetic narrative handed down from of old' and collected (rather than written or even significantly redacted) by J, E and P.[24] Gunkel goes out of his way in his opening chapter to explain the value and purpose of stories: 'story is not life', he insists, 'it is rather a particular type of poetical writing'. He draws on contemporary literary criticism of secular folk-tales to demonstrate that such 'poetical narrative is much better suited than simple prose to convey ideas'; they are also 'deeper, freer and truer than chronicles and histories'.[25] Stories of this kind are not about great political events but about ordinary people; they are not realistic, often involving implausible events narrated without much concern for verisimilitude. So the 'first woman was not surprised when the snake began to talk to her; the narrator did not ask how Noah managed to get the animals into the ark, and so on'.[26] The God portrayed in the oldest of these folktales is completely anthropomorphic: he

---

21 *Ibid.*, pp.188-9.

22 R.E.Clements, *A Century of Old Testament Study*, Revised Edition (Guildford: Lutterworth Press, 1983), pp.10-11.

23 *Ibid.*, p.12.

24 Hermann Gunkel, *The Stories of Genesis*, trans. John Scullion, ed. William Scott (Vallejo, CA: Bibal Press, 1994). This is a translation of the introduction to the third edition of Gunkel's commentary on *Genesis*, the first edition of which appeared in 1901. The original English translation by W.S.Carruth of the introduction to the first edition was entitled *The Legends of Genesis* (1901). The third edition contains much more comparative reference to secular literature and literary criticism. The Translator's Introduction to the 1994 edition has a useful discussion of the nuances of Gunkel's terms *Märchen, Sage, Legende, Saga* and *Mythos* on pp.xvii-xviii.

25 *Ibid.*, p.2.

26 *Ibid.*, p.5.

strolls in the garden, forms human beings with his own hands, closes the door of the ark himself, enjoys the smell of Noah's sacrifice, appears to Abraham in the form of a traveller and speaks 'as one person to another'. We moderns may smile at such a naïve conception of God but, once we have understood their conventions, can recognise that these stories 'are perhaps the most beautiful and most profound ever known on earth'.[27]

There is a difference, Gunkel explains in his second chapter, between the 'primeval stories' of the first eleven chapters of Genesis, which portray God in this anthropomorphic manner, and the 'patriarchal stories' of the rest of the book, which present Him as hidden, mysterious, only to be discerned through dreams and visions. The primeval stories are mainly mythical, attempting to answer basic questions:

> The creation story asks: Where heaven and earth come from? Why is the Sabbath holy? The garden narrative asks: Whence the human intellect and the fate of death? Whence the human body and spirit? Whence language? Whence the love between the sexes (Gen. 2:24)? How is it that the woman experiences such pain in childbirth and that the man has to till the recalcitrant land…?[28]

Other stories have more precise particular functions of an etiological, etymological or cultic kind, explaining the origin of certain words or practices.

Perhaps the most important chapter in Gunkel, in the context of later revisions to these stories by modern novelists, is the third, which explores 'The Artistic Form of the Stories in Genesis', making constant comparison between the kinds of story produced by an oral culture and more modern forms of written narrative. One of the distinguishing features of an oral story (and one of the criteria therefore for dating the oldest material in the Book of Genesis), Gunkel argues, is its independence: *'The more independent a narrative, the more certainly it is preserved in its old form'*.[29] Individual stories of this kind can be dominated by totally different moods: emotion in the sacrifice of Isaac, humour in the deception of Isaac, awe in the destruction of the tower of Babel. They can also be very short, often extending only for a few verses. Such conciseness, however, also brings benefits, since the storyteller has 'to focus all of his or her artistic power onto one tiny spot', increasing the intensity of insight.[30]

Such terse narratives have to focus on a few characters at a time: 'the ancient story-teller did not require the listeners to fix their attention simultaneously on several characters, as does the present-day novelist'. There are thus:

> two persons in the narrative of the separation of Abraham and Lot (Gen. 13), of Esau's sale of his birthright (Gen 25:29ff), and in the story of Penuel (Gen. 32:23ff). There are three characters in the story of the creation of the woman (God, the man, the woman), in the story of Cain's fratricide (God, Cain, Abel), in the story of Lot in the cave (Gen. 19:30ff), and in that of the sacrifice of Isaac (Gen. 22).[31]

---

27   Ibid., pp.6-8.
28   Ibid., p.12.
29   Ibid., p.33.
30   Ibid., p.34.
31   Ibid., pp.35-6.

Even when there are more characters involved in the whole story, it is one of the 'laws of folk narrative' that 'only two persons ever appear on the stage at the same time'. In the story of Ishmael's expulsion, therefore, in Genesis chapter 21,

> we see successively: Sarah as she hears Ishmael laughing and as she takes up the matter with Abraham, Abraham as he expels Hagar, Hagar alone with the child in the desert, and finally the rescue by the angel. The story of Jacob's trickery (Gen. 27) deals first with Isaac and Esau, then with Rebekah and Jacob, next with Jacob and Isaac, then with Esau and Isaac, then with Esau's hate for Jacob, and finally with Rebekah's advice to Jacob.[32]

Each episode focuses attention on the two central figures in this particular part of the story.

Even the description of these characters and their emotions, Gunkel argues, is 'remarkably meagre by our standards'. 'We are used to modern writers who, as far as possible, present each character as a complete individual'. The ancient storytellers by contrast focus only on a few characteristics, sometimes just one, even for major characters: Cain's envy, for example, Lot's avarice, or the snake's cunning.[33] Characterisation is entirely subordinate to action: 'The modern creative writer is wont to spend a long time in tracing the development of his characters' thought and moods' but in Genesis 'little is said about the inner being of its heroes'. Genesis is mostly silent about motive:

> Nothing is said of the reasons why the snake wanted to seduce the first couple. There is not a word about Abraham's feelings as he left his homeland (Gen. 12), nor of Noah's as he entered the ark (Gen 7:7). We hear nothing of Noah's anger at Canaan's shamelessness (Gen. 9:24), of Jacob's disappointment when Laban deceived him with Leah (Gen. 9:24)....[34]

These reactions on the part of the characters have to be supplied by the listeners or readers (or by later writers who take up the same stories).

The detailed psychological analysis of a Flaubert or a George Eliot, of course, is not the only means of conveying or suggesting emotion. Gunkel marvels at the 'art of indirect portrayal of people by means of actions that above all makes the stories so vivid'. Dialogue is another means: 'Two masterpieces of character portrayal by means of dialogue are the story of the temptation of the first couple (Genesis 3), and the conversation between Abraham and Isaac on the way to the mountain (Gen. 22:7-8).'[35] The ancient storytellers rarely provide detailed description of 'attendant circumstances'. There is no mention of Cain's murder weapon, no lavish description of the Garden of Eden. There is always, however, a strong 'narrative thread', a 'tight internal coherence, which makes the stories not only plausible but 'inescapable'. In Genesis 16, for example,

---

32 *Ibid.*, p.37.
33 *Ibid.*, pp.38-9.
34 *Ibid.*, p.42.
35 *Ibid.*, pp.44-5.

Sarah was barren, but wanted to have children....*Therefore* she gave her maid to Abraham as a concubine. Hagar conceived, and *as a consequence* looked with contempt on her mistress. *This* offended the proud lady of the house deeply. *As a result,* Hagar ran away from Sarah into the desert. *There*, however, God took pity on her and promised her a son.[36]

Each episode leads directly into the next, drawing its readers ever deeper into the story.

These stories, in other words, are not 'rough narratives, carelessly thrown together'. They are 'glittering, twinkling works of art'.[37] Gunkel also recognises that some of the later cycles of stories such as those surrounding Joseph are more extensive in their attention to detailed description and characterisation. These he labels 'novelettes' (*Novelle* in German).[38] He also notices developments in their religious and moral elements, the later stories displaying more complex ideas of God, taking less open delight in the cunning and deceit of the patriarchs. The older stories are 'often quite earthy' in their humour, for instance in the manner of Rachel's outwitting of her father by playing on his embarrassment at her bodily functions (Gen. 31:33).[39] It may be impossible finally to distinguish between the stories collected by J and E, which 'were in essence taken over by the collectors as they found them', but in general, Gunkel suggests, 'J has the liveliest and most picturesque narratives', E has some 'moving and tearful stories'[40] and P, by contrast, is factual rather than poetic, concerned with formulas and religious instruction. Gunkel ends by celebrating the variety of the whole book, which he compares with a great cathedral 'in whose form and adornment the spirit of many generations expresses itself'.[41] It is not the product of any individual but the combined achievement of a multitude of voices.

Later commentators on Genesis such as Gerhard von Rad inherit from Gunkel a notion of J as a collector of stories: 'With him began the writing down of those poetic or cultic narratives which previously had circulated orally and without context among the people'.[42] But his (or her) contribution is not limited simply to collection. Von Rad celebrates the 'artistic mastery' and 'creative genius' of the Yahwist:

> Wonderful clarity and utter simplicity characterize the representation of the individual scenes. The meagreness of his resources is truly amazing, and yet this narrator's view encompasses the whole of human life with all its heights and depths. With unrivalled objectivity he has made man the subject of his presentation— both the riddles and conflicts of his visible acts and ways of behaving as well as the mistakes and muddles in the secret of his heart. He among the biblical writers is the great psychologist.

---

36 *Ibid.*, pp.48-50.
37 *Ibid.*, pp.54-6.
38 *Ibid.*, pp.59-60.
39 *Ibid.*, pp.82-7.
40 *Ibid.*, pp.95 and 101.
41 *Ibid.*, p.119.
42 Gerhard von Rad, *Genesis*, revised edition, trans. John H.Marks (Philadelphia: Westminster Press, 1973), p.17. This edition is based on the ninth German edition of 1972, the introduction having been 'very extensively rewritten' from the original version, which first appeared in German in 1949 (Publisher's Note, p.9).

> However,…he subjects the great problems of humanity to the light of revelation: creation and nature, sin and suffering, man and wife, fraternal quarrels, internal confusion, etc. But above all, he investigates God's activities in the beginnings of Israel, both their visible wonders and their hidden mysteries.[43]

The cultic material of the ancient traditions is thus transformed, raised 'high above their sacred, native soil', by 'what seems to us like a cool breath from the freethinking era of Solomon'.[44] Material which may have 'existed popularly for a long time in more worldly narratives' was thus transformed within the tradition itself: 'the later the version of the saga, the more theologically reflective and less naïve'.[45] Von Rad limits 'the measure of freedom' which J or E or P would have have allowed themselves with this material, 'freedom…much more limited than any modern Western author would be permitted to claim for himself'. The 'individuality of the Yahwist', he claims, 'his basic theological conceptions, are much less apparent within the individual narratives than in the character of the composition as a whole', the way the separate stories are linked and harmonised.[46] But while recognising that the 'long process of tradition' which many of the narratives had undergone necessarily left traces in the final form of the text of Genesis, von Rad ends his introduction to his commentary on Genesis by urging critics to abandon the attempt to identify the earliest levels of the tradition, searching as in New Testament scholarship for authentic historical elements. Rather, 'we should turn once again to exegesis of the texts in their present form', uncovering the meaning of this 'great narrative complex' as it stands.[47]

Claus Westermann moves in the same direction, away from Gunkel's focus on individual stories, treating 'the classical criteria for source division with much greater caution' than previous critics, towards a consideration of the whole text.[48] He still recognises that this 'whole' would have taken some time to form, J and P probably working first with 'a clearly recognizable circle of stories which dealt with the primeval period or with the beginnings of the world and of humankind' and then with another group of patriarchal stories.[49] He makes J sound like an ancient Dostoevsky in the way he organises his primeval 'Narrative of Crime and Punishment'. While P, 'in accordance with the priestly theology, is interested only in the decision to destroy', J's interest

> is directed to the reason for the destruction, the capacity of God's creatures to turn against him. J, as always, is vitally interested in the person, in the individual's potential and limitations. Consequently his treatment of the material which belongs to the stories of the origins is concerned on the one hand with the person's capabilities and accomplishments,

---

43 *Ibid.*, p.25.
44 *Ibid.*, p.29.
45 *Ibid.*, p.36.
46 *Ibid.*, pp.37-9.
47 *Ibid.*, pp.41-2.
48 Claus Westermann, *Genesis: An Introduction*, trans. John Scullion (Minneapolis: Fortress Press, 1992), p.83. First published in English as the introduction to Westermann's three-volume commentary on Genesis (German 1974-82, English 1984-6).
49 *Ibid.*, p.62.

and on the other with the story of crimes and punishment and the terrifying possibility that a human being, created free, can revolt against God the creator.[50]

J may only be an 'heir' to pre-existing traditions but he is still able to impose his own concerns upon them:

> J is interested in the concrete and hence in variety...He is obviously concerned with people's all-round ability to defy their human state and so to act against the will of their creator...J is not aware of an abstract notion of sin according to which individual transgressions would be but manifestations of the one sin, nor of a notion of the fall, which only appeared in late Judaism.[51]

J is interested in people, their feelings and emotions, and this carries over into his treatment of God.

Developments in biblical scholarship since Westermann, as Clare Amos explains in the introduction to her recent commentary on Genesis, have moved even further towards reading the text as a whole:

> There has been an increased concern to look at the Bible and its individual books more holistically, exploring the story they are trying to tell us as a whole rather than engaging in the kind of 'excavative' scholarship which was overconcerned to break down the material into smaller units and spend time continually delving for sources.[52]

The scholarly consensus over the documentary hypothesis seems now to have disappeared. However the final form of the text was produced (and we will never be certain about this), the point is that we have to read it as we now find it, entering into the world of the story as it is presented in the final form of the text. In David Clines' words,

> What is offered in the story is a 'world'—make-believe or real....To the degree that the hearer or reader of the story is imaginatively seized by the story, to that degree she 'enters' the world of the story. That means that the reader of the story, when powerfully affected by it, becomes a participant of its world.[53]

Biblical critics themselves, in other words, have returned to the necessity of responding to the text as it stands, albeit with a greater insight into ancient generic conventions and more awareness of the possible reasons for some of the confusions and contradictions within it. It is the power of the stories of Genesis, both individually and as a whole, which continues to attract readers, drawing them so much into their world that they remain there, interpreting and recreating them in terms of their own particular concerns and questions. This probing of the text in terms of its contemporary context (the time of reading), I will argue in the following section

---

50 *Ibid.*, p.53.
51 *Ibid.*, p.99.
52 Clare Amos, *The Book of Genesis* (Peterborough: Epworth, 2004), p.xvi.
53 David Clines, *The Theme of the Pentateuch* (Sheffield: JSOT Press, 1978), p.102, cited in John Rogerson, *Genesis 1-11* (Sheffield: JSOT Press, 1991), p.28.

of this chapter, is a feature of reading the Bible which links the ancient practice of midrash with more recent literary-critical practices.

Generating New Stories: Midrash and Intertextuality

Midrash is a complex and controversial term, which has been defined in a variety of ways. Most interpreters begin with its derivation from the Hebrew verb *darash*, to seek or probe and thus to interpret. Harper's Bible Dictionary calls it 'the type of biblical interpretation found in rabbinic literature' of the early centuries of the Common Era which 'pays close attention to the meanings of individual words..., elucidates one verse by another verse, and relates the teachings of rabbinic Judaism to the biblical text'. 'In a wider sense', however, the entry continues, 'the word midrash is employed for any interpretation which...assumes that the biblical text has an inexhaustible fund of meaning that is relevant to and adequate for every question and situation'.[54] The entry ends with that instruction so beloved of all dictionaries, '**see also** Haggadah', which is in turn defined as 'the interpretation of the historical and religious passages of Jewish Scripture that are not legal in character' but 'often supplement the biblical narrative' in a 'rich variety of Jewish "retelling" of the tradition'.[55] Midrash, in other words, involves the belief that one of the best ways of understanding a story is to retell it, to augment the original narrative with additional details which 'answer' the questions it raises.

Jacob Neusner, who has probably written more about midrash than any other scholar, sees it as providing 'a paradigm of creative and profound response to the biblical record', 'a valuable alternative' to the dominant literalism that 'enjoys the authority of true religion'. He celebrates in *The Midrash* a literature which writes not *about* Scripture but '*with* Scripture', by which he means that the Bible itself is the starting point for 'a writing bearing its own integrity and cogency, appealing to its own conventions of intelligibility, and, above all, making its own points'.[56] Attempting to answer the question, *What is Midrash?*, Neusner defines it as 'a term given to a Jewish activity which finds its locus in the religious life of the Jewish community'. He appends a footnote to the effect that he distinguishes between 'midrash' and 'exegesis' only 'by assigning the former word to activity within the Israelite community'. He admits, however, that 'there may be extensive parallels between midrash which occurs within an Israelite context and exegesis which occurs in other religious and cultural systems' (10).[57] It is clearly debatable whether or not one should use the term midrash in this analogous sense, but it is this kind of exegesis, to some extent modelled upon midrash, that I want to explore in this book. Some of the novelists under discussion are Jewish and refer self-consciously to the

---

[54] Paul J. Achtemeier, ed., *Harper's Bible Dictionary* (San Francisco: Harper and Row, 1985), p.635.

[55] *Ibid.*, p.366.

[56] Jacob Neusner, ed., *Genesis and Judaism: The Perspective of Genesis Rabbah* (Atlanta, GA: Scholar's Press, 1985), pp.ix-xiii.

[57] Jacob Neusner, *What is Midrash?* (Philadelphia: Fortress Press, 1983), p.10.

rabbinic tradition; others can be shown to be aware of the tradition but would see their work as related to it only in the broadest possible way.

Midrash, as David Stern somewhat sceptically comments, became something of a 'hot topic' during the deconstructive, inter-disciplinary 1980s. Its 'predilection for multiple interpretations' and blurring of boundaries between literature and commentary were seized upon by disciples of Derrida (and others) as offering an alternative to the Greek 'logocentric' tendency towards the fixing (and therefore limiting) of meaning to a single essence or transcendent signified. Stern compares the excitement generated by literary and theoretical interest in midrash in the 1980s with the 'Bible as Literature' movement of the previous decade promoted by literary critics such as Alter and Kermode.[58] While rightly emphasising the need for a proper understanding of midrashic practice within its original historical context, he fails, I would argue, to do justice to what it is about midrash which continues to appeal to modern critics beset with similar problems to those of the ancient rabbis: how to make sense in their own time of these enigmatic and terse biblical texts, how to respond to these powerful but mysterious stories.

The real purpose of midrash, James Kugel insists, is interpretive. In exploring midrash therefore, 'one ought first to determine what it was in the biblical text itself that had originally caused an ancient author to create a particular narrative expansion'.[59] The first of the "Nine Theses" at the back of his book *In Potiphar's House* states,

> Most of the narrative expansion found in rabbinic midrash have as their point of departure some peculiarity in the biblical text itself. That is to say, these expansions, whatever other motives and concerns may be evidenced in them, are formally a kind of biblical exegesis.[60]

This is certainly the case in *Genesis Rabbah,* a collection of midrashim upon the Book of Genesis put together around the end of the fourth century of the Common Era. Why, for example, does God create Eve from Adam's rib (Gen. 2: 21)? Rabbi Joshua of Sikhnin supplies one possible answer, probing God's inner motives:

> He thought to Himself, 'We should not create her beginning with the head, so that she be not frivolous, nor from the eye, that she be not a starer, nor from the ear, that she be not an eavesdropper, nor from the mouth, that she not talk too much, nor from the heart, that she be not jealous, nor from the foot, that she be not a gadabout, but from a covered up place on man. For even when a man is standing naked, that spot is covered up.[61]

His interlocutors agree that this is a good theory, even if 'things did not work out as he had planned': Sarah listening at the tent door (Gen. 18.10), Rachel envying

---

58 David Stern, *Midrash and Theory* (Evanston, Illinois: Northwestern University Press, 1996), pp.3-10.
59 James L. Kugel, *In Potiphar's House: The Interpretive Life of Biblical Texts* (Cambridge, Mass.: Harvard University Press, 1994), p.6.
60 *Ibid.*, p.247.
61 Jacob Neusner, trans., *Genesis Rabbah: The Judaic Commentary to the Book of Genesis*, 3 vols (Atlanta, GA: Scholar's Press, 1985), I 191.

her sister (30:1) and stealing from her father (31:19), and even Dinah, who 'went out' (34:1) are all invoked as examples of women undermining God's intentions in this respect.[62] The blatant misogyny of these readings make this midrash comic to modern eyes but the original question (why from the rib?) remains valid.

Genesis Rabbah asks equally valid questions of other elements in the biblical narrative. 'Where was man [Adam]', asks one of the rabbis, 'when this conversation [between Eve and the snake] was going on?', to be told that he may have been in a post-coital sleep or that God was giving him a tour of the world.[63] What were Cain and Abel arguing over, they ask, coming up with three possible solutions: land, religion or a woman.[64] Why does God tell Noah to make three floors to the ark (Gen. 6:16)? The answer may appear arbitrary: 'The bottom floor was for the manure, the second floor for him and his family and the animals that fall into the classification of clean, and the third floor for the ones that fall into the classification of unclean'.[65] Again, it is not necessarily the answer a modern reader would give (it would make more sense to put the dirty animals into the floor immediately above the manure) but the question still arises.

The rabbis continue to probe away at the significance of similar details in the Book of Genesis almost in the manner of 'close readers' trained in the principles of New Criticism. Why, for example, does Genesis 22:7 repeat the word 'father': 'And Isaac said to Abraham *his* father and said, "*My* father"'? Why thus: "his father...my father?"'. The answer comes, 'It was so that he should be filled with mercy for him'.[66] The rabbis go beyond criticism to a more creative form of interpretation when they make Abraham continue his argument with God, initiated in chapter 18, when he had bargained with God for the salvation of Sodom on account of its righteous inhabitants:

> A. Said R.Aha, '[Abraham said to God,] "Are there jokes even before you? Yesterday you said to me, 'For in Isaac shall seed be called to you' (Gen.21:12). And then you went back on your word and said, 'Take your son' (Gen. 22:2). And now: 'Do not lay your hand on the lad or do anything to him.'" [What's next?]
>
> B. 'Said the Holy One, blessed be he, to him, "Abraham, 'My covenant I will not profane' (Ps. 89:35). 'And I *will* establish my covenant with Isaac' (Gen. 17:21)."
>
> C. "True, I commanded you, 'Take now your son' (Gen. 33:2). 'I will not alter what has gone out of my lips' (Ps.89:35). Did I ever tell you to kill him? No, I told you, 'Bring him up'."
>
> D. "Well and good! You did indeed bring him up. Now take him down.[67]

---

62 *Ibid.*
63 *Ibid.*, I 201.
64 *Ibid.*, I 253.
65 *Ibid.*, I 324.
66 *Ibid.*, II 280-1.
67 *Ibid.*, II 284.

This is a good example of the way the rabbis bring prooftexts from elsewhere in the Bible to unlock the meaning of these verses. Modern readers are unlikely to be impressed with God's somewhat casuistical logic but they will admire Abraham's courage (further developed by Jenny Diski in her two novels on the Akedah).

Later midrash develops the story still further. *Midrash Tanhuma,* not collected until the ninth century though clearly incorporating earlier material, has Satan come to tempt Isaac to disobey his father:

> R. Abbin Berabbi the Levite said: While they were walking, Satan came to Isaac on his right hand and said, 'Alas, wretched son of a wretched woman, how many fasts did your mother fast until you came? Now the old man has gone mad in his old age and here he is going to slaughter you. Isaac turned back and said to his father: Look at what this one is saying to me! He said to him: He has come to confuse you, but the Holy One shall not confuse us, as stated (in Gen. 22:8): GOD WILL SEE TO THE LAMB FOR A BURNT OFFERING.[68]

This is clearly a highly creative way of attempting to understand the story, entering into the mind of Isaac, imagining his probable initial response, in the way the biblical text could be said to demand.

Further questions put to the biblical narrative in *Genesis Rabbah* include 'Why did Jacob weep?' after kissing Rachel in Genesis 29:12. Some of the answers are subtle: for example 'Because he foresaw that she would not be buried with him'. Others reveal an apparent obsession with sex: 'Because he saw that men were whispering with one another, saying, "Has this one now come to create an innovation in sexual licentiousness among us?"'.[69] When Dinah is raped in Genesis 34 the rabbis seem more concerned with her lack of modesty in daring to go out than in Shechem's taking advantage of her. They again seem obsessed with what actually happened, interpreting 'he...lay with her' and 'humbled her' (Genesis 34:2) as indicating vaginal and anal sex respectively. This may seem an example of over-reading, reading too much into the details of the text. But the principle, of course, is that nothing in the text is without significance, a principle with which any literary critic would agree.

Modern critics and writers who develop biblical stories in similarly imaginative ways can thus be seen to be engaging in a similar process to that of midrash. An anthology of *Modern Poems on the Bible*, which prints a wide range of twentieth-century poems on a variety of subjects taken from the Hebrew Bible opposite the relevant scriptural verses (their biblical intertexts), claims precisely this. David Curzon, the editor, goes so far as to argue, 'Whether the poets knew it or not, and some of them did, they were writing midrash'.[70] That, I would suggest, may be to stretch the term too far. The poets need surely to be aware of rabbinic midrash to be said to be following its conventions. Geoffrey Hartman and Sanford Budick, in their

---

68 John Townsend, trans., *Midrash Tanhuma* (Hoboken, NJ: Ktav Publishing House, 1989), pp. 129-30.
69 Neusner, trans., *Genesis Rabbah*, III 36.
70 David Curzon, ed., *Modern Poems on the Bible: An Anthology* (Philadelphia: Jewish Publication Society, 1994), p.3.

highly-influential study of *Midrash and Literature*, make some equally bold claims for the extent to which many western modes of reading and writing have historically been modelled upon midrash. While the 'authorized interpreters— in church and university— ...remained oblivious to its influence, ignoring midrash as a subject and misconceiving or misappropriating the Hebraic elements in our culture', they argue, 'the great poets who wrote out of the western tradition somehow evidenced its existence in our collective literary imagination'.[71] The 'somehow' here, I would suggest, is a little problematic, appearing to gloss over the question 'how', while the Jungian connotations of the 'collective...imagination' may appear designed to excuse scholars from the historical research necessary to demonstrate the precise routes along which such knowledge has been transmitted. Budick himself, however, in an essay on Milton in the same volume, works hard to establish the historical and textual connections between the typology of the Epistle to the Hebrews and the midrashic terms employed by Philo of Alexandria, links earlier noted by Milton's friend, the Dutch scholar Hugo Grotius.[72] Others have explored the likelihood of Milton's having read contemporary Latin translations of midrashic material.[73] In cases such as this historical research can confirm the likely contribution of midrashic interpretation to one of the most famous literary reworkings of the Book of Genesis. In the case of the modern novelists to be studied in this book I will make similar efforts to gauge the extent of their familiarity with midrash, to establish intertextual links with the rabbis, leaving the 'collective imagination' as an argument of last resort.

Hartman and Budick themselves claim that 'many profoundly ingrained habits of western reading...are historical derivatives of midrash'.[74] They also note 'resemblances' between midrash and contemporary literary theories of intertextuality. They may be joking when they refer to Reb Derrida and Reb Kermode (not to mention Reb Milton and Reb Borges). But their point, like the kind of literary and critical 'play' they advocate, is a serious one, that this mode of interpretation, 'long lost to literary study' and neglected even by 'students of Judaica', needs to be recovered because 'it quickens our understanding of textual production' both in reading and in writing. It also addresses our postmodern predicament, our precarious relationship to religious and literary traditions:

> The canon is transmitted and even extended by an intertextual reflection that has accepted the task of memory and preservation while adding a spacious supplement that derives from its primary source a strength and daring which is anything but secondary - which is, indeed, 'literary' in the modern sense.[75]

---

71 Geoffrey H. Hartman and Sanford Budick, eds, *Midrash and Literature* (New Haven: Yale University Press, 1986), p.x.

72 *Ibid.*, pp.206-8.

73 Golda Werman, *Milton and Midrash* (Washington, DC: Catholic University of America Press, 1995). See also Cheryl H.Fresch, '"As the Rabbines Expound": Milton, Genesis, and the Rabbis', *Milton Studies* 15 (1981) 59-79.

74 Hartman and Budick, *Midrash and Literature*, p.x.

75 *Ibid.*, p.xii.

I will argue in a moment that one of Derrida's main concerns is the nature of the ambiguous 'supplement' to the canon which slips from being merely an addition to the biblical original to becoming a replacement of it. Rabbinic midrash, always reverent towards the biblical text, gives way in later literature (certainly in many of the twentieth-century novels I will analyse) to a more liberated rewriting of the original, a freer form of intertextuality, a relationship to the tradition which is less reverent and more appealing to postmodern readers.

'Midrashim are not novels', of course, as Harold Fisch, another contributor to the volume on *Midrash and Literature* insists. Exploring midrashic elements in *Robinson Crusoe* and *Joseph Andrews*, however, Fisch notes that the two types of writing shed light on similar literary processes, 'the way in which stories or hints of stories are generated by the art of interpretation'.[76] He prefers to restrict the term midrash to a mode of rabbinic interpretation operating under constraints related to its function within a believing community for which the primary text has 'unlimited authority' as revelation. Midrash always comes back with a 'joy of recognition' to its primary text, he suggests, rather than struggle, as Harold Bloom would have it, to escape the anxiety of its influence.[77] Fisch develops both the similarities and differences between midrash and the novel in his book *New Stories for Old*. Retelling stories, he notes, whether in midrash or in fiction, 'achieves two functions simultaneously— it gratifies the fundamental human need for novelty and also for sameness, for a constancy of meaning'.[78] Midrashic reading and rewriting of the Bible, however, can never be an 'extravagant' exercise; it involves an 'elaboration of meanings which the text seems to authorize and even to invite'. The result is 'something between interpretation and a new invention, for biblical narratives, by virtue of their polyphonic character, as well as their pregnant silences, are peculiarly suited to beget other narratives'. Such novels, Fisch claims, may therefore 'be viewed as an extension of the midrashic mode, which combines an act of reading with the fertile play of the imagination'. They are both the effect of 'an interpretive bounty, whereby new and independent narratives are generated out of the dialogic encounter with the prime text of the Bible'.[79] *Joseph Andrews* can thus be seen as 'a kind of 'midrash' on the biblical story of Joseph and his brothers' while Thomas Mann's 'famous trilogy[sic]...is even more obviously a "midrash"'.[80] Fisch will not allow himself to use the term 'midrash' without qualifying inverted commas or adjectives, for instance when he notes that 'Mann is writing a modern, somewhat sceptical midrash', even though it is clear that Mann himself 'made frequent use of actual midrashic materials'.[81]

The point about midrash and anything which can be said to resemble it, Fisch insists, is that it allows the Bible to exercise a certain constraint upon the imaginative

---

76 Harold Fisch, 'The Hermeneutic Quest in *Robinson Crusoe*', in Geoffrey H.Hartman and Sanford Budick, ed., *Midrash and Literature* (New Haven: Yale University Press, 1986), pp.213-35 (p.228).

77 *Ibid.*, pp.231-2.

78 Harold Fisch, *New Stories for Old: Biblical Patterns in the Novel* (Basingstoke: Macmillan, 1998), p.4.

79 *Ibid.*, p.18.

80 *Ibid.*, pp.18-19.

81 *Ibid.*, p.100.

freedom with which it can be retold. It remains 'an unsubverted, indeed obsessive point of reference', asserting its authority 'with a certain importunacy'.[82] There is therefore a difference between 'midrashic polysemy', the openness of the biblical text to multiple interpretations, and postmodern 'indeterminacy'. In the former, 'the biblical source is more than a model on which one may base one's own free invention'; it is a text which 'exercises authority'. It may possess

> a power which energizes and liberates the imagination, but it also has an authority which limits and compels. It is this dialectic of freedom and authority in the relation of the late-born author to an originary text which is never lost sight of, that distinguishes 'midrash' from other freer modes of invention or reinvention.[83]

Fisch is therefore careful to refer to novels as 'midrashic' or employing 'a kind of midrash'; they can never be mistaken for the genuine article.

Fisch is also careful to explore the extent to which the novelists he studies were aware of the midrashic tradition or had access to midrashic sources. In his analysis of the way in which *Joseph Andrews* reworks not only the account in Genesis of Joseph's attempted seduction by Potiphar's wife but also (in Abraham's grief over the reported death of his son) the story of Abraham and Isaac, he makes a strong case for Fielding's being familiar with William Whiston's translation of Josephus' *Antiquities of the Jews*, published five years before the novel. Josephus, according to Fisch, tones down the 'nakedness' of biblical narrative, that harshness and intensity to which Auerbach drew attention, balancing it with 'Hellenized' gentility (reflected in the Augustan flavour of Whiston's translation). Just as Josephus introduced a certain 'smoothness' to his midrashic sources, so Fielding balances the raw intensity of the biblical narrative with a more classical comic epic quality, reflecting his own ambivalence towards the Bible as an authoritative text.[84] Saul Bellow's *Herzog*, for all its complex layers of allusion to the Akedah, is seen by Fisch to depart even further from midrashic reverence towards the Bible, representing 'a naturalistic, secularized transformation of the [biblical] pattern' rather than a genuinely midrashic interpretation.[85] Contemporary modern novelists, according to Fisch, rarely submit themselves to the Bible in the manner of true midrash. An American Jew such as Malamud can be 'influenced' by the Bible (among other things), 'looking around for appropriate models in a supermarket of mythic patterns'. For him (and his readers) 'the Bible has become, at the most, a fruitful source of ideas and images'.[86] For Modern Hebrew writers, by contrast, such as A.B.Yehoshua and S.Y.Agnon, the Bible remains all-powerful. Agnon's acceptance speech on being awarded the Nobel Prize for Literature explicitly recognised his debt not only to the Bible but to the 'Mishnah, Talmud, Midrash and Rashi's commentary on the Bible', material which he spent much time collecting and editing. All his works have biblical titles while

---

82   *Ibid.*, p.20.
83   *Ibid.*, pp.59-60.
84   *Ibid.*, pp.53-5.
85   *Ibid.*, p.139.
86   *Ibid.*, p.130.

The Day Before Yesterday clearly qualifies as 'a kind of modern midrash', seeking as it does to interpret not only the Akedah but other trials of Abraham.[87]

What western literary critics celebrate in midrash is its imaginative freedom, its ability seriously and creatively to play with the biblical text. A lecture on 'Biblical Narratives and Novelists' Narratives' by the South African Critic and novelist Dan Jacobson compares a passage from the *Midrash Rabbah* with material from Kierkegaard's *Fear and Trembling* and Thomas Mann's *Joseph and His Brothers*, similarly based upon biblical originals. All three passages, he argues, share a profound respect for the original text, a recognition of their own relative provisionality and a celebration of imaginative truth. Jacobson concludes,

> The spirit of imaginative speculation and self-projection, out of which all our richest fictions, in all ages, have emerged, is by no means as irreconcilable as it might seem to be with the biblical writers' conception of their task as sacred historians. Precisely because they have such confidence in the indefeasible veracity of the larger, overarching story they are telling, they are able to grant an autonomy, a dramatic presence, a psychological inwardness and coherence, to all or any of the participants in their tales.[88]

Elsewhere, in his wide-ranging study of the Bible, *The Story of the Stories*, Jacobson discusses the way in which he discovered for himself, while writing his midrashic novel *The Rape of Tamar*, that 'every phrase, virtually every word, in the relevant chapter of 2 Samuel was like a seed...capable of astonishing growth'.[89] Reading the biblical text seemed almost to require rewriting it, teasing out its compressed or implicit meanings.

The Bible itself, as Michael Fishbane and others have demonstrated, is full of midrashic material or 'inner-biblical exegesis', accretions to the canon within the canon as a result of a continuing process of self-reflexive commentary. We should distinguish between this 'intratextuality' within the canon and the more extensive 'intertextuality' between the Bible and non-canonical texts. But the process is the same, allowing for the continual supplementation and renewal of the tradition. 'Aggadic exegesis', in Fishbane's words, is not simply 'content to supplement gaps in the *traditum* [the sacred text] but characteristically draws forth latent and unsuspected meanings from it,...its fullness of potential meanings and applications'.[90] This, he explains in *The Garments of Torah*, is how 'cultures renew themselves hermeneutically',[91] retaining reverence for the text while subjecting it to 'a daring reinflection of the traditional sense', often signalled in midrash by a phrase such as *kivyakhol*, 'as it were', thus acknowledging its own boldness and daring along

---

87 *Ibid.*, p.193.
88 Dan Jacobson, *Biblical Narratives and Novelists' Narratives* (London: University of London, 1989), p.6.
89 Dan Jacobson, *The Story of the Stories: The Chosen People and Its God* (New York: Harper and Row, 1982), p.131.
90 Michael Fishbane, *Biblical Interpretation in Ancient Israel* (Oxford: Oxford University Press, 1985), p.283.
91 Michael Fishbane, *The Garments of Torah: Essays in Biblical Hermeneutics* (Bloomington: Indiana University Press, 1989), p.ix.

with its own limitations.[92] Fishbane indicates the continuity between ancient midrash and modern literary theory in referring as he does to 'midrashic *differance*',[93] a Derridean phrase which points to the absence or gap in a supposedly stable or fixed sign which allows for (or even requires) further interpretation, thereby stimulating the generation of fresh meaning.

All reading, as Daniel Boyarin explains, can thus be said to share with midrash in the process of intertextuality, involving an actualisation or completion of gaps in the text in accordance with the readers' 'own intertext— that is, the cultural codes which enable them to make meaning and find meaning'.[94] This is particularly the case in reading the Bible. In the words of an article on 'Midrash and Allegory' by Gerald Bruns in Alter and Kermode's *Literary Guide to the Bible*, 'The Bible always addresses itself to the time of interpretation; one cannot understand it except by appropriating it anew'.[95] Far from deploring the freedom with which modern intertextuality treats the original text, Bruns goes on to celebrate the 'astonishing examples of midrashic extravagance' which can be found even among the rabbis, an extravagance which makes 'many scholars construe midrash as a literary rather than as a hermeneutical phenomenon'. Since it 'cannot be taken seriously as a interpretation', they argue, 'it can be appreciated only as literature or art; it is creativity rather than commentary'.[96]

The term intertextuality, of course, is as slippery as the word midrash, covering an equally broad spectrum of writing. It is used, M.H.Abrams explains, in a general sense

> to signify the multiple ways in which any one literary text echoes, or is inseparably linked to, other texts, whether by open or covert citations and *allusions*, or by the formal and substantive features of an earlier text, or simply by participation in a common stock of literary and linguistic procedures and conventions.[97]

Abrams moves quickly from the specific relationship of one text to another to the broader process by which all texts within a particular period might be said to be related to each other. The helpful glossary in Danna Fewell's study of *Reading Between Texts: Intertextuality and the Hebrew Bible* also notices the way intertextuality overlaps with cognate (and more conventional) terms such as allusion, echo and poetic influence as well as more recent notions of the trace.[98] It has clearly come to signify a very broad range of possible relationships between texts.

---

92 *Ibid.*, p.28.

93 *Ibid.*, p.22.

94 Daniel Boyarin, *Intertextuality and the Reading of Midrash* (Bloomington: Indiana University Press, 1990), p.16.

95 Gerald L.Bruns, 'Midrash and Allegory', in Robert Alter and Frank Kermode, eds, *The Literary Guide to the Bible* (London: Collins, 1987), pp.625-46 (pp.627-8).

96 *Ibid.*, p.629.

97 M.H.Abrams, *A Glossary of Literary Terms*, Fifth Edition (New York: Holt, Rinehart and Winston, 1988), p.247.

98 Danna Fewell, ed., *Reading Between Texts: Intertextuality and the Hebrew Bible* (Louisville, Kentucky: Westminster/John Knox Press, 1992).

Most accounts of intertextuality[99] begin with Kristeva's seminal article 'Word, Dialogue, and Novel', written in 1966, which in turn celebrates the way in which

> Bakhtin was one of the first to replace the static hewing out of texts with a model where literary structure does not simply *exist* but is generated in relation to *another* structure. What allows a dynamic dimension to structuralism is his conception of the 'literary word' as an *intersection of textual surfaces* rather than a *point* (a fixed meaning), as a dialogue among several writings: that of the writer, the addressee (or the character) and the contemporary or earlier cultural context.[100]

Any text, in other words, can be seen to have been 'constructed as a mosaic of quotations; any text is the absorption and transformation of another'.[101] The earlier texts, according to Bakhtin, continue to carry with them the historical 'baggage' they have acquired; they carry with them at least some of the 'taste' of their original use. But they can be 're-accented', acquiring new adifferent meanings, in their new context.

There is something of a problem about the use of Bakhtin in the context of biblical intertextuality, however. Not only does he appear to have been unaware of the midrashic tradition but he positively denies the possibility of such creative re-interpretation of the Bible, which he sees as an example of the 'authoritative word', which is monological and demands complete acceptance rather than opening itself to dialogue. The 'word of the fathers', he claims, is semantically 'static and dead', coming to us 'fully complete' with an authorized 'single meaning', demanding not a 'free appropriation and assimilation' but 'unconditional allegiance'.[102] Quite why Bakhtin refused to believe that the Bible was capable of generating new stories is hard to understand; I have argued elsewhere that it may have been the way in which powerful institutions of Bakhtin's time, such as the Russian Orthodox Church or the Stalinist state, controlled the 'authorized' use of official language that made him so wary of the Word.[103] His model of the creative tension between different discourses in a text, I would suggest, may contribute something to the study of biblical intertextuality in the modern novel in spite of his own disavowal of the possibility of the Bible lending itself to such fruitful interaction. In what follows, for example, Mark Twain will be seen struggling to overcome the doctrinal 'baggage' (for instance the notion of the Fall), the historical 'accents' with which the story of Adam and Eve comes.

Perhaps more relevant to the study of biblical intertextuality is the work of a number of Jewish critical theorists, all of whom draw upon the midrashic tradition

---

99 See Judith Still and Michael Worton, eds, *Intertextuality: Theories and Practice* (Manchester: Manchester University Press, 1990) and Graham Allen, *Intertextuality* (London: Routledge, 2000).

100 *The Kristeva Reader*, ed. Toril Moi (Oxford: Blackwell, 1986), pp.35-6.

101 *Ibid.*, p.37.

102 *Ibid.*, p.343.

103 For a fuller discussion of this question, see my forthcoming chapter 'The Word in the Novel: Bakhtin on Tolstoy and the Bible', in Mark Knight, ed., *Biblical Religion and the Novel* (Aldershot: Ashgate, 2006).

and therefore take a more positive view of the possibility of the Bible generating fresh stories. Harold Bloom, as we have seen, celebrates *The Book of J* as an ancient precursor of the modern novel. His understanding of intertextuality, like that of Bakhtin, recognises some of the conflicts and tensions, the sheer struggle, of the creative process. *The Anxiety of Influence* portrays the relationship of poets to their precursors as always one of struggle, a wrestling to avoid submission to the poetic father, the poet who first awakened creativity:

> Poetic influence— when it involves two strong, authentic poets— always proceeds by a misreading of the prior poet, an act of creative correction that is actually and necessarily a misinterpretation. The history of poetic influence...is a history of anxiety and self-serving caricature, of distortion, of perverse, wilful revisionism without which modern poetry as such could not exist.[104]

After spelling out a variety of ways in which poets escaped the control of the their precursor, whether by completion, repetition, or swerving (the details of Bloom's somewhat arcane set of terms, derived from Alexandrian Gnostics, matter less than the general principle that there are such different modes of intertextuality), Bloom insists that creative writing (not criticism) is the most appropriate response to an earlier work of literature.

A Map of Misreading and *Kabbalah and Criticism*, develop this general theory with specific reference to Jewish revisionism, the way rabbinic and kabbalistic writers have re-interpreted and rewritten their sacred texts. *A Map of Misreading* spells out the general principle of intertextuality, or 'poetic influence', as he prefers to call it, 'that there are *no* texts, but only relationships *between* texts' and that all criticism involves the 'misreading or misprision, that one poet performs upon another'. Bloom takes Lurianic Kabbalism as 'the ultimate model for Western revisionism' in terms of 'its work of *interpretation*, of revisionary replacements of Scriptural meaning by techniques of *opening*'.[105] The details of Isaac Luria's rewriting of *Genesis*, involving firstly 'the Creator's withdrawal or contraction so as to make possible a creation that is not himself', then the breaking of the vessels of divine light, giving birth to base matter, and finally redemption (the release of the imprisoned sparks of light by the action of righteous human beings) is again less important than the model it provides for later revision of the biblical narrative. It provides an account of creation, fall and redemption which Bloom (like Thomas Mann) finds attractive not only as theology but as 'the best paradigm available for a study of the way poets war against one another'.[106]

Bloom explains that Kabbalah literally means 'tradition', that which has been 'received' and that tradition etymologically means 'a carrying-over of influence'. But *traditio*, Bloom argues, 'is Latin only in language; the concept deeply derives from the Hebraic *Mishnah*, an oral handing-over, or transmission of oral precedents'

---

104 Harold Bloom, *The Anxiety of Influence* (Oxford: Oxford University Press, 1973), p.30.

105 Harold Bloom, *A Map of Misreading* (Oxford: Oxford University Press, 1975), pp.3-4.

106 *Ibid.*, p.5.

and applies to the written and the literary as much as to oral tradition.[107] Midrash too began as an oral tradition but became written, a mode of seeking for the Torah, interpreting and developing it.[108] Bloom adds Kierkegaard's notion of repetition, a compulsion to recover the prestige of origins, the vision of the fathers, and Nietzsche's view of interpretation as the will to power, a struggle for control, to his rabbinic models to create a model of relating creatively to tradition which goes well beyond the 'weak' reading permitted by orthodox institutions. For Bloom, famously, there are no 'correct' or 'incorrect' readings, only 'weak' or 'strong' ones (with Bloom himself apparently acting as the arbiter).

Kabbalah and Criticism takes the Jewish tradition as a model not only 'for the processes of poetic influence' but for a radical mode of criticism, breaking down the boundaries so carefully preserved in the Talmud between text and commentary. 'This line', to quote Bloom, 'wavers and breaks in the Zohar', allowing for the creation of a magnificent poem which acted as 'a collective, psychic defence... against exile and persecution'.[109] Bloom stresses both the literary and theological motives of the Kabbalists, who suffered 'an overwhelming anxiety-of-influence' in response to Scripture as well as a need to reinterpret in the light of experience, which made Gnosis and Kabbalah 'the first Modernisms'.[110] Scripture, most notably at the end of the Book of Revelation, invokes a curse upon anyone who dares add to the canon;[111] the Kabbalists defy that curse and the control of normative institutions, producing a supplement to the canon which is both interpretive and creative.

The Breaking of the Vessels (1982) also employs Kabbalistic mythology in order to dramatise the process of poetic influence, the way in which individual writers and readers relate to their tradition. T.S.Eliot makes the process sound very benign in his famous essay on 'Tradition and the Individual Talent', which allows for the new work to be happily incorporated in the existing canon. Bloom points out that a less well-known review written by Eliot only a few weeks before that essay and never subsequently reprinted, recognises the ambivalence any poet feels towards a precursor, how 'the awareness of our debt naturally leads us to hatred of the object imitated, a personal "crisis" which changes our whole personality'.[112] Bloom considers other followers of the path of Jacob (maimed as well as blessed by the angel with whom he wrestled in Genesis 32), including 'Wrestling Waldo [Emerson], heroically confronting all the cultural past' and insisting that all products of the human intellect, including the Bible, are 'revisable, corrigible, reversible',[113] and 'Wrestling Sigmund', whose struggle with the Yahwist, 'is the largest and most intense of our century'.[114] The 'poetic tales of Yahweh and the Patriarchs', Bloom claims, are so strong, so strange and original, and so encrusted with traditional

---

107 *Ibid.*, pp.31-2.
108 *Ibid.*, p.42.
109 *Ibid.*, pp.52-3.
110 *Ibid.*, pp.71 and 79.
111 *Ibid.*, p.99.
112 Harold Bloom, *The Breaking of the Vessels* (Chicago: Chicago University Press, 1982), pp.19-20.
113 *Ibid.*, pp.27 and 35.
114 *Ibid.*, p.47.

misreading, that 'we simply cannot read them'.[115] We certainly cannot read them simply but need to resort to complex modes of rewriting and revision in order to make our own sense of them.

A number of the essays in *Poetics of Influence* (1988) develop Bloom's theory of influence with particular reference to poets and their relationship with the Bible. 'The Covering Cherub' considers a triad of wrestling matches, between Jacob and Jehovah in Genesis 32, between Milton and Urizen in Blake's poem *Milton* and between Blake and Milton, who for many an eighteenth-century poet was 'the Covering Cherub blocking a new voice from entering Paradise'.[116] 'Martin Buber on the Bible' develops Bloom's critique of orthodox biblical scholarship as 'inadequate' literary criticism which fails to grasp the power of the original text.[117] *Ruin the Sacred Truths* (1989) continues Bloom's celebration of the literary strength of J,[118] the earliest strand of the Pentateuch, for which, as we have seen, Bloom proceeded to provide an interpretation and commentary. Bloom remains a great believer in the western literary canon, much of which he sees as a creative response to the Bible, continuing the great struggle with this most powerful of precursors. His study of *Genius* (2002), for example, divides its *Mosaic of One Hundred Exemplary Creative Minds* (which, incidentally, include both Twain and Mann) into ten sections named after the *Sefirot* of the Kabbalah. This may appear far-fetched, imposing a Jewish model onto such evidently gentile figures, but Bloom's model of the tensions and conflicts involved in the creative struggle helps to explain the violence of the relationship between the novels I will study and their biblical original, which often goes well beyond the passivity of 'influence' as conventionally understood.

Another theorist who draws upon the model of midrash to shed light on the nature of later intertextuality is Bloom's former Yale colleague, Jacques Derrida, the founder of deconstruction.[119] Deconstruction has been called boring from within (in more than one sense) because it is concerned with understanding and to some extent dismantling a tradition using terms and methods derived from that tradition. Derrida, like Bloom (albeit in a more indirect and detached manner) wrestles with traditions, whether religious, philosophical or literary. *Specters of Marx*, for example, is an attempt to read Marx's will, to work out what remains of the spirit of Marx for his political heirs. Derrida suggests that Marx tried to exorcise too many ghosts too quickly, spirits of the past that should have been acknowledged and allowed a continuing voice. Derrida has learnt from Levinas the way repetition can bring out the alterity, the otherness to be found within traditional terms when they are repeated in new contexts.[120]

---

115 *Ibid.*, pp.50-1.

116 Harold Bloom, *The Poetics of Influence* (New Haven, CT: H.R.Schwab, 1988), p.87.

117 *Ibid.*, p.325.

118 *Ruin the Sacred Truths: Poetry and Belief from the Bible to the Present* (Cambridge MA: Harvard University Press.

119 For a fuller study of both Bloom and Derrida's relationship to the rabbinic tradition, see Susan A.Handelman, *The Slayers of Moses: The Emergence of Rabbinic Interpretation in Modern Literary Theory* (Albany: State University of New York Press, 1982).

120 For Derrida's reading of Levinas, see Simon Critchley, *The Ethics of Deconstruction* (Oxford: Blackwell, 1992).

Introduction: Wrestling with the Book of Genesis

For Derrida, of course, everything is textually mediated. As Vincent Leitch explains it, 'Everything gets textualized. All contexts...become intertexts; that is, outside influences and forces undergo textualization', becoming the prooftexts which a reader brings to the original.[121] The clear dividing line between what is inside and what is outside the text has been broken down, since all signs contain traces of their other, opposites against which they are defined, differential traces which account for the generation of meaning. The process of reading a text becomes for Derrida

> a kind of cabal or cabala in which the blanks will never be anything but provisionally filled in, ...open to the play of permutations, blanks rarely glimpsed as blanks, (almost) pure spacing, going on forever and not in the expectation of Messianic fulfillment...there exists a whole interpretation of spacing, of textual generation and polysemy, of course, revolving around the Torah. Polysemy is the possibility of a 'new Torah' capable of arising out of the other.

Derrida quotes a Hasidic Rabbi promising that God will eventually 'unveil the white in the Torah', the spaces between the letters. For the present, however, we have to fill them in for ourselves, opening the biblical text to 'an indefinitely disseminated transformation'.[122] That, I would claim, could be said to characterise what is happening in the work of all the novelists considered in this book, who open up the blank spaces of the biblical text to new interpretations.

Derrida's works often dramatise the meanings generated by blanks or spacing within or between texts. 'The Double Session', for example, and *Glas* place literary and philosophical texts opposite each other, Plato opposite Mallarmé, Hegel opposite Genet, allowing the juxtaposition itself to create meaning. 'Living On: Border lines' has a continuous footnote, rather like a Talmudic commentary, supplementing the main text. The word 'supplement' here brings out Derrida's concern with citation and repetition (with difference) as a mode of generating meaning. As he explains in *Of Grammatology,* the supplement has two senses: it both adds to and replaces, often sliding from being an interpretation to become a substitute for the original object. Writing, for example, begins as a supplement to speech, only brought in to replace the absent speaker, but ends up by supplanting it and producing surplus meaning, that excess of the signifier, irreducible to a single signified, which characterises literature.[123]

Derrida often employs horticultural metaphors to suggest how this intertextual process works. The graft in writing, as in horticulture, is a quotation introduced within a text, which generates new meaning: 'A notch is marked there, one that again opens onto another text and practices another reading'.[124] *Limited Inc* uses another botanical metaphor, dehiscence, referring to 'the divided opening, in the growth

---

121 Vincent B.Leitch, *Deconstructive Criticism: An Advanced Introduction* (London: Hutchinson, 1983), p.122.

122 Jacques Derrida, *Dissemination*, trans. Barbara Johnson (Chicago: Chicago University Press, 1981), pp.344-5.

123 Jacques Derrida, *Of Grammatology*, trans. Gayatri Spivak (Baltimore: Johns Hopkins University Press, 1976).

124 Derrida, *Dissemination*, pp.203-4.

of a plant', which 'makes production, reproduction, development possible'.[125] Dehiscence, like citation and iterability, makes pure repetition impossible, introducing the contamination of fresh growth, new interpretation. A mark or a sign can never be completely reproduced without difference since it always occurs in new contexts with different intertexts. Hence the notion of the re-mark, as explained by Rodolphe Gasché:

> The re-mark...is a form of the general law of supplementarity, which dislocates all presence, plenitude, or propriety. As the re-mark demonstrates, supplementation always consists of adding a mark to another mark.[126]

The word re-mark exemplifies what it represents, that repetition with difference characteristic of all signifying systems and all traditions. However hard institutions may try to control and regulate meaning, to delimit 'proper' interpretation, Derrida insists, all linguistic signs will open themselves to fresh meanings as they collide with different intertexts.

Derrida illustrates this kind of creative intertextuality in practice in *The Gift of Death,* which comes close to producing a form of midrash in its commentary upon Kierkegaard's comments upon the Akedah in *Fear and Trembling.* The mysterious, ungraspable otherness of God is particularly evident in the story from Genesis upon which Kierkegaard chooses to dwell, in which this 'secret, hidden, separate, absent, or mysterious God...decides, without revealing his reasons, to demand of Abraham that most cruel, impossible, and untenable gesture: to offer his son Isaac as a sacrifice'.[127] Derrida is particularly intrigued by Abraham's truthful but (at the time) equivocal answer to Isaac's question where the sacrificial lamb is to be found: 'God will provide a lamb for the holocaust' (Gen. 22:8). This, as Derrida points out, is not exactly a lie but it is economical with the truth; not only does Abraham fail to tell his son anything about God's demand but he keeps his secret bargain from his wife too. That is why, in the Midrash Tanhuma discussed above, Satan tells Isaac what is going on in attempt to destroy Abraham's secret.

Kierkegaard relates Abraham's silence to Christ's command to hate one's family, offering them the same gift of death as the Father extends to the Son within Christian theology. Derrida picks up on the scandalous paradox of this command before engaging in his own supplementary midrashic additions to the biblical narrative, imagining what Abraham felt like, wanting to tell the whole truth to Sarah and Isaac and to comfort them but fearing that they will then demand he renegotiate with God.[128] Derrida extends the midrashic reading of this story from Genesis to incorporate New Testament material and Christian theology. His relationship to his own Jewish religious tradition, particularly clear in the 'Circumfession' he

---

125 Jacques Derrida, *Limited Inc*, ed. Gerald Graff (Evanston, Illinois: Northwestern University Press, 1988), p.59.

126 Rodolphe Gasché, *The Tain of the Mirror: Derrida and the Philosophy of Reflection* (Cambridge, MA: Harvard University Press, 1986), p.217.

127 Jacques Derrida, *The Gift of Death*, trans. David Wills (Chicago: Chicago University Press, 1995), p.58.

128 *Ibid.*, pp.73-4.

attaches as a running footnote to Geoffrey Bennington's book *Jacques Derrida*,[129] is complex and problematic. Like Bloom, he reads it in ways which run counter to the conventions of normative Judaism. There is a peculiar blend of continuity and discontinuity in their readings of the tradition, a necessary ambivalence which is part of the postmodern condition, entailing both a modernist critique of the normative canon *and* a re-assertion or re-reading of that tradition which retains at least some of its component elements.

There is a particular problem for modern (and postmodern) *women* in their relation to the biblical tradition. In spite of the surprising strength of the women characters in Genesis, which makes Bloom's speculation that they were the product of a woman writer at least plausible, the Bible is undeniably imbued with the patriarchal attitudes of the society within which they originated. *The Woman's Bible* of 1895, edited by Elizabeth Cady Stanton, highlighted the extent to which 'modern' women found it difficult to accept the passive role models held out to them, setting out accordingly to 'revise…those texts…referring directly to women'.[130] Stanton's work, as we shall see, was much admired by Twain and seems to have fed into his understanding of Eve. More recent practitioners of such revisionary reading of the Bible include Alicia Suskin Ostriker, another Jewish critic and poet who appropriates the midrashic tradition from a decidedly feminist perspective. Among the 'disappearing women of the Bible' who show glimpses of enterprise and initiative before making way for male protagonists she lists Rebecca (retiring from sight after ensuring that Jacob receives his father's blessing in Genesis 25), Rachel and Leah (who both vanish after the birth of Benjamin, though only Rachel dies in childbirth in Genesis 35), Tamar (who outwits Judah with spectacular daring and thus ensures marriage to his son and the consequent survival of her particular tribe in Genesis 38) and Potiphar's wife (the attempted seducer of Joseph and indirect cause of his later career in Genesis 39). This 'startlingly recurrent pattern in biblical narrative', Ostriker claims, has not previously been recognised 'because everyone *takes it for granted* that women must be rejected in order for the story of male maturity, male leadership, male heroism, to take place'.[131]

Ostriker also appropriates Bloom's metaphor of the need to wrestle with the biblical text, like Jacob with the angel, and 'wrest a blessing' from it.[132] To this image she adds her own metaphor of the need for women to 'enter the tents/texts, invade the sanctuary, uncover the father's nakedness'.[133] Anita Diamant, as we shall see, does precisely this in *The Red Tent*, attempting to fill the gaps in the biblical narrative, to provide the women's perspective on these events. This is enabled, Ostriker insists, by the fact that the original biblical text is 'a radically layered,

---

129 Jacques Derrida, 'Circumfession', in Geoffrey Bennington, *Jacques Derrida* (Chicago: Chicago University Press, 1993).

130 Elizabeth Cady Stanton, *The Woman's Bible* (Amherst: Prometheus Books, 1999), p.5.

131 Alicia Suskin Ostriker, *Feminist Revision of the Bible* (Oxford: Blackwell, 1993), pp.47-9.

132 *Ibid.*, p.15.

133 *Ibid.*, p.9.

plurally authored, multiply motivated composite, full of fascinating mysteries, gaps and inconsistencies, a garden of delight to the exegete...a paradise of polysemy'.[134] In midrash and in more recent revisionist rewriting of the Bible, Ostriker argues, these gaps in the Bible can be made to 'yield new meanings to new generations', in particular to 'liberate Torah's positive meanings for women'.[135] Again, this is what a novelist such as Anita Diamant could be said to be doing in *The Red Tent*.

If Ostriker's *Feminist Revision of the Bible* focuses on modern women poets who have engaged intertextually with the Bible from Emily Dickinson and H.D. to Eleanor Wilner and Enid Dame, her later work, *Nakedness of the Fathers*, practises her own brand of midrash on a range of biblical narratives, many from the Book of Genesis. 'Rabbinic tradition itself', she claims, 'leads us to expect that the process of understanding the Bible's meaning will and should continue through history'. 'It is this tradition to which I hope to belong.'[136] Some of her readings of passages in Genesis self-consciously incorporate material from ancient midrash. In "Isaac, or Laughter", for example, in imagining Isaac's response to the events, she refers to the midrash 'that God sent an angel to speak to Abraham because he was too embarrassed to do so personally', only for Abraham to insist that he tell him himself and promise 'to forgive his children whenever they retell this tale'.[137] Ostriker even gives 'The Opinion of the Ram' on all this. But her main concern, of course, is to give voice to the otherwise silenced women, to Sarah, Rebecca, Rachel and Leah.

Not all of the novelists to be analysed in the chapters that follow are quite so self-conscious about the rabbinic tradition. Mark Twain's knowledge of midrash, for example, is likely to have been limited (though it is highly probable that he was aware of it, given that his own publishing firm published a collection of *Stories from the Rabbis*). John Steinbeck's acquaintance with the midrashic tradition was also probably indirect, through the mediation of Louis Ginzberg. Jeanette Winterson is also unlikely to have studied the midrash themselves, though she reviewed *The Book of J.* The other novelists in question, however, from Jennifer Diski and Anita Diamant to Thomas Mann, can be seen to have engaged directly with midrashic material, employing it not only as a source but as a model for their own writing. Their intertextual engagement with the biblical texts can therefore be seen as thoroughly midrashic; they can be said self-consciously to follow the tradition of the rabbis, wrestling with the original biblical narrative in order to wrest from it a 'blessing' or at least a significance for their own time.

---

134 *Ibid.*, p.62.
135 *Ibid.*, p.10.
136 Alicia Ostriker, *The Nakedness of the Fathers: Biblical Visions and Revisions* (New Brunswick, NJ: Rutgers University Press, 1997), pp.xii-xiii.
137 *Ibid.*, p.87.

Chapter 2

Adam, Eve and the Serpent: Mark Twain

Twain against God: Refiguring the Fall

Twain's 'many attempts to rewrite and supplement the biblical account of Creation and its aftermath', as the editors of *The Bible According to Mark Twain* explain, 'range from farce to fantasy to biting satire'.[1] As early as 1869 he had written about the deluge in the form of a diary kept by Shem in which the carpenters laughed at Noah 'for an old visionary'.[2] In 1877 he had written 'Adam's Expulsion', an unpublished piece in which Adam's children ask him to write about his experiences in paradise, only for him to procrastinate and finally find himself unable to remember '*that woful day that saw me banished thence*'.[3] He would return to the subject again and again, particularly in the last two decades of his life before he died in 1910. *The Diaries of Adam and Eve* may appear relatively gentle in their satire but some of his writing in his final years was so savage in its satire of Christian orthodoxy that it could not be published. *Letters from the Earth*, for example, supposedly sent by Satan to his fellow-archangels Michael and Gabriel, did not eventually appear in print until 1962, when they still caused considerable controversy. I will begin this chapter by outlining Twain's religious development, paying particular attention to passages in his work which address the question of the Fall. The second section will then focus on his sustained rewriting of the first three chapters of Genesis in *The Diaries of Adam and Eve* and in his many pieces about Satan, including *Letters from the Earth* and the different versions of *The Mysterious Stranger*.

Twain's intellectual formation was very much a nineteenth-century one (he was born in 1835), but there is something very 'modern' about it. John Hays, in his account of *Mark Twain and Religion*, notes that, having abandoned Calvinist Christianity 'fairly early in his life, he was put in the modern position of finding an alternative'. His whole life, in fact, culminating in his repeated retelling of the early chapters of Genesis, has been called 'a quest for that alternative', mirroring the development of American religious thought 'up to and through his own time'. The very confusion of his final period for Hays shows 'someone spiritually alive', not yet fixed in his beliefs.[4] Sholom Kahn also challenges the earlier view, to be found

---

1   Howard G. Baetzhold and Joseph B. McCullough, eds, *The Bible According to Mark Twain: Writings on Heaven, Eden, and the Flood* (Athens, GA: University of Georgia Press, 1995), p.xvi.
2   Edgar M. Branch, Michael B.Frank and Kenneth M.Sanderson, eds, *Mark Twain's Letters* (Berkeley: University of California Press, 1988-2002),6 vols, III 311.
3   Baetzhold and McCullough, *Bible According to Mark Twain*, pp.111-5.
4   John Q.Hays, *Mark Twain and Religion: A Mirror of American Eclecticism* (New York: Peter Lang, 1989), p.12.

in biographers from Paine and Kaplan to Hamlin Hill,[5] that Twain's late writing was 'morbid and eccentric'. On the contrary, Kahn claims, 'by writing "not for publication" he seems to have released energies that enabled him to reach new, profound, rich levels of literary achievement'. This 'posthumous Mark Twain' can thus be regarded as 'one of the liveliest and most modern of contemporary writers'.[6]

The only full-length book on *Mark Twain and the Bible*, by Alison Ensor, is strangely unsympathetic towards Twain's 'Adam complex'. Ensor accepts that 'no other American author has ever thought and written so much about…the first chapters of Genesis' but argues (rather oddly) that his 'use' of them is 'far out of proportion to the importance of that section to the Bible as a whole'. According to Ensor, he had no 'informed understanding of biblical scholarship' and 'not much originality' in what he said about it.[7] Later critics have disagreed, notably Stanley Brodwin, who calls Twain a 'counter-theologian', by which he means someone who explored his own 'intensely personal relationship to the Garden of Eden' in order to demonstrate how the churches had misread the Bible.[8] Twain's 'obsession with the history of the fall', Brodwin notes, was both 'lifelong' (from his first publication of 1853 to his last of 1910)[9] and more than merely 'literary'; it was a matter of 'correcting' a 'false' understanding of the stories.[10]

Twain, it should be noted, must have known about the midrashic tradition. His library included a volume of *Stories from the Rabbis* by a New York Professor of German and Hebrew, Abram Isaacs, published by Twain's own firm, Charles Webster, in 1893, the year of his first Adamic Diary. The stories are described in Webster's catalogue as 'entertaining tales in popular style from legends of the Talmud and Midrash'.[11] Isaacs insists in his introduction that the rabbis were not 'abstruse pedants' but 'admirable storytellers' whose tales had been a source of 'solace and inspiration' to the Jews for centuries and could provide a similar resource to the 'intelligent reading public…of our own age'.[12] Among the many examples of midrash in this volume is a story taken from Rabbi Joshua ben Levi exploring the double-edged nature of God's cursing and consolation of Adam in Genesis chapter 3:

---

5 Albert Bigelow Paine, *Mark Twain: A Biography*, 4 vols (New York: Harper, 1912); Justin Kaplan, *Mr.Clemens and Mark Twain* (New York: Simon and Schuster, 1966); Hamlin Hill, *Mark Twain: God's Fool* (New York: Harper, 1973).

6 Sholom J.Kahn, *Mark Twain's Mysterious Stranger: A Study of the Manuscript Texts* (Columbia: University of Missouri Press, 1978), pp. viii and 7.

7 Alison Ensor, *Mark Twain and the Bible* (Lexington: University of Kentucky Press, 1969), pp.44 and 99-101.

8 *Ibid.*, pp.235-6.

9 Stanley Brodwin, 'The Humour of the Absurd: Mark Twain's Adamic Diaries', *Criticism* 14 (1972) pp.49-64, (p.52).

10 Stanley Brodwin,'The Theology of Mark Twain: Banished Adam and the Bible', in Louis J.Budd, ed., *Critical essays on Mark Twain, 1910-1980* (Boston: G.K.Hall, 1983), pp.176-93 (pp.178-9).

11 Abram Samuel Isaacs, *Stories from the Rabbis* (New York: Charles Webster, 1893) advertising quoted from the *Publishers Trade List Annual* for 1893 in Alan Gribben, ed., *Mark Twain's Library: A Reconstruction*, 2 vols (Boston: G.K.Hall, 1980), I 347.

12 Abram S. Isaacs, *Stories from the Rabbis* (London: Osgood, McIlvaine and Co., 1893), pp.7-9.

When God spoke to Adam the words, 'Thorns and thistles will grow for you,' tears gushed from his eyes, and he said, 'Shall I then eat with my ass from one crib?' Quickly God replied, 'In the sweat of thy countenance shalt thou eat bread.' Then Adam was soothed. His soul was comforted in its affliction. He saw in labour compensation and consolation for life's bitterness and sin.[13]

The same, of course, can be said of Twain himself, who turned to his writing in the 1890s in similar compensation for the increasing bitterness of his life. His interest in (and identification with) Adam clearly predated his knowledge of the midrashic tradition but his own retelling of Adam's stories from 1893 onwards may well have gained impetus from this volume. At the very least, it establishes some awareness on his part of the rabbinic tradition of retelling biblical narrative.

Before I proceed to discuss Twain's Adamic texts themselves, however, I want briefly to trace his religious development, paying special attention to his attitude to the Bible in general and the opening chapters of Genesis in particular. Twain was brought up within the 'frontier Protestant fundamentalism' satirised in *The Adventures of Tom Sawyer* and *Huckleberry Finn*.[14] His mother, who had switched from Methodism to Presbyterianism in 1843, and his sister were perpetually urging him to read his Bible daily,[15] making his boast to have 'read the Bible through' before he was fifteen at least credible.[16] His *Autobiography*, however, records that he was prepared to read it critically even as 'a Sunday school scholar':

> I was greatly interested in the incident of Eve and the Serpent, and thought Eve's calmness perfectly noble. I asked Mr.Barclay [the teacher] if he had ever heard of another woman who, being approached by a serpent, would not excuse herself and break for the nearest timber.[17]

This critical attitude was no doubt encouraged by his father, who remained a classic freethinker of the Enlightenment tradition, fed on writers such as Voltaire and Paine. Twain himself reportedly read Thomas Paine's *Rights of Man* while working as a pilot on the Mississippi River, a period during which he appears to have adopted the attitudes of an eighteenth-century deist and even (for a short time) a Freemason.[18]

Twain's ambivalence towards the Bible is evident in one of his first books, *Innocents Abroad* (1869), an account of a visit to Europe and the Holy Land in the company of some elderly pilgrims who were mostly so pious that they 'thought they could have saved Sodom and Gomorrah' itself.[19] Twain's many references to the

---

13 *Ibid.*, pp.152-3.
14 Harold K.Bush, 'A Moralist in Disguise: Mark Twain and American Religion', in Shelley Fisher Fishkin, ed., *A Historical Guide to Mark Twain* (Oxford: Oxford University Press, 2002), p.56.
15 Branch, Frank and Sanderson, eds, *Mark Twain's Letters*, I 148.
16 Bush, 'Moralist in Disguise', p.57.
17 Mark Twain, *Autobiography* (New York: Harper, 1923) p.307.
18 R.Kent Rasmussen, *Mark Twain A to Z* (Oxford: Oxford University Press, 1996), p.325.
19 Mark Twain, *Travelling with the Innocents Abroad: Mark Twain's Original Reports from Europe and the Holy Land*, ed. Daniel M.Mckeithan (Norman, Oklahoma, 1958), p.310.

Bible in this book are often irreverent, especially in the original version, which was toned down to avoid causing offence. He famously sheds tears at the tomb of 'poor old Adam',[20] but he is at times sharply critical of what Paine termed 'mental lying' on the part of his fellow-pilgrims, who refuse to see what is before them, inventing a 'Presbyterian Palestine' which bears no relation to the realities of the Middle East.[21] Some of the journal entries he wrote at the time are even more outspoken, referring to the people of the region 'in the Bible' as 'just as they are now – ignorant, depraved, superstitious, dirty, lousy, thieving vagabonds':

> Seen afar off – as far as from America to the Holy Land – the ancient children of Israel seem almost too lovely & too holy for this coarse earth; but seen face to face, in their legitimate descendants, with no hope of distance to soften their features & no glamour of Sabbath school glory to beautify them, they are like any other savages.[22]

Writing in his journal rather than for the public, he can be savagely subversive of the conventional pieties.

Courtship and marriage to the Congregational Olivia Langdon, however, brought another phase in Twain's theological development, as he briefly 'reinvented himself as a Christian husband and parishioner'.[23] *The Love Letters of Mark Twain* show him dutifully reading the Bible under her instruction though his remarks show him refusing to accept the Genesis account as literal: the six days, he insists, 'must be six immensely long periods', given the complexities of the processes involved.[24] 'Religion seems far away and well nigh unattainable', he wrote to her at the end of 1868. But he studied 'the Testament every night', reading 'anything that touches upon religion that comes my way' even though it often left him cold.[25] Twain soon had to admit to his wife that their daily chapter of Bible reading was 'making me a hypocrite. I don't believe in this Bible'.[26] They continued nevertheless to rent a pew at the Asylum Hill Congregational Church at Hartford from the time they moved there in 1871 until they left twenty years later. This exposed Twain to the very liberal brand of Protestantism promoted by products of Yale Divinity School such as Horace Bushnell and the Beecher family. Henry Ward Beecher, for example, in *Evolution and Religion* (1885), one of many contemporary attempts to reconcile Genesis and science in which Twain took a great interest, dismissed the doctrine of 'the fall of Adam' (with more bravado than accuracy) as 'a bastard belief of the

---

20   *Ibid.*, p.273.
21   Ensor, *Mark Twain and the Bible*, pp.25-6.
22   Frederick Anderson, Michael B.Frank and Kenneth M. Sanderson, eds, *Mark Twain's Notebooks and Journals*, 3 vols (Berkeley, LA: University of California Press, 1975), I 424-5.
23   Bush, 'Moralist in Disguise', p.61.
24   Dixon Wecter, ed., *The Love Letters of Mark Twain* (New York: Harper, 1949), pp.133-4.
25   Branch, Frank and Sanderson, eds, *Mark Twain's Letters*, I 363-4.
26   Paine, *Mark Twain*, I 411.

Jews'.[27] Jewish theologians, as Paul Carter points out, citing a contemporary reform rabbi, Isaac Wise, were more likely to insist that 'the fate of humanity was not decided in some long-lost Eden' but that man was 'free to do good and overcome his original depravity'.[28] Nevertheless, the liberal Congregationalism to which Twain was exposed at this time had clearly travelled a long way from Calvinism. By the mid-nineteenth-century most New England theological schools, where the ministers of Hartford, including Twain's close friend Joseph Twichell, had been trained, had accepted the findings of Higher Criticism.[29] Kenneth Andrews suggests Twain may have gone 'further than most in his rejection [of Calvinism], but he was on the same road'.[30]

One book which appears to have deepened and broadened Twain's understanding of religion was a six-volume commentary entitled *The Bible for Young People* originally written by three Dutch scholars in the 1870s. It is mentioned in Twain's notebook for August to October 1878, when he sent a copy of the American edition (entitled *The Bible for Learners*) to his brother Orion, who was writing 'a refutation of the Old and New Testaments'.[31] The Preface to the volumes dealing with the Old Testament (the responsibility of Dr.H.Oort, Professor of Oriental Languages at the University of Amsterdam) explains that the Bible is 'a mine of gold' in which some parts are 'priceless' but others failed to give 'a pure reflection of God's being and God's will'. For 'the writers of the books of the Bible were men— constantly going astray...in their search for the way to God'. There were also plenty of 'legends' and 'myths' which had to be read as such, as literary 'vehicles for religious truths' rather than literally and historically accurate.[32]

Chapter two, entitled 'Paradise' exemplifies Oort's critical approach. Having explained the documentary hypothesis, that this account was 'not written by one man' but 'put together from works of very different date', he proceeds to acknowledge that 'the idea of the woman being made out of a rib of the man strikes us as almost ludicrous' but 'the people of antiquity' clothed their thoughts 'in tangible forms'. He adds, in a passage which would find many an echo in Twain's writing, 'Each of us has lived in a paradise like this; for as long as we were children we were ignorant, and, therefore, innocent'. Maturity, however, as Genesis taught, involved growing up morally, learning about good and evil.[33] The following chapter, entitled 'Paradise Lost', launches a severe attack on the way 'the teachers of the Christian church have run up a whole block of doctrinal edifices on the basis of this story', in particular the doctrine of 'original sin'. Yet 'not a word of all this is to be found in our story'.

---

27 Quoted in Paul Carter, *The Spiritual Crisis of the Gilded Age* (DeKalb: Northern Illinois University Press, 1971), p.47.

28 *Ibid.*

29 Ferenc Morton Szasz, *The Divided Mind of Protestant America, 1880-1930* (Alabama: University of Alabama Press, 1982), p.18.

30 Kenneth R.Andrews, *Nook Farm: Mark Twain's Hartford Circle* (Seattle: University of Washington Press, 1969), p.57.

31 Anderson, Frank and Sanderson, eds, *Mark Twain's Notebooks and Journals*, II 209

32 H.Oort, I.Hooykaas and A.Kuenan, *The Bible for Young People*, trans. Philip H.Wicksteed, 6 vols (London: Williams and Norgate, 1873-1879), I 2-5.

33 *Ibid.*, pp.52-7.

For a start, he insists, in arguments which will also find expression in Twain, 'the first human beings...were not perfect, since they did not even know the difference between good and evil'. There is also no devil in the biblical account, only a serpent. Finally, 'Nothing is said of a fall, but only of a progress'. Although 'innocence' might be a 'happier' state than 'moral knowledge', Oort insists, it is morally and theologically 'lower'.[34]

Oort, like Twain, has a number of criticisms to make of the character of Yahweh in this part of Genesis:

> We cannot conceal the fact that the serpent, when speaking to the woman, tells nothing but the truth. Yahweh had really deceived the man and the woman when he threatened them with death if they ate of the tree of knowledge. Not death, but the gift of distinguishing evil from good, by which they were made like to God, was the result of their tasting this fruit.[35]

The 'whole conduct of Yahweh' in the story of the flood, in which He repents that He had made man and therefore destroys him, appears to Oort full of 'unedifying anthropomorphism'. It may be the case that when men forget about God, their structures are swept away but this kind of destruction is not something which a loving God would willingly bring about.[36] The similarities between these arguments and those to be found in Twain (to be considered shortly) suggest that this commentary helped significantly to shape his attitudes to the early chapters of Genesis, which should not be regarded as the ramblings of a bitter old man but rather as the result of quite wide reading and reflection.

That Twain's private theological views were distinctly unorthodox is apparent in a document dating from the early 1870s which contrasts the 'God of the Bible' with the 'God of the Present Day' (as revealed by science). The main difference is in scale. The biblical God, according to Twain, exercised 'his sole solicitude' over 'a handful of truculent nomads':

> He worried and fretted over them in a peculiarly and distractingly human way. One day he coaxed and petted them beyond their due, the next he harried and lashed them beyond their deserts. He sulked, he cursed, he raged, he grieved, according to his mood and the circumstances, but all to no purpose; his efforts were all vain, he could not govern them.

He was also unfair, particularly in the case of Adam, whom he commanded (to continue Twain's lower-case irreverence towards this anthropomorphic figure) 'not to eat of the tree of the knowledge of good and evil'. For Twain, disobedience of this command 'could not be a sin, because Adam could not comprehend a sin *until* the eating the fruit should reveal to him the difference between right and wrong'.[37]

Twain, like Oort, is altogether unimpressed by the cavalier fashion in which the God of the Bible decides to drown his creation. To trust this God, Twain argues, 'is to trust an irascible, vindictive, fierce, and ever fickle and changeful master' whereas to

---

34 *Ibid.*, pp.60-3.
35 *Ibid.*, pp.65-6.
36 *Ibid.*, pp.94-8.
37 Baetzhold and McCullough, eds, *Bible According to Mark Twain*, p.315.

trust the true God revealed by science 'is to trust a Being...whose beneficent, exact, and changeless ordering of the...universe is proof that he is at least steadfast to his purposes'.[38]

'Three Statements of the Eighties' express Twain's continuing critique of the Bible. The first begins by acknowledging that 'the Old and New Testaments were imagined and written by man' and are therefore riddled with human errors. The second recognises that the kind of religion preached at Hartford,

> latter-day Protestantism, by selecting the humaner passages of the Bible, and preaching them to the world, whilst allowing those of a different sort to lie dormant, has produced the highest and purest and best individuals which modern society has known. Thus used, the Bible is the most valuable of books.

The third repeats his belief not only that the Bible was not 'written by God, but was not even written by remarkably capable *men*'.[39] Twain's notebooks from this period contain even more unorthodox entries on how 'unhappy' God must be at seeing his creatures suffering 'unspeakable miseries', how the notion of 'special providence... nauseates me' and how the doctrine of the Trinity involves a 'curious combination of thug, theological student, & and spectre'.[40] As in his earlier journals Twain allows himself in these notebooks to express a frustration with Christian orthodoxy which he would have been unable to voice in public.

Twain's critical attitude to the Bible also emerges in an equally unpublishable essay entitled 'Bible Teaching and Religious Practice' written in 1890. Here he likens the Bible to 'a drug store. Its contents remain the same; but the medical practice changes'. Treatment in the past had been heavy-handed:

> The dull and ignorant physician day and night, and all the days and all the nights, drenched his patient with vast and hideous doses of the most repulsive drugs to be found in the store's stock; he bled him, cupped him, purged him, puked him, salivated him, never gave his system a chance to rally, nor nature a chance to help. He kept him religion sick for eighteen centuries, and allowed him not a well day during all that time.

The stock itself, Twain estimates, comprises 'about equal portions of baleful and debilitating poisons, and healing and comforting medicines'. Only recently, however, has the patient begun to revolt against the system, restricting the power of the church to act as the 'infallible expounder of his Bible' and limiting the amount of medicine he would swallow. The world, Twain claims, has thus 'corrected the Bible', forcing the physicians (the clergy) to follow suit.[41] It is an allegory that encapsulates his continuing attempt to salvage what he believed still of value in the Bible.

Twain's views darkened considerably in the 1890s as his personal life began to unravel. Up to the 1880s, as Hamlin Hill admits, everything he touched seemed to

---

38 *Ibid.*, pp.316-7.
39 Mark Twain, *What is Man? And Other Philosophical Writings*, ed. Paul Baender (Berkeley: University of California Press, 1973), pp.56-8.
40 Anderson, Frank and Sanderson, eds, *Mark Twain's Notebooks*, III 149, 246 and 411.
41 *Ibid.*, pp.71-5.

turn to gold,[42] but financial and personal problems mounted in the 1890s culminating in the illness of his wife and the death of his daughter Susie from spinal meningitis in 1896. Twain's comments on God, religion and the Bible from this point on take on a Job-like rage, a blasphemous intensity which can still be recognised as the product of a genuinely religious temperament but finds expression in savage notebook comments such as one attacking the whole concept of the atonement, in which he could see 'nothing rational', only an 'anger against Adam' which has grown 'so uncontrollable...that nothing but a sacrifice of life can appease it'.[43] It is God, rather than Adam, Twain writes in another indignant entry, who should 'recognize in Himself the Author and Inventor of Sin'.[44] Twain continues to have little time for the God of the Old Testament, who is 'jealous, trivial, ignorant, revengeful', unlike the 'real' God of science, 'the One who created this majestic universe'.[45] Later entries refer to the Old and New Testament respectively as 'the Jekyll and Hyde of sacred romance'.[46] Adam meanwhile can be seen as 'man's benefactor' for giving him 'all he has ever received that was worth having— Death'.[47] These comments, of course, should not be taken literally but serve as a vehicle for letting off steam, venting his suppressed anger at the smug pieties of the conventional.

Twain's most sustained attack on the way in which conventional Christianity had closed some of these questions came in the passages he dictated for his autobiography in 1906, passages which he knew would get his heirs 'burnt alive if they venture to print it this side of 2006 A.D'. But, he told William Howells, 'I got them out of my system, where they had been festering for years'.[48] They would find their first publication as 'Reflections on Religion' in the *Hudson Review* in 1964.[49] Passages relating to the God and the Bible have also been reprinted as an appendix to *The Bible According to Mark Twain*. One of these continues Twain's critique of the character of God as represented in the Bible: 'He is always punishing— punishing trifling misdeeds with thousandfold severity'. The worst example of God's 'inexcusable treachery' for Twain occurs in the opening chapters of Genesis:

> That beginning must have been invented in a pirate's nursery, it is so malign and childish. To Adam is forbidden the fruit of a certain tree— and he is gravely informed that if he disobeys he shall die. How could that be expected to impress Adam?...in knowledge and experience he was in no way the superior of a baby of two years of age; he could have no idea of what the word death meant; he had never heard of a dead thing before.

Yet, according to the doctrine of the Fall, not only Adam but his descendants were then punished for this supposed 'trespass':

---

42 Hill, *Mark Twain*, p.xviii.
43 A.B.Paine, ed. *Mark Twain's Notebook* (New York: Harper, 1935), p.290.
44 *Ibid.*, p.,301.
45 *Ibid.*, pp. 360-1.
46 *Ibid.*, p.392.
47 *Ibid.*, p.381.
48 Baetzhold and McCullough, eds, *Bible According to Mark Twain*, p.318.
49 Mark Twain, 'Reflections on Religion', ed. Charles Neider, *Hudson Review* 16 (1963-4) 332-52.

> For thousands and thousands of years, his posterity, individual by individual, has been unceasingly hunted and harried with afflictions in punishment of the juvenile misdemeanour which is grandiloquently called Adam's sin. And during all that vast lapse of time, there has been no lack of rabbins and popes and priests and parsons and lay slaves eager to applaud this infamy....[50]

Twain's contempt for this teaching, like Henry Ward Beecher's, makes no distinction here between Judaism and Christianity, although it is only the latter, most famously through St. Augustine, which developed the full-blooded doctrine of original sin.

These dictated passages continue to accuse the Bible of 'an almost pathetic poverty of invention',[51] to mock the notion of its God 'making pets' of 'a thimbleful of Jew microbes',[52] and to discount the possibility that this God has human qualities, that he cares for individuals, listens to their prayers, given that he allows so much pain, misery and disease to enter the world.[53] It is possible to see in some of these outbursts the influence of thinkers such as Thomas Paine and W.E.H.Lecky. Baetzhold and McCullough point out, for example, that chapters 13 to 15 of Paine's *Age of Reason* include similar contrasts between the God of the Bible and the 'real' God.[54] Brodwin finds in Twain's copy of Lecky's *History of European Morals* two underscored passages on the Fall and its alleged consequences:

> The [philosophers] taught that death is a law and not a punishment; the [fathers] taught that it is a penal affliction introduced on account of the sin of Adam, which was also the cause...of all convulsions in the material globe...the first [the philosophers] represented man as pure until his will had sinned; the second [the fathers] represented him as under a sentence of condemnation at the very moment of his birth.[55]

It is often difficult, of course, to attribute 'influence' this precisely but it is important to notice how widely Twain read, to see through his own projected mask as a man of no education, an innocent.

Many of Twain's novels, it should be noted, also raise questions about the opening chapters of Genesis. The whole point of *The Adventures of Tom Sawyer* (1876), as of *Huckleberry Finn* (1885), is that the boys possess a natural innocence which the hypocritical adults attempt to stamp out. This emerges explicitly in some of the maxims of *Pudd'nhead Wilson* which serve as epigraphs to the early chapters of that novel of 1894. These probe the biblical text in characteristically idiosyncratic ways, for instance in chapter 2:

---

50 Baetzhold and McCullough, eds, *Bible According to Mark Twain*, pp.319-20.
51 *Ibid.*, p.322.
52 *Ibid.*, p.323.
53 *Ibid.*, pp.323-8.
54 *Ibid.*, p.313.
55 Brodwin, 'The Theology of Mark Twain', p.185.

Adam was but human – this explains it all. He did not want the apple for the apple's sake; he wanted it only because it was forbidden. The mistake was in not forbidding the serpent; then he would have eaten the serpent.[56]

The epigraph to chapter 3 repeats the sardonic joke that we owe 'a debt of gratitude' to Adam for bringing death into the world while that for chapter 4 reckons the 'principal' of Adam and Eve's 'many advantages' to have been that 'they escaped teething'.[57] This is the public voice of Twain, altogether less savage about the Bible than in the notebooks.

Even the public Twain, however, allows himself a little subversion of orthodoxy. *Extracts from Captain Stormfield's Visit to Heaven,* first conceived in 1868 and worked on sporadically until its eventual publication in 1909, incorporates a few sideswipes at the whole Christian concept of creation, the androcentrism, for example, in the biblical account of God having to rest after creating earth.[58] As the head clerk Peters explains to Captain Stormfield, 'People take the figurative language of the Bible... for literal', expecting harps, haloes and a welcome from the patriarchs when they arrive in heaven.[59] They find it all very different when they arrive, he warns, even in the small Christian corner of heaven where Adam can still draw a crowd (even he, however, 'has to walk behind Shakespeare', a clear indication of the superiority of writers to patriarchs).[60]

Twain's publications in the last decade of his life became increasingly outspoken in their critique of Christianity. *What is Man?*, published anonymously in 1906, takes its title, of course, from the Psalms (8:4) though one suspects that Twain, like Job, finds it genuinely difficult to believe that God does 'magnify' man (Job 7:17). The book takes the form of a dialogue between a believing Young Man and a sceptical Old Man, who argues that everything is predetermined by scientific laws. In some of the drafts of the book dating from around 1898, in which the interlocutors are given numbers rather than names, Twain pursues the possibility that the Fall may have been 'upwards', exemplifying moral progress rather than a calamitous decline. No.1 asks whether God 'holds in dearer affection and approval the animal that lacks the Moral Sense than the animal that has it', given that Adam and Eve began 'pure and sinless, like the beasts and the angels', but then fell. No.2 replies that the word 'fell' does not 'mean that they fell to a lower moral estate; it merely means that they fell from His grace and approval'. No. 1 presses him finally to decide which way the pair went, up or down, forcing him to acknowledge that by acquiring 'the Moral Sense' they 'rose to an estate which was higher and better than their former one'. For No.1 this means that 'they fell up'. The problem was that this caused God to be 'so angered that He punished them calamitously— and their whole race after them'.[61]

---

56 Mark Twain, *Pudd'nhead Wilson*, ed. Malcolm Bradbury (Harmondsworth: Penguin, 1969), p.61.

57 *Ibid.,* pp.69 and 75.

58 Ray Browne, ed., *Mark Twain's Quarrel with Heaven* (New Haven: College and University Press, 1970), p.16.

59 *Ibid.*, pp.65-6.

60 *Ibid.*, pp.80 and 84.

61 Twain, *What is Man?*, pp. 470-1.

The argument is repeated in another draft fragment in which the disputants have now acquired names. The Old Man asks if Adam 'was a good man', to which the Young man replies that 'he was not merely good, up to the Fall, he was perfect—absolutely perfect; and could have remained so if he and Eve had listened to God their friend instead of to Satan their enemy'. The Old Man then presses the question further, whether 'God wanted to have him remain as he was?—preferred him so', to which the Young Man replies, 'Infinitely. He loved him, He walked and talked with him; when he fell He drove him from the Garden and turned his back on him.' Having forced his young opponent to admit that God preferred Adam without the Moral Sense, the Old Man concludes after all that 'he didn't rise, but fell'.[62]

In yet another fragment the Old Man again presses the Young Man to admit that God did not want Adam and Eve to 'eat of the fruit of the tree of knowledge and find out the difference between good and evil'. He asks whether God 'knew they would disobey' and that 'they would be tempted by the serpent and that they would yield'. In that case, could He not, for example, 'have cut the tree down or removed it to a straight place in heaven'. 'All things are possible with God', replies the pious Young Man, to which the Old Man retorts, 'Except square dealing, apparently. And common consistency'. For him God's behaviour seems grossly unfair:

> He created a weak Adam when He could have created a strong one, then laid a trap for him which He foreknew he would fall into. Then He punished him when He was solely responsible for Adam's crime Himself.[63]

The remorseless logic of the Old Man, on to whom Twain seems to have projected his own rationalist tendencies, once again triumphs over the rather feeble arguments of the orthodox youth.

One particularly interesting note included among the supplements to *What is Man?* refers to *The Woman's Bible* (1895), a feminist commentary on the women in the Bible, edited by Elizabeth Cady Stanton. Here Twain appears to chastise himself for too quickly subjecting the project to satire:

> We laughed at Elizabeth Cady Stanton when she devoted her noble spirit and applied her fine powers to quite as valuable a work as the founding of a religion; after that, whom shall we revere and what new thing shall we respect?[64]

Stanton herself observes of Eve that the 'unprejudiced reader must be impressed with the courage, the dignity, and the lofty ambition of the woman'. The serpent, Stanton notes, must have valued her 'high character', for he 'did not try to tempt her from the path of duty by brilliant jewels, rich dresses, worldly luxuries or pleasures, but with the promise of knowledge', which she clearly preferred to 'picking flowers and talking with Adam'. Stanton proceeds to deplore 'the curse pronounced on woman', which was 'inserted in an unfriendly spirit to justify her degradation and subjection to man', and to laugh at the way Adam 'whines' to God about Eve giving him the

---

62 *Ibid.*, pp.473-4.
63 *Ibid.*, p.491.
64 *Ibid.*, p.517.

apple, 'trying to shield himself at his wife's expense'.[65] Stanton's comments here may well have served as a model for the way in which Twain himself would re-tell this particular story in the Adamic Diaries (those parts of them at least that were written after 1895).

Three other late works by Twain return more or less directly to the question of Adam and his supposed Fall. 'A Monument to Adam' of 1905 recounts the story of what had been an ongoing joke for Twain, the plan to erect a monument to the Father of the Human Race, a project which first surfaced in 1879 when he drafted a deliberately florid petition for such a monument which was actually signed by 94 of the leading citizens of Elmira before being withdrawn.[66] He had also written to the *New York Times* in February 1883 to suggest that the statue of liberty then being built might be more appropriately dedicated to Adam.[67] In May of that year he delivered a speech 'On Adam' in Montreal attributing to him the invention of sin.[68] An article on the subject for *Harper's Weekly* in 1905 envisaged such a monument as a tribute to Eve as well, 'a token of her loyalty to him in this dark day of his humiliation when his older children were doubting him and deserting him' for the theory of evolution.[69] 'Refuge of the Derelicts', an unfinished novel written in 1905, fictionalises the project as the brainchild of a poet George Sterling who tries to persuade an Admiral and his motley house-guests (the derelicts themselves) of the justice of such an attribute to the first human being. The derelicts are not initially in favour: '*He brought life into the world*', exclaims one, 'I hate him'.[70] Even the Admiral ranks him only with 'the minor sacred characters' but George defends his hero stoutly: 'How was he going to know what "surely die" meant? *Die!* He hadn't ever struck that word before; he hadn't even seen a dead creature'.[71] The admiral admits that he is impressed with Adam's ability to find names for all the animals and also with the way he and Eve wandered around 'naked and unashamed': 'They had the right kind of modesty, to my mind— the kind that ain't aware of itself'.[72] So the project is unanimously carried (though the novel itself was never finished).

The latest reference to Adam in Twain's work occurs in 'The Turning Point of My Life', published in *Harper's Bazar* in 1910 as part of a series of essays on this subject. Twain characteristically goes all the way back to the beginning, to the Garden of Eden for 'the real turning point of my life (and of yours)': 'It was there that the first link of the chain was forged that was ultimately to lead to the emptying of me

---

65 Elizabeth Cady Stanton, ed., *The Woman's Bible* (Amherst, N.Y.: Prometheus Books, [1895] 1999), pp.24-7.

66 See Howard G.Baetzhold, 'Monument to Adam, A', in J.R. LeMaster and James D.Wilson, ed., *The Mark Twain Encyclopedia* (New York: Garland, 1993) p.522 and the relevant documents in John S.Tuckey, ed., *Mark Twain's Fables of Man* (Berkeley: University of California Press, 1972), pp.449-52.

67 Anderson, Frank and Sanderson, ed., *Mark Twain's Notebooks*, III 13.

68 *Ibid.*, p.15. See *Mark Twain's Speeches*, ed. Albert Bigelow Paine (New York: Harper and Brothers, 1923), pp.93-7.

69 Mark Twain, *The Diary of Adam and Eve* (London: Hesperus Press, 2002), p.90.

70 Tuckey, ed., *Mark Twain's Fables of Man*, p.201.

71 *Ibid.*, pp.208-9.

72 *Ibid.*, p.220.

into the literary guild'. On one level, of course, this is quite literally true: much of Twain's writing can be seen as a direct response to the opening chapters of Genesis. But he also proceeds to locate Adam in a deterministic framework which sees all actions, including that of the first man, as the result of unchangeable circumstance and temperament:

> Adam's *temperament* was the first command of the Deity ever issued to a human being on this planet. And it was the only command Adam would *never* be able to disobey. It said, 'Be weak, be water, be characterless, be cheaply persuadable.' The later command, to let the fruit alone, was certain to be disobeyed. Not by Adam himself, but by his *temperament*— which he did not create and had no authority over.

There is no point therefore in lamenting that those first two human creatures were 'afflicted with temperaments made out of butter' or wishing that Martin Luther and Joan of Arc had been in their place ('By neither sugary persuasions nor by hellfire could Satan have beguiled *them* to eat the apple'). For there would then have been 'no human race' (and no Mark Twain).[73]

Even without his more sustained reworkings of the story of Adam and Eve to be considered in the following section, it would be fair to conclude that Twain was obsessed with the figure of Adam, the unfairness of God's treatment of him and the faulty logic of the doctrine of the Fall. The comments I have extracted so far from journals, notebooks, books and manuscripts, however, are random responses to questions provoked by the early chapters of the Book of Genesis. The texts I want now to explore, although just as critical of orthodoxy, provide a more coherent rewriting of the biblical text.

The Diaries of Adam and Eve and *Letters from the Earth*

Adapted as they are to a readership expecting 'vintage, funny "Mark Twain"', *The Diaries of Adam and Eve* have been seen to lack both the 'complexity and pathos' of Twain's later writing on the topic, and the pointed satire of *Letters from the Earth* and *The Mysterious Stranger*.[74] Stanley Brodwin calls them 'sophisticated folktales':

> They serve not only as seemingly naïve (or radically innocent) commentaries on one of the most influential stories in Western literature and religion, but also supply an imaginatively instructive alternative...to the Sunday school Bible images that Twain had rejected.[75]

There is an appropriateness, in other words, in Twain's choice of genre here, matching the original folktales of the early chapters of Genesis with his own.

'Extracts from Adam's Diary' first appeared as part of *The Niagara Book*, a souvenir of the Buffalo World Fair of 1893. Unsuccessful in placing his original text elsewhere, Twain deliberately added material relating to Niagara Falls (which, of

---

73 Twain, *What is Man?*, p.464.
74 William Macnaughton, *Mark Twain's Last Years as a Writer* (Columbia: University of Missouri Press, 1979), p.219.
75 Stanley Brodwin, 'Extracts from Adam's Diary', *Mark Twain Encyclopedia*, p.274.

course, contains a fortuitous pun on the central theme of the diary). The 'Extracts' have a complex textual history, reappearing as a separate work (complete with Strothman's illustrations) in 1904 and together with 'Eve's Diary' as *The Private Lives of Adam and Eve* in 1931. Neither of these editions, however, incorporated the revisions Twain had made in 1893 so it was not until 1995, in *The Bible According to Mark Twain*, that 'Adam's Diary' appeared in the form Twain wanted.[76] Even the Oxford edition of *The Diaries of Adam and Eve* of 1996 and the Hesperus Press *Diary of Adam and Eve* of 2002 reprint the Niagara version.

This version of Adam's Diary, as well as having frequent references to the Falls,[77] attributes the Fall not to the eating of an apple but the making of an 'old chestnut', a 'mouldy joke' in which Adam says the Falls would be even more wonderful if the water fell upwards.[78] This has been variously construed as an act of pride (mocking the Creator's work)[79] or even a confession on Twain's part that humour was the 'sin' which prevented him from being a 'great' writer.[80] 'To attribute man's fallen condition and the source of his suffering to a bad joke', as Joseph McCullough argues, certainly 'undermines the tragic consequences of the event'.[81] But it does not work particularly well either as a theological strategy or as a joke.

Removing these elements in the Niagara version, as Twain wanted, increases the pathos of 'the first couple as innocent victims of an incomprehensible prohibition' but leaves the 'Extracts' primarily as a comedy.[82] There are plenty of gender jokes: Eve is the first to use the word 'we' (thus inventing relationships), the first to cry (in Adam's defamiliarising words, to 'shed water out of the holes it looks with') and also, as Adam complains, she 'is always talking'.[83] He is later relieved to report that she 'has taken up with a snake' (even though this illustrates her over-trusting nature) because the snake talks back 'and this enables me to get a rest'.[84] The jokes are not merely misogynistic, however: Eve is shown to have more initiative than Adam (he finds her 'trying to clod apples out of that forbidden tree'[85]) and more intellectual curiosity. According to Adam,

> She engages herself in many foolish things— among others to study out why the animals called lions and tigers live on grass and flowers, when as she says, the sort of teeth they wear would indicate that they were intended to eat each other.

---

76 Baetzhold and McCullough, pp.4-7.
77 Twain, *Diary of Adam and Eve*, pp.3-4.
78 *Ibid.*, p.12.
79 Joseph B.McCullough, 'Mark Twain's First Chestnut: Revisions in "Extracts from Adam's Diary"', *Essays in Arts and Sciences* 23 (1994) pp.49-58 (p.54).
80 Laura E.Skandera-Trombley, 'Afterword', in Mark Twain, *The Diaries of Adam and Eve*, ed. Shelley Fisher Fishkin (Oxford: Oxford University Press, 1996), p.5.
81 McCullough, 'Mark Twain's First Chestnut', p.56.
82 *Ibid.*, p.55.
83 Twain, *Diary of Adam and Eve*, p.5.
84 *Ibid.*, p.10.
85 *Ibid.*, p.7.

'That is foolish', Adam insists, 'because to do that would be to kill each other' and introduce 'death' into the Park.[86] Twain apparently told a friend that he had been reading commentaries on Genesis, one of which claimed that 'the meat-eating animals on the ark became vegetarians during the voyage', conjuring up the image in his mind of a Barbary lion calling on Noah to bring him a bale of hay.[87] There is a serious point, however, behind the carnivorous teeth of the lions, which clearly suggest that the Fall was predetermined. Later, when Adam hears 'a tempest of frightful noises' and sees that 'every beast was destroying its neighbour', he realises that Eve's observations were well founded, that death has indeed 'come into the world'.[88] He has no qualms about eating the apple himself, not out of any great Miltonic magnanimity but because he was 'so hungry. It was against my principles, but I find that principles have no real force except when one is well fed'.[89] Twain again subverts the high-minded tragedy conventionally associated with the Fall, making Adam the unwitting advocate of a materialist position. It is also apparent that Adam finds it hard to attach so much importance to the eating of a piece of fruit.

The gender differences continue after the Fall with the stuffy and rather pompous Adam objecting to the way in which the postlapsarian Eve 'tittered and blushed', which he finds 'unbecoming and idiotic'.[90] He proceeds to express complete bafflement over Cain, whom he first sees as a kind of fish, then as 'some kind of a bug', then as a kangaroo or possibly even a bear. He continues for ten years to puzzle over 'this unclassifiable zoological freak' but does eventually come to recognise the merits of his partner, acknowledging that 'it is better to live outside the Garden with her than inside without her'.[91] Human companionship is made to outweigh theological correctness. This 'message' having been acknowledged, it must also be admitted that what satire there is in this first diary is very mild, executed in what Twain called 'a kind of friendly and respectful way that will commend him [Adam] to the Sunday schools'.[92] Most of the key action takes place off stage (the command, the temptation, even the Fall itself) while God remains respectfully invisible. Reading between the lines, it is possible to see that Adam at least (if not Eve) has improved as a result of his Fall. But Twain's contemporaries could hardly take offence at what was written in so unprovocative a manner.

The same could be said of 'Eve's Diary', written for the Christmas issue of *Harper's Magazine* in 1905, the year Twain's wife Olivia died. It was reprinted the following year with line-drawings by Ralph Lester. At least one library, however, withdrew the book from its shelves because of the nudity depicted, which may have been 'a trap for the committees of decency', since 'to denounce nudity in *Eve's Diary* was to contradict the Bible'.[93] In the text Eve tells the story of her encounters

---

86   *Ibid.*, p.8.
87   Ensor, *Mark Twain and the Bible*, p.115, n.48.
88   Twain, *Diary of Adam and Eve*, p.10.
89   *Ibid.*, p.11.
90   *Ibid.*, p.11.
91   *Ibid.*, p.15-18.
92   Branch, Frank and Sanderson, eds, *Mark Twain's Letters*, II 591-2.
93   Skandera-Trombley, 'Afterword', pp.6 and 24.

with Adam both before and after the Fall. The gender jokes of the first diary continue with Eve wanting to tidy everything up, including the landscape. She also makes a somewhat garrulous and gushing narrator, insisting that 'the core and centre of my nature is love of the beautiful'.[94] This is partly to excuse her hankering after stars to put in her hair, tiger-skins to wear, and butterflies for 'wreaths and garlands'.[95] To begin with, she is quite critical of Adam, 'the other Experiment', who likes resting, 'has low tastes and is not kind'.[96] When he admires her, however, she finds it 'very agreeable' and when he tries to avoid her, she feels her 'first sorrow'. She also notices that 'He talks very little. Perhaps it is because he is not bright, and is sensitive about it'.[97] Eve spends her time admiring her reflection in the water while Adam fishes. It is Eve who invents religion, coming to the conclusion that she was made 'to search out the secrets of this wonderful world and be happy and thank the Giver of it all for devising it'. Even after the Fall she does not seem to suffer much, consoling herself for the loss of her garden with an increased closeness to Adam: 'I have found *him*, and am content. He loves me as well as he can; I love him with all the strength of my passionate nature'.[98] The final line, supposedly written by Adam beside Eve's grave, underlines the fact that he too has learned to love: 'Wherever she was, *there* was Eden'.[99] The theological point, softened by sentiment as it is, appears, as in some of the fragments of *What is Man?*, to be that Adam and Eve have risen, have matured morally and emotionally, as a result of the supposed Fall.

'Eve Speaks', written in the early 1900s but not published until 1923, adopts an entirely different tone, displaying more of the private, less acceptable side of Twain's thinking. It opens three months after the Fall with Eve still burning with indignation at her treatment:

> They drove us from the Garden with their swords of flame, the fierce cherubim. And what had we done? We meant no harm. We were ignorant and did as other children might do. We could not know it was wrong to disobey the command, for the words were strange to us and we did not understand them.

Eve repeats the arguments to be found elsewhere in Twain that without the Moral Sense it was impossible for them to know right from wrong and therefore unfair for God to punish them. She is also scathing about the 'knowledge' the fruit of the tree has gained for them:

> We were ignorant then; we are rich in learning, now— ah, how rich! We know hunger, thirst, and cold; we know pain, disease, and grief; we know hate, rebellion, and deceit; we know remorse, the conscience that prosecutes guilt and innocence alike, making no distinction; we know weariness of body and spirit, the unrefreshing sleep, the rest which rests not, the dreams which restore Eden and banish it again with the waking; we know misery; we know torture....

---

94 Twain, *Diary of Adam and Eve*, p.22.
95 *Ibid.*, pp.22-3 and 29.
96 *Ibid.*, pp.23-4.
97 *Ibid.*, pp.26-7.
98 *Ibid.*, pp.37-8.
99 *Ibid.*, pp.39-40.

This ironic list of benefits reaches an apparent climax in 'the rich product of the Moral Sense', with which she wishes 'we could degrade the animals'.[100] The remainder of 'Eve Speaks' dramatises her discovery of the meaning of death. At first she thinks Abel is merely sleeping but finally grasps the fact that she will never be able to wake him, that this is the 'death' which is their punishment for eating the forbidden fruit. The final irony, however, is left to Satan, who observes sardonically, 'The Family think ill of death' but 'will change their minds'.[101]

The longest of the Adamic papers is 'Eve's Autobiography', which Twain began writing in 1901 or 1902. The manuscript originally numbered some 98 pages with Eve as narrator throughout but Twain then decided to recast the material, assigning some of it to different narrators.[102] Some of this material was included by DeVoto in 'Papers of the Adam Family' in *Letters from the Earth* when that was published in 1962 but the fullest version can be found in *The Bible According to Mark Twain*. It is supposedly written by Eve around the year 900 AC (After Creation) as she rereads her old diaries and worries about the approaching Flood. Quite how carefully Twain studied the biblical text while writing it is apparent from the extensive planning notes which he wrote on the back of page 41 of the manuscript. These are reprinted in the notes to *The Bible According to Mark Twain* (although the fact that the editors refer to 'items 9 and 16' serves almost to conceal the allusion here to the verse numbers of Chapter 2 of the Book of Genesis).[103]

Twain's notes begin with 'a line squeezed in above the original first line': 'II 10 Before Eve's birth— forenoon, Jan.1', which shows him working hard on the chronology of the story. He notes from verse 15 that 'Adam is to "dress the garden & keep it"— but he doesn't fatigue himself'. Then come a series of notes from other verses in Genesis chapter 2:

9. Tree of life & knowledge

16. The Prohibition.

17. Shalt die

19. Naming the things.— Before Eve's birth

'But for Adam (the others had mates)

This last quotation is not closed in the manuscript presumably because what begins as a quotation from verse 20 ('but for Adam there was not found an help meet for him') becomes a summary in Twain's own words. Twain then moves on to chapter 3, 'In the Garden', where he has Eve say 'What is die?', presumably adding his own dialogue to verse 3, in which she summarises for the serpent's benefit God's

---

100 *Ibid.*, pp.73-4.
101 *Ibid.*, pp.75-6.
102 Howard G.Baetzhold, Joseph B.McCullough and Donald Malcolm, 'Mark Twain's Eden/Flood Parable: "The Autobiography of Eve"', *American Literary Realism* 24 (1991), pp.23-38 (p.24).
103 Baetzhold and McCullough, *Bible According to Mark Twain*, p.337.

command that they must not eat of 'the fruit of the tree which is in the midst of the garden...lest ye die'. Twain then turns his attention to the command 'Be fruitful' (Gen. 1:28) and to the phrase 'as the gods', which is part of the serpent's argument that 'God doth know that in the day ye eat thereof...ye shall be as gods' (3:5). The rest of the notes develop Twain's own ideas, for instance that Adam kept a diary but it was 'not reliable' and he 'couldn't spell'.[104] Twain's development of the story, it is worth noticing, like that of the rabbis, begins with close analysis of the original text before proceeding to supplement its narrative with his own.

'Eve's Autobiography', the final product of all this planning, begins with an older, sadder Eve re-reading the diary entries she wrote immediately after creation. The first entry shows her asking urgent questions both about her identity and about her strange predicament: 'Who am I? What am I? Where am I?' A week later these 'questions remain unanswered' while after a fortnight, not yet having encountered Adam, she starts to register just how 'lonely' and 'tedious' her life is. She gazes longingly at her own reflection in a pool, admiring her Miltonic 'slender white body' and long 'yellow hair',[105] all of which makes her jealous of the other animals, which have mates (Twain here transferring to Eve the feelings he had attributed to Adam in his note on Genesis 2:19 cited above). She derives some pleasure from playing with the animals, whose sheer exuberance and sense of fun make her 'laugh till the tears come'. She also occupies herself classifying the observable flora and fauna and continuing to ask questions about who she is and why she was created.[106]

These original diary entries are interrupted at this point by the older, sadder and wiser Eve recalling 'the splendid enthusiasm of youth' with some nostalgia.[107] The pattern for the whole autobiography is now established, with details of the young Eve's early adventures in the 'enchanted valley' of Eden interspersed with the older Eve's mournful reflections, for instance after the Fall. She recalls the day she managed to enter that valley but found no one there:

> This faded manuscript is blurred by the tears which fell upon it then, and after ten centuries I am crying over it again. Crying over it for pity of that poor child; and from this far distance it seems to be not me, but a child that I have lost— *my* child.[108]

The diaries continue into Eve's second year, when she encounters an Adam who is not only beautiful ('Curly brown hair, tumbling negligently about his shoulders— oh, *so* handsome') but unattached ('Such a bewitching boy— and all mine!').[109] Her passionate kisses, however, succeed only in frightening him away, leaving her as lonely as before. Adam meanwhile occupies himself by making 'a lot of fossils'. Eve appears to think these will help to reconcile Science and the Scriptures (a satirical

---

104 *Ibid.*

105 *Ibid.*, p.42. See the note on p.335 for the description of Eve's 'golden tresses' and 'slender waist' in *Paradise Lost* IV 304-5 and 458-9.

106 *Ibid.*, pp.44-6.

107 *Ibid.*, p.47.

108 *Ibid.*, p.49.

109 *Ibid.*, p.50. See the note on p.336 for the description of Adam's 'hyacinth locks' in *Paradise Lost* IV 301-3.

sideswipe by Twain at some of the more implausible creationist arguments, including the idea that the fossil record was designed by God at the moment of creation to make it appear that the world had been in existence for a long time).[110]

The young Eve continues in her diary to recount her oscillating but eventually successful endeavours to re-unite herself with Adam while the older postlapsarian Eve looks back with nostalgia at her idyllic life in the days before pain, disease or sorrow. There was instead the pleasure of constantly learning about the world: the older Eve recalls the scientific pride with which the young Adam formulated his Law of Fluidic Precipitation (that all water flows downhill) and her younger self discovered that lions were not designed to be vegetarians. In another extract from the young Eve's diary, however, Twain introduces the figure of God, or at least of a disembodied 'Voice' heard by Adam, who attributes it to 'the Lord of the Garden' and reports its command not to eat the fruit of the tree of the knowledge of good and evil lest we should die. The couple engage in an extended debate over the meaning of these new words: good, evil and death, concluding that the only way to discover their meaning is to eat of the fruit. Ironically, Adam is just 'reaching for the apple when a most curious creature came floundering by', distracting him and consequently postponing the Fall as the two natural scientists pursue it.[111] In Twain's version of Genesis, in other words, the Fall is at least temporarily 'postponed *because of* intellectual curiosity rather than brought about because of it'.[112]

This particular rewriting of Genesis has the children arriving before rather than after the Fall. Adam again has some difficulty in working out what they are but by year 10 Eve can report that they have nine of them, including the incongruously named Gladys and Edwina. Since the Fall has not yet occurred, they can wander around eating poisonous berries without any ill effects. Cain is particularly bright, 'really expert at making the simpler kinds of fossils'.[113] Here the manuscript 'breaks off abruptly in mid-sentence',[114] as if Twain could not bring himself to write directly about the unspoken event which looms large throughout the autobiography, the Fall itself. An attempted continuation of the narrative, much of it deleted and reassigned to other 'Diaries Antedating the Flood', appears as an appendix to *The Bible According to Mark Twain*. In this we learn that Gladys dies, victim of 'a famine reinforced by pestilence', and that Adam too 'is gone from us' as a result of scenes over which Eve wishes to draw a veil: 'they were not becoming to him'.[115] A mad prophet called Reginald Selkirk tells Eve about the catastrophes in store for the human race, including the Flood, foreknowledge of which succeeds only in sending her into despair:

---

110 *Ibid.*, pp.50-1. The note on p.336 explains that Twain would have encountered these arguments in Andrew Dickson White's *History of the Warfare of Science with Theology*.
111 *Ibid.*, p.58.
112 *Ibid.*, p.338.
113 *Ibid.*, p.62.
114 *Ibid.*, p.339.
115 *Ibid.*, pp.264-5.

> For a while my mind was thronged and oppressed with pathetic images of that coming calamity— appealing faces, imploring faces, despairing faces— multitudes upon multitudes, the rocks and crags and mountain ranges dense with them, and all bone of my bone, flesh of my flesh...I could not bear it![116]

This manuscript ends with Reginald the Mad Prophet reading an extract from a first edition of Eve's diary, which again breaks off abruptly.[117] The memories of happier past times seem too painful to continue, both for Eve herself and for Twain.

The final perspective from which Twain rewrites the early chapters of Genesis is that of Satan. As early as 1856, according to Brodwin, Twain had read and admired Milton, finding 'the greatest thing in *Paradise Lost*— the Arch-Fiend's terrible energy'.[118] His own Satan, the narrator of 'That Day in Eden', written in the early 1900s but not published until 1923, is characterised rather by his sympathy for Adam and Eve than by the ferocity of his opposition to God. His account of events surrounding the Fall begins with a lyrical description of the first couple:

> Long ago I was in the bushes near the Tree of Knowledge when the Man and Woman came there and had a conversation. I was present, now, when they came again after all these years. They were as before – mere boy and girl – trim, rounded, slender, flexible, snow images lightly flushed with the pink of the skies, innocently unconscious of their nakedness, lovely to look upon, beautiful beyond words.[119]

They are still puzzling over the words 'good', 'evil', and 'death' so Satan tries to explain these concepts along with related ideas such as 'fear' and 'pain'. 'It is impossible for you to do wrong', he explains to Eve, 'for you have no more notion of right and wrong than the other animals have'. He also cautions her against acquiring the dreaded Moral Sense: because 'it is a degradation, a disaster', having 'but one office, only one— to teach how to do wrong'. He cannot prevent Eve reaching for the apple, however, lamenting its consequences in Miltonic vein:

> Oh farewell, Eden and your sinless joys! Come poverty and pain, hunger and cold and heartbreak, bereavement, tears and shame, envy, strife, malice and dishonour, age, weariness, remorse, then desperation and the prayer for the release of death, indifferent that the gates of hell yawn beyond it.

Satan watches in horror as Adam observes the immediately visible changes in Eve (her skin loses its 'satin lustre', her hair turns grey, and wrinkles form around her eyes and mouth) but 'loyally and bravely' chooses to join her in exile.[120]

Satan becomes even more outspoken in his attack on God's injustice in *Letters from the Earth*, which was written in 1909, actually prepared for publication in 1939 (when Twain's daughter Clara refused permission), but not finally published until 1962. 'This book will never be published', Twain wrote sarcastically to a friend,

---

116 *Ibid.*, p.272.
117 *Ibid.*, p.274.
118 Brodwin, 'Humor of the Absurd', p.58.
119 Twain, *Diary of Adam and Eve*, p.65.
120 *Ibid.*, pp.66-70.

'for it has much Holy Scripture in it of the kind that…can't properly be read aloud, except from the pulpit and in family worship'.[121] As with many of these late works, it is primarily concerned to draw attention to absurd or unjust elements in the biblical text, obscured for many readers by their familiarity with it. *Letters from the Earth* begins with the creation of the universe, observed by the archangels Satan, Michael and Gabriel, who are all suitably impressed. A hundred million years pass and they observe the creation of the animals, all with their own laws, including 'the masterpiece— *Man!*' Banished from heaven 'on account of his too flexible tongue', Satan travels to the earth to 'see how the Human-Race experiment was coming along',[122] sending letters back to his fellow-archangels.

Satan's initial reports emphasise what a 'strange place' earth is, especially its inhabitants, who 'are all insane', imagining that the Creator cares for each of them and listens to their prayers, beliefs in which they are encouraged by 'salaried teachers' who tell them that God is loving, kind and merciful.[123] Satan has much fun at the expense of conventional Christianity and of the Bible, a book he describes as 'full of interest. It has noble poetry in it; and some clever fables'. Its history, however, is somewhat 'blood-drenched' and some of its morality 'execrable'. It also contains 'a wealth of obscenity; and upwards of a thousand lies'. Constructed 'mainly out of the fragments of older Bibles that had their day and crumbled to ruin', it 'noticeably lacks in originality'.[124] Satan finds the early chapters of Genesis particularly entertaining, with their absurdly anthropocentric account of God spending five days creating the Earth and 'only *one* day to make *twenty million suns and eighty million planets!*'[125]

Satan's most profound amazement, however, is reserved for the biblical account of the Fall, which he summarises satirically for the benefit of his fellow-archangels. He makes Twain's usual complaint that Adam and Eve could not possibly have understood God's warning about death before explaining why they were so open to the serpent:

The serpent said the forbidden fruit would store their vacant minds with knowledge. So they ate it, which was quite natural, for man is so made that he eagerly *wants to know*: whereas the priest, like God, whose imitator and representative he is, has made it his business from the beginning to keep him *from* knowing any useful thing.

Satan appears somewhat envious of the couple's discovery of 'the art and mystery of sexual intercourse' but continues to entertain his fellow-angels with further 'Biblical curiosities':

Naturally you will think the threat to punish Adam and Eve for disobeying was of course not carried out, since they did not create themselves, nor their natures nor their impulses nor their weaknesses, and hence were not properly subject to any one's commands, and

---

121 Paula Garrett, 'Letters from the Earth', in *The Mark Twain Encyclopedia*, pp.461-3 (p.461).
122 Baetzhold and McCullough, *Bible According to Mark Twain*, pp.218-21.
123 *Ibid.*, pp.221-2.
124 *Ibid.*, p.227.
125 *Ibid.*, p.228.

not responsible to anybody for their acts. It will surprise you to know that the threat *was* carried out. Adam and Eve were punished, and that crime finds apologists unto this day. *The sentence of death was executed.*[126]

He proceeds to recount some of the later events recorded in Genesis in an equally ironic manner, expressing envy of the Sons of God who 'had wonderful times with those hot young blossoms', the daughters of men, in the opening verses of Genesis chapter 6. Like Eve, he feels sympathy for all the victims of the Flood,

the multitude of weeping fathers and mothers and frightened little children who were clinging to the wave-washed rocks in the pouring rain and lifting imploring prayers to an All-Just and All-forgiving and All-Pitying Being who had never answered a prayer since those crags were built....[127]

He even somewhat mischievously suggests that the reason Noah went back to collect a fly that had been left behind was so that providence could complete its collection of diseases in store for the survivors. He also brings God's confession, 'I the Lord thy God am a jealous God' (Exodus 20:5), as a prooftext to explain his behaviour towards Adam and Eve:

The fear that if Adam and Eve ate of the fruit of the Tree of Knowledge they would 'be as gods,' so fired his jealousy that his reason was affected, and he could not treat those poor creatures either fairly or charitably, or even refrain from dealing cruelly and criminally with their blameless posterity.[128]

Satan will later argue that the Old Testament 'gives us a picture of these people's Deity as he was before he got religion', though he also has some harsh things to say about the ideas of hell entertained by the supposedly gentle Jesus.[129]

Adopting Satan as a persona clearly freed Twain to be as outspoken as he liked about those aspects of the biblical account of creation and the Fall which he found hard to accept. It is clear nevertheless throughout *Letters from the Earth* that it is not God as such whom Satan attacks but the depiction of Him in the Bible. This fits in with Twain's repeated distinction between the God of the Bible and the 'real' God. Reading the first three chapters of Genesis entirely on their own terms, as a story involving characters called 'God', 'Adam' and 'Eve', Satan cannot help coming to the conclusion that God's treatment of the first human couple is unfair.

Twain employed what Brodwin calls 'The Masks of Satan'[130] in several other places. In an essay 'Concerning the Jews', for example, he claimed to have

no special regard for Satan; but I can at least claim that I have no prejudice against him. It may be that I lean a little his way, on account of his not having had a fair show. All

---

126 *Ibid.*, p.231.
127 *Ibid.*, pp.235-6.
128 *Ibid.*, pp.237-8.
129 *Ibid.*, pp.250-1.
130 Stanley Brodwin, 'Mark Twain's Masks of Satan: The Final Phase', *American Literature* 45 (1973-4) pp.206-27.

religions issue bibles against him, and say the most injurious things about him, but we never hear *his* side.[131]

More importantly, Twain could use the mask of Satan against the Bible, as he does in the various versions of *The Mysterious Stranger* on which Twain worked from 1897-1908.[132] It is not the archangel Satan himself but his nephew who appears in 'The Chronicle of Young Satan', written between November 1897 and 1900. Young Satan insists that it was only the original Satan 'who ate of the fruit of the tree and then beguiled the man and the woman with it', the rest of the family being 'without blemish'.[133] Young Satan has miraculous powers, able like the young Jesus to make animals out of clay and bring them to life (Twain apparently encountered an 1820 edition of *The Apocryphal New Testament* in a New York Library in 1867).[134] His knowledge of the early chapters of Genesis, however, is not without the occasional inaccuracy, as when he re-creates the Garden of Eden and has model figures within it re-enact the murder of Abel.[135]

In 'Schoolhouse Hill' (1898) the Satan figure, the son of the original archangel, is called 44, possibly named after two Jewish brothers called Levin (nicknamed twenty-two by their schoolfellows in Hannibal because they were two times 'eleven')[136] or alternatively twice the number of letters in the Hebrew alphabet, which is of mysterious significance in the Kabbalah.[137] Whatever the origins of his name, 44 has a keen interest in the theology behind the Fall: 'No Adam in any of the millions of other planets', he explains, 'had ever disobeyed and eaten of the forbidden fruit'. Nor was there any 'tempter until my father ate of the fruit himself'. 44 himself, who was 'away when it happened' and returned to find his father so upset that 'he could not bear to talk about the details', engages like Satan in the classic midrashic practice of using one biblical text as a prooftext to unlock the meaning of another, although (again characteristically of his family) he significantly alters Job 5:7: 'Yet man is born unto trouble, as the sparks fly upward'. His father's error, he explains, lay 'in supposing that a knowledge of the difference between good and evil was *all* that the fruit could confer':

> Consider the passage which says *man is prone to evil as the sparks to fly upward*....It is not true of the men of any other planet. It explains the mystery. My father's error stands revealed in all its nakedness. The fruit's office was not confined to conferring the mere knowledge of good and evil, it conferred also the passionate and eager and hungry

---

131 Charles Neider, ed., *The Complete Essays of Mark Twain* (Garden City, NY: Doubleday, 1963), pp.236-7.

132 Sholom J.Kahn, 'The Mysterious Stanger', in *The Mark Twain Encyclopedia*, pp.530-3 (p.530).

133 William M.Gibson, ed., *Mark Twain's Mysterious Stranger Manuscripts* (Berkeley: University of California Press, 1969), p.49.

134 *Ibid.*, p.16.

135 *Ibid.*, p.134.

136 *Ibid.*, p.472.

137 Sholom J.Kahn, *Mark Twain's Mysterious Stranger: A Study of the Manuscript Texts* (Columbia: University of Missouri Press, 1978), p.206.

*disposition to DO evil....*Ah, my father's error brought a colossal disaster upon the men of this planet. It *poisoned* the men of this planet poisoned them in mind and body.[138]

This 'fundamental change in man's nature' the young 44 sees as unrectifiable but he sets himself 'earnestly' to lift 'part of its burden of evil consequences' from the human race.[139]

The final version of the story, 'No.44, The Mysterious Stranger', written between 1902 and 1908, relocates the story to Eseldorf, Switzerland, in 1490 and casts the young Satan as a 'printer's devil' given the task of completing a Bible. This particular fragment ends with 44 uttering a violent attack on

> a God who could make good children as easily as bad, yet preferred to make bad ones; who could have made every one of them happy, yet never made a single happy one, who made them prize their bitter life, yet stingily cut it short...who created man without invitation, then tries to shuffle the responsibility for man's acts upon man, instead of honourably placing it where it belongs, upon himself.[140]

Gibson's edition of *The Mysterious Stranger* also includes in the Appendix several fragments of 'Working Notes and Related Matter', including several that return to the subject of the Fall, probably written between 1899 and 1900. In one of these, a drunk Satan is inveigled into eating the half-eaten apple thrown away by Adam in order 'to give him the Moral Sense & Christianise him':

> When sober he recognizes what has happened, & bitterly reproaches them. His great powers are gone, disease invades him, becomes swiftly old & feeble; people no longer afraid of him; he is persecuted, but remains a heretic; so they torture him, convict him, damn him & burn him.[141]

Other fragments repeat Twain's complaints about the injustice of traditional teaching on the Fall, suggesting that 'Adam acquired the Moral Sense from the apple in a diseased form – *insanity* of mind & body'. The angels, by contrast, have the Moral Sense in a '*healthy* way', giving them a 'disposition to avoid evil & dislike it. They are sane'.[142]

That Twain was indeed obsessed with the early chapters of Genesis should by now have been established. His writings return again and again to this foundational story, examining it from every possible angle, from Adam's perspective, from Eve's, from Satan's and even from that of the other animals. His imagination manages constantly to find new ways of dramatising it, teasing out fresh questions, new implications. Some of his outbursts against God may appear to border themselves on the insane; like Nietzsche, he challenges the boundaries of the thinkable. What is undeniable, I would claim, is that Twain's many reworkings of the story, like those of the rabbis (though more subversively) force readers to confront the many questions which the biblical narrative raises.

---

138 Gibson, *Mark Twain's Mysterious Stranger Manuscripts*, p.216.
139 *Ibid.*, p.217.
140 *Ibid.*, p.405.
141 *Ibid.*, pp.420-1.
142 *Ibid.*, p.442.

Chapter 3

Cain and Abel: John Steinbeck

The Growth of a Novel: Ginzberg, Campbell and Fromm

To treat *East of Eden* (1952), John Steinbeck's fictional account of the family history of some Californian settlers, as a form of midrash may appear to stretch that term too far. But Steinbeck, as I will demonstrate, not only drew on the work of Joseph Campbell and Eric Fromm, who were both familiar with the midrashic tradition, to explore this 'symbol story of the human soul'.[1] He also got his editor Pascal Covici to consult Louis Ginzberg (Professor of Talmud at the Jewish Theological Seminary in New York and author of the pioneering anthology of midrash, *The Legends of the Jews*), about the crucial Hebrew word *timshol* (thou mayest conquer) in Genesis 4:7. The whole novel, it can be argued, is built upon this. For in this verse God tells Cain that he has a choice; sin lies in wait but he can triumph over it, he does not need to give in to his anger and resentment against his brother. Steinbeck, no Hebrew scholar himself, carved the Hebrew letters of the word *timshol* on the cover of the wooden box he gave Covici (as recorded in the epigraph to the novel).[2] He persisted somewhat unfortunately on transliterating the Hebrew word *timshel*, but he clearly understood the significance of the freedom and with it the moral responsibility with which it endows the human race. Far from being an 'assault on the big book of his tradition', as David Wyatt claims in the introduction to the Penguin edition of the novel,[3] *East of Eden*, I will argue, follows the midrashic tradition (whether consciously or unconsciously) in providing both a commentary upon Genesis 4 and a supplementary narrative based upon it.

The terse and enigmatic tale of the murder by Cain of his brother, as Ricardo Quinones has shown, is uniquely important in Western culture. It is not only about sibling rivalry, the symbolic slaying of the competitor-brother necessary for individual development; it is about violence and discord in history, the 'fracture at the heart of things'.[4] The killing of a brother, many commentators have felt, is a more resonant symbol of the fallen human condition than the theft of an apple.[5] The pain Cain suffers on the rejection of his offering also speaks volumes to those who have experienced similar rejection of what they have to offer, whether as a person or as

---

1   John Steinbeck, *East of Eden* (London: Mandarin, 1990), p. 300.
2   Jackson J.Benson, *The True Adventure of John Steinbeck, Writer* (New York: Viking Press, 1984), p.687.
3   David Wyatt, 'Introduction' to John Steinbeck, *East of Eden* (Harmondsworth: Penguin, 2000), p.xvi.
4   Ricardo Quinones, *The Changes of Cain: Violence and the Lost Brother in Cain and Abel Literature* (Princeton: Princeton University Press, 1991), p.3.
5   *Ibid.*, p.251.

an artist. In Steinbeck's words, 'this one story is the basis of all human neurosis'(*JN* 104).[6]

The biblical account is characteristically reticent about motive, about why God rejects Cain's offering and why Cain takes his anger out on his brother. Cain, as we have seen, is told by God in verse 7 that he has a choice, that he can master sin and overcome his resentment, but on this occasion he fails to do so. God's reaction to Cain's murder of his brother, however, is strangely ambivalent: he both curses him (in verse 11) and marks him with a sign of protection (in verse 15). Cain's reaction to his curse is in turn ambiguous: 'My punishment is greater than I can bear', he says (in verse 13), though the Hebrew for punishment, *hawon,* could also be translated as guilt or iniquity, which would make a significant difference. Much, of course, depends on the tone in which he says this, which could be whining, defiant, or simply desperate. He is sent out as a wanderer, 'a fugitive and a vagabond', in verse 12, driven 'away from the presence of the Lord...east of Eden' (verse 16) but by verse 17 he has recovered sufficiently to have founded a city. In settling outside the gates of paradise, Cain occupies dangerous territory, leading a life which demands the continued exercise of moral choice. But this, the biblical narrative would appear to suggest, reflects the human condition in the wake of the 'Fall'.

There are additional complexities in these first seventeen verses of Genesis 4, for instance the role of Eve. Her triumphant cry on giving birth in the opening verse, 'I have gotten a man from the Lord'(with the verb *qanithi* containing a pun on the name of her child) could be read as a sign of arrogance, appropriating for herself the power to give life as her son will arrogate to himself the right to take it away. One midrash, as we shall see, attributes her child to a very different father (the serpent), suggesting a clear genealogy of evil. The passage also introduces the theme of brotherhood often seen as central to the whole book.[7] The word 'brother' recurs throughout the passage, six times in verses 8-11, the conflict between Cain and Abel anticipating later tensions between Isaac and Ishmael, Jacob and Esau and Joseph and his brothers. So these seventeen verses can be seen to introduce crucial elements in the whole Book of Genesis.

There are two midrashic traditions mentioned by Ginzberg in *The Legends of the Jews* which seem particularly relevant to what Steinbeck will eventually make of the story. The first concerns Eve and her sexuality. God, Ginzberg writes in his summary of the midrashic commentary upon this part of Genesis, had warned Adam and Eve 'against carnal intercourse with each other. But after the fall of Eve, Satan, in the guise of the serpent, approached her, and the fruit of their union was Cain'. What she says in the opening verse therefore amounts to a confession: 'I have gotten a man through an angel of the Lord'.[8] A lengthy footnote in the fifth of Ginzberg's seven volumes explores a tradition 'independent of the legend concerning Eve's sexual intercourse with the serpent...that the original sin consisted in this that the serpent

---

6   John Steinbeck, *Journal of a Novel* (London: Heinemann, 1970), p.104.

7   See, for example, J.P.Fokkelman's chapter on 'Genesis', in Robert Alter and Frank Kermode, eds, *The Literary Guide to the Bible* (London: Collins, 1987), pp.36-55.

8   Louis Ginzberg, *The Legends of the Jews*, trans. Henrietta Szold, 7 vols (Philadelphia: Jewish Publication Society, 1909-25), I 105.

had awakened in her a sexual desire'.[9] After her seduction by the serpent, Ginzberg's summary continues, Eve 'left her husband and journeyed westward, because she feared her presence might continue to bring him misery' while 'Adam remained in the East' until his wife's lamentations 'miraculously reached his ear'. Even more interestingly in the light of Steinbeck's novel, in which Cal grows beans in order to please his father, is the way Ginzberg continues his narrative, here drawing on the apocryphal *Life of Adam*:

> Now Adam took Eve and the boy to his home in the east. God sent him various kinds of seeds by the hand of the angel Michael, and he was taught how to cultivate the ground and make it yield produce and fruits, to sustain himself and his family and his posterity.[10]

It is perfectly possible, of course, for Steinbeck to have developed the biblical tradition in these directions independently of the midrashim summarised by Ginzberg. The similarities, however, as I hope to demonstrate, are interesting and the imaginative process of interpretation at least analogous.

Among other midrashic traditions enumerated by Ginzberg is an explanation of God's rejection of Cain's gift: that he offered only 'what was left over, a few grains of flax seed. As though his offence had not been great enough in offering unto God fruit of the ground which had been cursed by God!'[11] Ginzberg, as Elie Wiesel notes in his chapter on Cain in *Messengers of God*, comes up with at least three midrashic motives for the struggle between Cain and Abel: property, love and religion. The first involves Cain and Abel dividing the world between them, Cain to receive all the land and Abel all the chattels. Cain tells Abel to get off his land, only for Abel to reply by insisting that Cain remove all his animal skins.[12] In Neusner's rendering of the dialogue in his 'New American Translation' of *Genesis Rabbah*,

> The one said, 'Strip.'
>
> The other said, 'Bug off.'
>
> And, as matters played themselves out...Cain rose up against his brother and killed him.[13]

The rejection of Cain's gift, Ginzberg continues,

> was not the only cause of Cain's hatred toward Abel. Partly love for a woman brought about the crime. To ensure the propagation of the human race, a girl, destined to be his wife, was born with each of the sons of Adam. Abel's twin sister was of exquisite beauty, and Cain desired her. Therefore he was constantly brooding over ways and means of ridding himself of his brother.[14]

---

9   *Ibid.*, V 133.
10   *Ibid.*, I 106.
11   *Ibid.*, I 107-8.
12   Elie Wiesel, *Messengers of God: Biblical Portraits and Legends* (New York: Summit Books, 1976), p.48.
13   Jacob Neusner, trans., *Genesis Rabbah: The Judaic Commentary to the Book of Genesis*, 3 vols (Atlanta, GA: Scholar's Press, 1985), I 247.
14   Ginzberg, *Legends of the Jews*, I 108.

This again anticipates, if it did not actually suggest, Steinbeck's development of a rivalry between the brothers at least partly based upon their loving the same girl. The third motive (the midrash has them vying to build a temple) could also be said to play a part in Steinbeck's novel, with Aron, his Abel-figure, becoming an adherent of a particularly effete brand of Anglo-Catholicism. It is the rivalry of the twins for the love of their father and of Abra, however, which offers the strongest link between the midrash summarised by Ginzberg and Steinbeck's novel.

The murder of Abel also raises questions explored in both midrash and novel about the origins of evil, questions not altogether answered by the earlier chapters of Genesis. Ginzberg cites some of the rabbinic expansions of Cain's famous reply to God in Genesis 4: 9:

> Am I my brother's keeper? Thou art He who holdest watch over all creatures and yet Thou demandest account of me! True I slew him, but Thou didst create the evil inclination in me. Thou guardest all things; why, then, didst Thou permit me to slay him?[15]

Ginzberg brings together a number of details from different midrashic accounts of the manner in which Cain kills Abel, most of which involve pelting with stones. He also describes the consequences of God's curse as portrayed in midrashic sources: the earth quakes under Cain and a range of animals gather to devour him. At this point Cain claims to repent, bringing home to Adam the benefits of confession.[16] *Genesis Rabbah* describes an encounter between Cain and his father in which Adam celebrates 'the power of repentance' and starts to recite Psalm 92.[17] These themes, as we shall see, also recur in *East of Eden* in Cal's attempts to confess his true feelings both to his father and to Lee. Again, I should acknowledge that it is possible that Steinbeck developed the story along the same lines as the midrash completely independently. But his consultation of Ginzberg about the Hebrew makes it at least likely that he also consulted the *Legends*.

Steinbeck is not normally regarded as having much interest in religion; he was certainly out of sympathy with theological creeds and dogma. His acceptance speech on the award of the Nobel Prize for Literature in 1964 ends by urging the race to 'seek in ourselves for the responsibility and the wisdom we once prayed some deity might have'. It is significant, however, that this speech reaches its climax with a paraphrase of St. John's Gospel: 'In the end is the *word*, and the word is *man*, and the word is *with* man'.[18] Steinbeck, it seems, can only go beyond the Bible by citing it, albeit with major modifications. 'I am not religious', he told his doctor in the same year, explaining that he had no fear of hell or hope of heaven.[19] Interpreters, however, have not always agreed; Lester Marks, for example, argues that both Steinbeck and

---

15 *Ibid.*, I 110.
16 *Ibid.*, I 111-2.
17 Neusner, *Genesis Rabbah*, I 254.
18 Jay Parini, *John Steinbeck: A Biography* (London: Heinemann, 1994), p.537. Steinbeck's Nobel Prize Acceptance Speech is reproduced in full in John Steinbeck, *America and Americans and Selected Nonfiction*, ed. Susan Shillinglaw and Jackson J.Benson (New York: Viking, 2002), pp.172-4.
19 Parini, *John Steinbeck*, p. 575.

his characters reveal not only a deep yearning for religion but a recognition that this yearning requires some form of expression in creed, ritual and ethical codes, however inadequate they may be.[20]

Steinbeck's work certainly evinces a deep reverence for the Bible, a respect presumably inherited from his mother and grandmother on the Hamilton side of the family, whose history he recorded for his sons and posterity in the novel. *East of Eden,* appropriately enough, is the name of the restaurant which now occupies the building attended by the young Steinbeck when it was St. Paul's Episcopal Church. He soon rebelled, however, against the church of his upbringing. He also allegedly interrupted a Methodist Christmas service attended with a fellow-student at Stanford, muttering that it was a 'lot of crap'. 'Yes, you all look satisfied here', he is supposed to have shouted, 'while outside the world begs for a crust of bread or a chance to earn it!' (46).[21] But even this rebellion, it could be argued, follows biblical precedent, imitating Christ in the Temple. His characters too, most famously Jim Casey, the preacher who loses his faith but sacrifices his life in defence of the oppressed strikers in *The Grapes of Wrath,* can be seen to follow Christ's example in unorthodox ways.

Many of Steinbeck's beliefs were framed by the respect for science which he absorbed at Stanford University, where one of his favourite teachers, Harold Brown, taught that philosophy should address the world revealed by science, distrusting all closed philosophical systems, all systems of thought not open to disproof by experience. This was a position reinforced by his friend and mentor, Ed Ricketts, the marine biologist celebrated in *Cannery Row* and *The Sea of Cortez*. It is in the latter log-book of a voyage with Ricketts that Steinbeck explains a distinction they both made between teleological or goal-directed thinking, with its 'sometimes intolerant refusal to face facts as they are', and non-teleological thinking, which 'concerns itself primarily not with what should be, or could be, or might be, but rather with what actually "is"'.[22] Non-teleological or 'is' thinking, Steinbeck continues in what has been called his Easter Sunday sermon (it is dated Easter Sunday in the log-book and encapsulates his own 'credo'), is not limited to the narrowly empirical or positivistic; it involves 'an all-embracingness', the 'love and understanding of instant acceptance', a reverence and humility before 'the infinite whole', which 'is unknowable except by *Being* in it; by living into it', a worldview very different from the 'mechanical-model world of the Victorian scientists'.[23]

The Sea of Cortez is awash with references to archetypes and symbols, of which the sea is the most central: 'For the ocean, deep and black in the depths, is like the low dark levels of our minds in which the dream symbols incubate and sometimes rise up to sight like the Old Man of the Sea'.[24] It is this need for symbolic significance which

---

20 Lester Marks, *Thematic Design in the Novels of John Steinbeck* (The Hague: Mouton, 1971), pp.12-26.

21 Parini, *John Steinbeck*, p.46.

22 John Steinbeck, *The Log from the Sea of Cortez* (London: Mandarin, 1990), pp.197-8.

23 *Ibid.*, pp.208-10.

24 *Ibid.*, p.93.

for Steinbeck explains the 'fact' of religion. He writes sympathetically, for example, of the Mexican Indian reverence before a statue of Our Lady, which 'our [modern American] eyes...should find...gaudy' but instead find 'lovely in her dim chapel with the lilies of Easter around her. This is a very holy place', Steinbeck insists, 'and to question it is to question a fact as established as the tide'.[25] The unquestionable 'fact' of religious experience, in other words, is something that 'is' thinking must recognise.

Two thinkers who clearly contributed to Steinbeck's understanding of religion, providing significant intertexts between the Book of Genesis and *East of Eden*, are Joseph Campbell and Erich Fromm. In the remainder of this section therefore I will outline some of their ideas, in particular their recognition of the importance of midrash. I will also the consider *The Journal of a Novel*, the title given to the letters Steinbeck wrote to his editor Covic while writing *East of Eden*. *The Journal of a Novel* is an astonishingly full account not only of Steinbeck's reading of Genesis but of the genesis of his own novel in his response to the biblical narrative. Finally, in the second section of the chapter, I will consider *East of Eden* itself both as 'midrashic' commentary upon and supplementary reworking of the story of Cain and Abel.

Joseph Campbell became a close friend of Steinbeck's after moving to Monterey in December 1931, long before he was to become something of a cult figure as a result of his PBS television series on *The Power of Myth*. Most of Campbell's writing postdates his friendship with Steinbeck and, as with Ginzberg, it is difficult to prove that Steinbeck read it. But since they used to stay up all hours of the night discussing all aspects of life it is a fair inference that Steinbeck became familiar with Campbell's views on religion. It is also highly likely that he read his friend's work as it came out even after they parted company in June 1932 after Campbell fell in love with Steinbeck's first wife Carol. Campbell, a lapsed Catholic who had begun to question traditional doctrines as a student first at Dartmouth College and then at Columbia University, retained a deep respect not only for religion but for art, which he saw as performing in the modern world some of the same functions as myth. He had been a great admirer of Thomas Mann since his Columbia days and in a letter of July 1934 celebrated the publication in English of the first two volumes of *Joseph and His Brothers* as 'the most marvellous thing I've ever come across. It is a magnificent epic, the finest thing of my experience. It has made the connection that I have been looking for between *mythos* and the modern work of art'.[26] Mann, as I will show in chapter 7, can be seen to have modelled *Joseph* on midrash.

Campbell became famous after publishing *The Hero with a Thousand Faces* in 1949 (three years before *East of Eden*), in which there is an interesting discussion of the early chapters of the Book of Genesis, displaying an awareness of the whole midrashic tradition. After citing *Genesis Rabbah* on Adam's initial androgyny, he proceeds to build upon the separation of the first creature into two genders a theory of the origin of evil:

---

25   *Ibid.*, p.238.
26   Stephen and Robin Larsen, *A Fire in the Mind: The Life of Joseph Campbell* (New York: Doubleday, 1991), p.229.

The removal of the feminine into another form symbolizes the beginning of the fall from perfection into duality; and it was naturally followed by the discovery of the duality of good and evil, exile from the garden where God walks on earth, and thereupon the building of the wall of Paradise, constituted of the 'coincidence of opposites,' by which Man (now man and woman) is cut off from not only the vision but even the recollection of the image of God.[27]

It is 'the duality of good and evil', however, as we shall see in Steinbeck's *Journal of a Novel,* which gives man the moral responsibility celebrated in *East of Eden.* The Bible itself, along with other mythologies, Campbell argues, holds out the hope that the divine unity once so tragically lost can eventually be recovered, dissolving the walls of paradise, and restoring the ancient 'wisdom'. [28]

Campbell went on to write a four-volume account of *The Masks of God*, which devotes a volume each to Primitive, Oriental, Occidental and Creative Mythology respectively. The underlying assumption in all this is that 'mythological symbols' both ancient and modern, eastern and western, can contribute to human understanding and wonder at the universe. The creative mythology of individual artists, Campbell argues, 'springs not, like theology, from the dicta of authority, but from the insights, sentiments, thought and vision of an adequate individual, loyal to his own experience of value'.[29] *The Power of Myth* talks in similar fashion about looking at 'old stories' in 'new ways', 'stories that helped people discover again what it means to be spiritual'.[30] Although it is difficult to pinpoint precisely what Steinbeck took from Campbell in terms of direct 'influence' it is at least likely that he learnt from him to appreciate both the power of ancient eastern myth, in particular the Bible and the midrashic tradition, and of modern western myth, including fiction. *East of Eden* would certainly find 'new ways' to look at an old story.

Another significant 'intertext' between Genesis and *East of Eden* is Erich Fromm's *Psychoanalysis and Religion* (1950) which Steinbeck read shortly before beginning the novel. *Journal of a Novel* clearly follows Fromm in referring to the great figures from Plato and Buddha to Christ and the great Hebrew prophets, all of whom point to the same 'human reality', the same 'striving for love, truth and justice'.[31] Fromm explains that whereas Freud attacked religion as a collective neurosis and saw the unconscious as potentially dangerous, Jung celebrated the collective unconscious as a positive religious phenomenon, a source of revelation and a symbol for God Himself.[32] Fromm makes a distinction between 'authoritarian religion', which stresses obedience to a superior power, and 'humanistic religion', which celebrates human capacity for joy, self-realization and 'oneness with the All'. God for Fromm

---

27 Joseph Campbell, *The Hero with a Thousand Faces* (Princeton: Princeton University Press, 1972), pp.152-3.

28 *Ibid.*, p.154.

29 Larsen, *A Fire in the Mind*, pp.458-9.

30 *Ibid.*, p.550.

31 Steinbeck, *Journal of a Novel*, p.115. The passage from which he is borrowing can be found in Erich Fromm, *Psychoanalysis and Religion* (London: Victor Gollanz, 1951), p.70.

32 Fromm, *Psychoanalysis and Religion*, p.102.

is a 'symbol of man's own powers' rather than 'a symbol of force and domination having *power over man*'.[33]

At the beginning of the Book of Genesis, according to Fromm, God is depicted as authoritarian, an absolute ruler who forbids the eating of fruit and threatens death for disobedience. But the serpent is proved more accurate in his prediction than the authoritarian deity: Adam and Eve do not die but learn the difference between good and evil as a result of their choice. After the Flood, however, 'the relationship between God and man changes fundamentally': God promises respect for life, a promise to which Abraham will attempt to keep him, pleading in chapter 18 for the inhabitants of Sodom and Gomorrah. Fromm cites Rabbi Eliezer in the Talmud and passages from later Hassidic folklore as illustrating the humanistic elements to be found within the Jewish tradition, in which human beings exercise the right to challenge God if he fails to protect them. They refuse to remain 'slavishly dependent on God' and consequently 'alienated from themselves as in authoritarian religion'.[34]

Steinbeck clearly found Fromm's account of 'humanistic religion' sympathetic, particularly its emphasis on independence. Fromm notices, for example, two kinds of orientation among human beings, 'the orientation by proximity to the herd and the orientation by reason', the latter creating such demands that only a few individuals can stand the isolation: 'They are the true heroes of the human race but for whom we should still be living in caves'.[35] This belief in moral progress is reflected in *Journal of a Novel* in Steinbeck's claim,

> It is true that we are weak and sick and ugly and quarrelsome but if that is all we ever were, we would millenniums ago have disappeared from the face of the earth, and a few remnants of fossilized jaw bones, a few teeth in strata of limestone, would be the only mark our species would have left on earth...so that although East of Eden is not Eden, it is not insuperably far away.[36]

For Fromm (as for Steinbeck), the Book of Genesis tells a story of human emancipation and moral growth. The normative Jewish and Christian traditions may 'have ignored the fact that it is the emancipation from the security of Paradise which is the basis for man's truly human development', his knowledge of good and evil,[37] but Fromm (and Steinbeck) read Genesis against the grain of later 'authoritarian' traditions to stress the importance of individual moral responsibility.

Journal of a Novel, as well as revealing some of the sources of Steinbeck's beliefs, tells the story of his creative wrestling with Genesis chapter 4. It is a remarkable document, probably the fullest account of the genesis of a novel that we have, the fullest evidence of creative and intertextual processes unfolding in the mind of a writer. Steinbeck's biographer Jackson Benson claims that the journal may even come to be seen as greater than the novel itself, magnificent though that is.[38] It certainly sheds light

---

33   *Ibid.*, pp.42-5.
34   *Ibid.*, pp.53-8.
35   *Ibid.*, p.66.
36   Steinbeck, *Journal of a Novel*, p.116.
37   Fromm, *Psychoanalysis and Religion*, p.89.
38   Benson, *The True Adventures of John Steinbeck*, p.691.

upon the novel itself and on the way which it came into existence partly in reaction to the 'authoritarian' interpretation of Cain and Abel. The *Journal* begins by explaining that the novel will be addressed by Steinbeck to his sons, to explain their inheritance (both from the Hamilton family and from the human race, from Adam):

> I will tell them one of the greatest, perhaps the greatest story of all— the story of good and evil, of strength and weakness. Of love and hate, of beauty and ugliness. I shall try to demonstrate to them how these doubles are inseparable— how neither can exist without the other and how out of their groupings creativeness is born.[39]

He is aware, however, of the dangers of didacticism, of setting out too obviously to illustrate a moral. The *Journal* shows him grappling both with the meaning of what he calls 'that powerful, profound and perplexing story in Genesis of Cain and Abel' and the best mode of retelling it:

> There is much of it that I don't understand. Furthermore it is very short, but this story with its implications has made a deeper mark in people than any other save possibly the story of the Tree of life and original sin. Now since this is indeed my frame - is there any reason to conceal it from my reader? Would it not be better to let him know even in the title what the story is about?[40]

Steinbeck explains that he has gone back to Genesis itself in search of a title and come up with 'Cain Sign', a reference to 'the best known mark in the world', a mark both of punishment and protection. As a title, it strikes him as 'short, harsh, memorable', famous and 'pretty good-looking'.[41]

Steinbeck's enthusiasm for this title may have been short-lived (perhaps dampened by his editor) but his excitement about Genesis 4 visibly increases. He records copying out the first sixteen verses by hand and discovering in the process that

> the story changes with flashing lights when you write it down. And I think I have a title at last, a beautiful title, *EAST OF EDEN*. And read the 16th verse to find it. And the Salinas Valley is surely East of Eden. I could go on and write another page and perhaps it would be good, who knows. Or maybe not. What a strange story it is and how it haunts one.[42]

Steinbeck notes both the psychological damage such excitement can cause and its creative rewards. The entry for the next day records a 'restless night' which results in finding 'a key to the story', which will

> only be boring to people who want to get on with the plot. The reader I want will find the whole book illuminated by the discussion: just as I am. And if this were just a discussion of Biblical lore, I would throw it out but it is not. It is using the Biblical story as a measure of ourselves.[43]

---

39 Steinbeck, *Journal of a Novel*, p.4.
40 *Ibid.*, p.91.
41 *Ibid.*, p.91.
42 *Ibid.*, p.104.
43 *Ibid.*, p.105.

Steinbeck is clearly aware that it runs counter to the conventions of realism to interrupt the narrative with a lengthy discussion of a biblical passage. But in this novel, as in midrash, the Bible will be seen to have meaning not only for its own time but for the time of the reader.

Eight days later Steinbeck's journal records another sleepless night over this new-found 'key' to the novel, one of those 'nights of discovery' out of which 'comes the whole week's work'.[44] Steinbeck is now convinced that *East of Eden* will be 'the final title'. He also wants the biblical text 'And Cain etc.' 'in fairly large italics...at the bottom of the title page...There should never be any doubt in the reader's mind what the title refers to'. Here again he appears to have had second thoughts (again perhaps prompted by Covici). He proceeds to air some concerns to his editor about the different translations of verse 7:

> The King James says of sin crouching at the door, 'Thou shalt rule over it.' The American Standard says, 'Do thou rule over it.' Now this new translation [the Douai edition published in Manchester in 1812] says, 'Thou *mayest* rule over it'. This is the most vital difference. The first two are 1, a prophecy and 2, an order, but 3 is the offering of free will. Here is individual responsibility and the invention of conscience. You can if you will but it is up to you.[45]

If this last translation is accurate, Steinbeck feels, the King James version 'will turn out to be one of the most important mistranslations in the Old Testament'. The long-suffering Covici is commissioned to dig out some Hebrew scholarship on the matter since the precise meaning of the biblical verse, as in midrash, is absolutely crucial to the critical commentary and narrative augmentation. This, as we have seen, is where Ginzberg came in, approached by Covici to provide the necessary linguistic and theological expertise. Steinbeck seems to have valued the former above the latter, commenting that 'Dr Ginzberg, dealing in theology, may have a slightly different attitude from that of a pure etymologist'.[46]

Steinbeck, it should be admitted, seems neither to have been unduly in awe of the rabbinic tradition nor unduly modest about what he was doing: 'I do not think that the Cain-Abel story has ever been subjected to such scrutiny. Nor has any story been so fruitful of meaning'.[47] He continues to mull over the best possible translation of the Hebrew verb at the end of verse 7: 'May is a curious word in English. In the negative it is an order but in the positive it allows a choice. Thou mayest not is definite but thou mayest implies either way— do you see'.[48] Yet more on *timshol* follows two days later on July 6th while on the 13th Steinbeck explains how he is reversing the emphasis in the final section of the novel, which will fall on Caleb, who is 'my Cain principle', rather than on Adam Trask, 'who was the Abel' through whose eyes the first part of the novel had been told. This final part of the novel, Steinbeck insists, will be 'no repetition but an extension' of the first. 'There is the

---

44   *Ibid.*, p.106.
45   *Ibid.*, pp.107-8.
46   *Ibid.*, p.122.
47   *Ibid.*, p.115.
48   *Ibid.*, p.120.

plan', he announces, a plan about which he feels 'good because I think in myself I have access to both Cain and Abel'.[49] Whether the final result will bear out his confidence, he is not so sure.

The *Journal of a Novel* is very revealing not only of Steinbeck's sources, of the intertexts between himself and the Bible, but of his developing understanding of Genesis 4. That the particular verb *timshol* is the key to this understanding will become apparent in the novel, which foregrounds the whole interpretive process in a remarkable manner. It is entirely appropriate, I would claim, that Covici should have turned to Ginzberg for a fuller understanding of this verb because what Steinbeck is doing (whether he knows it or not) is very much in the spirit of midrash, unpacking the meaning of a particular detail of the text through a combination of commentary and supplementary narrative. Now, however, it is time to consider the novel itself.

East of Eden: The Choice between Good and Evil

East of Eden advertises its primary theme in its opening paragraphs, which describe the Salinas Valley, with its sunny Gabilan mountains to the east and broody Santa Lucias to the west, establishing in symbolic landscape 'the duality of good and evil' and the necessity of choosing between them. There are explicit echoes of Genesis later in the first chapter in the reference to six or seven years of plenty, as in the Joseph-narrative, being followed by a spell of dry years and lean harvests.[50] Although Steinbeck abandoned the plan of addressing his sons directly in the text, it is made immediately apparent that the first-person narrator, who later identifies himself as John Steinbeck, the son of Olive Hamilton and thus a minor character in the novel (in technical terms, a homodiegetic narrator, existing on the same level of discourse as the other characters), has little time for narrow attitudes to religion, whether on the part of the colonising Spaniards, collecting souls along with gold, or the 'dour Presbyterian mind' (10). There is also a clear indication of his 'humanistic' religious values (in Fromm's sense) at the end of the second chapter, which celebrates the moral strength of the early settlers, who 'could give God their own courage and then receive it back' (14). This 'God' is clearly to be understood as immanent rather than transcendent, a projection of human values rather than a metaphysical entity.

The narrator's unconventional and even irreverent attitude to institutional religion is also apparent in such passages as the second paragraph of chapter nineteen, which proclaims, somewhat provocatively, 'The church and the whorehouse arrived in the Far West simultaneously'. They both, according to Steinbeck, 'accomplish the same thing', taking 'a man out of his bleakness for a time', although one important difference is that the churches bring 'the Scripture on which our ethics, our art and poetry, and our relationships are built' (242). Steinbeck expresses a certain grudging admiration even for someone like Liza Hamilton, who reads nothing but the Bible: 'In that one book she had her history and her poetry, her knowledge of people and of things, her ethics, her morals, and her salvation'. The problem in her case is that

---

49 *Ibid.*, p.128.
50 John Steinbeck, *East of Eden* (London: Mandarin, 1990), pp.5-6. All subsequent page references, given in brackets in the text, are to this edition.

she has become so familiar with it that she cannot hear what it says: 'she knew it so well that she went right on reading it without listening' (47). It is not that the Bible is an inappropriate source for all these values; it is just that people like Liza interpret it too narrowly.

Liza's husband Samuel is a more critical reader of the Bible, receiving Liza's rebuke for 'picking at it and questioning it' (285). But he also has great reverence for it, which is why he takes it to his neighbour Adam Trask in order to find names for Adam's twins. There's a running joke in the way in which Samuel teases his wife by replying 'Here I am' every time she calls, playing the infant Samuel to her God. He explains to Adam, 'The man I'm named after had his name called clear by the Lord God, and I've been listening all my life. And once or twice I've thought I heard my name called— but not clear, not clear' (293). He does, however, claim to be able to judge character by the part of Scripture a person reads: 'Give me a used Bible', he tells Adam, 'and I will...tell you about a man by the places that are edged with the dirt of seeking fingers' (296). Samuel himself is clearly a Genesis man:

> 'Two stories have haunted us and followed us from our beginning,' Samuel said. 'We can carry them along with us like invisible tails— the story of original sin and the story of Cain and Abel...here it is— such a little story to have made so deep a wound (296-7).

He proceeds to read the first sixteen verses of Genesis 4 in the King James version, silencing the attempted interruptions by Adam and Lee, Adam's oriental factotum and philosopher, until he has finished reading the relevant verses.

At this point in the novel, as he admitted in the *Journal of a Novel*,[51] Steinbeck risks boring those readers who 'want to get on with the plot' still further by allowing these three characters to engage in prolonged biblical criticism. Samuel, closing the book 'almost with weariness', opens the discussion by commenting, 'I had forgotten how dreadful it is— no single tone of encouragement'. Lee then brings his oriental wisdom to bear upon the sacred text (and it is important that he doesn't belong to a western religious tradition, emphasising the universal nature of the Bible's moral truth): 'No story has power', he says, 'nor will it last, unless we feel in ourselves that it is true and true of us.' The three men discuss the story, in Samuel's words, 'as though it happened in King City yesterday', with Lee feeling its burden of guilt and Adam rebelling against God's arbitrary rejection of Cain's gift. Lee repeats his argument that the story has lasted 'because it is everybody's story...the symbol story of the human soul', employing the term symbol in the Jungian sense adopted by Campbell and Fromm. Lee too dwells on the psychological resonance of the tale, the effect upon Cain of God's rejection of his offering:

> The greatest terror a child can have is that he is not loved, and rejection is the hell he fears. I think everyone in the world to a large or small extent has felt rejection. And with rejection comes anger, and with anger some kind of crime in revenge for the rejection, and with the crime guilt— and there is the story of mankind (298-300).

---

51 Steinbeck, *Journal of a Novel*, p.105.

The three men have enough commonsense, however, not to burden the poor twins with the names Cain and Abel; instead they are called Caleb and Aron, after Joshua's captain and Moses' brother respectively (it is not made clear why the latter loses an a somewhere in the process).

There is a ten-year gap in the story-world (the action represented in Parts 2 and 3 of the novel) between the baptising of the twins and the next narrated meeting of the same three men (only a few pages later in the text), when they resume their discussion of Genesis 4. In this period, we are told, 'the story bit into' Lee so much that he 'went into it word for word', exploring the different translations, as Steinbeck himself had done, and even enlisting the help of four elderly Confucian scholars, who themselves become so intrigued by the passage that they engage a rabbi to teach them Hebrew. After two years of rabbinic instruction they feel equipped to approach the sixteen verses once more, at which point they alight upon the key Hebrew verb *timshel* (as Steinbeck continues to transliterate it). Lee explains the different translations of this verb:

> The American Standard translation [Do thou] orders men to triumph over sin, and you can call sin ignorance. The King James translation makes a promise in 'Thou shalt', meaning that men will surely triumph over sin. But the Hebrew word, the word *timshel*— 'Thou mayest'—that gives a choice...'Thou mayest!' Why, that makes a man great, that gives him stature with the gods, for in his weakness and his filth and his murder of his brother he has still the great choice. He can choose his course and fight it through and win...That makes a man a man. A cat has no choice, a bee must make honey. There's no Godliness there...(338-9).

A 'true story'such as this, Lee claims, transcends cultural differences: 'these sixteen verses are a history of humankind in any culture or race'. He adds, in terms which echo Campbell's similar advocacy of 'spirituality' above theology, that his reference to 'Godliness' should not be taken as 'theology. I have no bent toward gods. But I have a new love for that glittering instrument, the human soul' (336-40).

To devote such a large amount of a novel to detailed biblical exegesis is to impose an unusual burden on readers. Significantly, Lee as a character is excised completely from the 1955 film of *East of Eden* directed by Elia Kazan, which, as well as acting as a vehicle for James Dean, focuses entirely on the last part of the novel, playing down the biblical allusions in it. Adam is portrayed making his children read aloud from the Bible but this is more an index of his patriarchal authoritarianism than an encouragement to viewers to pursue the reference. What is remarkable about the novel is the sheer extent of its focus upon the Book of Genesis. Not only, as in midrash, is the biblical text itself reproduced in its entirety, with much discussion of individual words and with full critical commentary upon the contemporary relevance of the story. More significantly, and more persuasively as far as modern readers and critics are concerned, the novel as a whole can be seen as a narrative augmentation and interpretation of the story. The two main generations around whom the plot of the novel revolves dramatise the story of rejection, anger, crime and guilt embodied in the original narrative. The novel as a whole, in other words, embodies the moral teaching which Steinbeck believes to lie at the heart of the biblical text.

The first part of the novel focuses on Charles and Adam Trask— there's a C and A pattern in the names of all the characters in the novel which many critics have found too schematic, although, as Steinbeck explains in the *Journal*, this is designed as much to surprise readers, to frustrate their expectations, as to confirm them: readers will expect the final part of the novel simply to repeat the pattern of the first, which it does not. The first generation of Trask brothers, as in the biblical story, fall out over the difference their father makes in his reception of their gifts. Charles feels rejected because his present, that of a pearl-handed pen-knife, is counted as nothing beside Adam's gift of a puppy. He beats his brother almost to death in the first of many attempted murders in this most violent of novels. His letter to Adam at the end of chapter four, as Steinbeck revealed in *Journal of a Novel*, contains 'a number of keys' to the novel. 'If you miss this', he warned Covici, 'you will miss a great deal of this book'.[52] His pen loosened by drink, Charles pours out to his brother the feelings of rejection which lay behind his attack. 'I shouldn't be here', he adds. 'I ought to be wandering around the world' (40-1), a clear allusion to Genesis 4:12, in which Cain is condemned to be 'a wanderer and a vagabond'. It may seem a little surprising that Steinbeck should worry that his readers might miss the point, but they would not have read his journal, nor (on a first reading) the explicit discussion of Genesis 4 later in the novel. They would surely, however, have begun to put two and two together when Charles acquires a prominent scar on his forehead, taking a crowbar to a recalcitrant rock.

Adam, meanwhile, who cowers in a secret part of the garden like his namesake after the eating of the apple, remains loyal to his father long after the evidence of his fraud becomes undeniable. As he explains to Charles, 'The proofs that God does not exist are very strong, but in lots of people they are not as strong as the feeling that he does' (77). This is the only point in the novel where the connection between the earthly and the heavenly father is made explicit. Steinbeck himself is not concerned with metaphysical questions so much as symbolic ones (in the Jungian as well as the Freudian sense). He self-consciously brings modern psychoanalytic notions to bear upon family relationships and their relevance to the development of religious and moral belief. In *Totem and Taboo*, as Steinbeck would have read in Fromm, Freud attributes the development of religion and morality to the sense of guilt suffered by the murderers of the primal father whereas for Jung, altogether more positive about religion than his mentor, such archetypal symbols retain a certain validity.

The first generation of Trask brothers, then, are shown simply to repeat the pattern of Genesis 4, with Charles only just failing in his murderous desire to revenge himself upon his brother Adam for the preference their father bestows upon him. The second generation, however, develops the biblical story in unexpected ways, bringing out the significance of moral choice, the possibility of conquering sin. Caleb and Aron are presented at the beginning of the third part of the novel quarrelling over the hunting of rabbits, one of which Aron wants to give their father. 'Don't tell me you're a gardener?', says Samuel to Caleb, much to the annoyance of Lee, who has not spent ten years poring over Genesis 4 without an awareness of its potential application to the children in his care (334). The brooding Cal, as in the biblical

---

52   *Ibid.*, p.28.

narrative and its midrashic supplements, resents the fact that everyone, not only their father but Abra, the girl for whose affection they compete, seems to prefer the generous, open-hearted, golden-haired Aron to him: 'he punished because he wished he could be loved as Aron was loved' (388). He counters his feelings of rejection by building up a 'wall of self-sufficiency' (490). That he loves his father and craves love in return becomes painfully obvious. When Adam on a rare occasion listens to him and shows him affection, Cal quickly loses the 'poison of loneliness and the gnawing envy of the unlonely' (505). But he is forced firstly to recognise how jealous he is of Aron and secondly that his gift of money, the profits of his Cain-like bean-growing enterprise, is an attempt to buy his father's love (594).

The rejection of this gift (Adam finds it hard to accept profits arising from the war to which he has to send young men) threatens to turn Cal into another Cain, although Lee insists (having just had another discussion with Adam about *timshol*), 'You have a choice' (601). Cal finally takes his revenge upon Aron by revealing that their mother now operates a brothel, a revelation which makes him partly responsible for his brother's death, since Aron's response is to enlist for the war, where he is killed. The similarities with the biblical narrative are made very clear: 'Do you know where your brother is?' asks Adam, to receive the reply, 'Am I supposed to look after him?' (623), only a slight variation upon the exchange between God and Cain in Genesis 4. But the reader who is expecting the C and A pattern simply to repeat itself is in for a surprise. Not only is Aron shown to be the weaker of the two, unable to cope with the knowledge of evil, but Cal overcomes the strong sense of guilt which makes him confess to Lee, 'I killed my brother. I'm a murderer' (660). Lee manages to persuade him that he does indeed have a choice, that he doesn't have to repeat the cycle of violence. Lee also manages to persuade the dying Adam to give a final patriarchal blessing, as Isaac blessed Jacob and Joseph his children at the end of Genesis. 'Your son is marked with guilt...almost more than he can bear', Lee says, taking the words out of the biblical Cain's mouth. 'Don't crush him with rejection.' The scene is thus set for a final tableau in which the dying father blesses his errant son, uttering with his dying breath the word *timshel* (665).

It's a grand, almost operatic, ending, not actually how Steinbeck originally finished the novel in the first draft of the manuscript, which had Cal and Abra wandering off inconclusively into the country and the narrator hammering home the moral lesson by urging his own boys never to 'destroy any single thing good or bad by pretending that it does not exist' but rather to choose good in the knowledge of evil (Givoni 1987:16, 22).[53] The final version of the novel, which drops the direct address to the boys throughout, encapsulates its moral in the final tableau, very much in keeping with the Book of Genesis, which has the dying Jacob bless his sons in chapter 49.

It is not only the male characters in the early chapters of Genesis and its midrashic commentary whose significance is teased out in Steinbeck's novel. Ginzberg, as we have seen, dwells not only on the role of Eve but on the woman over whom Cain and Abel fight. These roles are played in *East of Eden* by the twins' mother, Catherine,

---

53 Mark M.Givoni, 'Symbols for the Wordlessness: The Original Manuscript of *East of Eden*', *Steinbeck Quarterly* 14 (1987) 14-23.

to some extent the 'Eve' of the novel, and by Abra, who eventually transfers her affections from the hopelessly idealistic Aron, unable to see her as she really is, to Cal. The film version of the novel, of course, centres upon this romantic theme, Hollywood (not for the first time) turning biblical epic into romantic melodrama.

Catherine, like Eve in the biblical and midrashic accounts, seems to be particularly open to the serpent's temptation; in some midrashim, as we have seen, she even has intercourse with the serpent, the fallen 'angel of the Lord'. In introducing Catherine, his embodiment of evil, in chapter 8 of the novel, Steinbeck calls her a 'monster' of depravity, a 'malformed soul', referring back to a 'time when a girl like Cathy would have been called possessed by the devil' before being 'exorcised to cast out the evil spirit' or even 'burned as a witch for the good of the community' (80-1). She proceeds to build a career upon the sexual weakness and credulity of men, beginning with the brothel-owning Mr Edwards, who is responsible for inflicting the scar that she too subsequently bears on her forehead. She brings out what Steinbeck not altogether ironically calls 'the glory' in Adam, whose dreams of a paradise in the Salinas valley are clearly rooted in the opening chapters of Genesis. He tells Samuel, in terms of the Genesis-code they enjoy using with each other, 'I mean to make a garden of my land. Remember my name is Adam. So far I've had no Eden, let alone been driven out'. Samuel in turn starts joking about apples, wondering whether his Eve will allow him not to have an orchard, only for Adam to insist, 'You don't know this Eve...I don't think anyone can know her goodness' (189).

This, of course, is painfully ironic for readers, who have privileged access to the earlier career of this Eve. Steinbeck himself, at this stage, backtracks a little on his earlier description of Cathy as a monster. Using a self-consciously textual metaphor which draws attention to the whole process of narrative characterisation (analogous to the midrashic practice of returning again and again to the text in order to tease out further meaning), Steinbeck questions his earlier characterisation of Cathy as monstrous: 'Now I have bent close with a glass over the small print of her and re-read the footnotes, and I wonder if it was true'. He discusses the strange behaviour of women in pregnancy, which 'was set down to the Eve nature still under sentence for original sin' (206), another explicit suggestion that Cathy is cast very much in the role of Eve, the mother of Cain and the source (in conjunction with the serpent) of evil. Part of Cathy's motivation, which becomes particularly apparent in her role as madam of a brothel, is that she likes to expose the evil in men, the hypocrisy of those who pretend to be good. As she tells Adam, when he visits her after Samuel's funeral, 'I love to rub their noses in their own nastiness'(359). Lee recognises that she is full of hatred : 'When the first innocence goes', he tells Cal, 'you can't stop', although when Cal insists 'I've got her in me', he won't allow him to take refuge in genetic determinism, insisting that he still has a choice between good and evil (494-5).This battle between good and evil, as Steinbeck proclaims somewhat sententiously at the beginning of Part IV of the novel, is 'the one story in the world...There is only one story', one question which it makes sense to ask of an individual's life (459). In Cathy's case, the answer clearly is that she's bad, although even she has her moments of goodness, for instance in wanting to protect Aron from all knowledge of her. Her final thoughts before swallowing the capsule that will make her disappear suggest that the others in the novel 'had something she lacked', a belief in the possibility of goodness which keeps them going (610).

The battle between good and evil is depicted on a grand scale in the lives of all the characters in *East of Eden*. Among the sons of Samuel Hamilton, for example, Will is able to sympathise with Cal because he too never gains his father's recognition for his business talents while Tom never comes to terms with the evil in the world, the final example of which is his sister's cancer. Steinbeck refrains from spraying more scars on foreheads or indulging in more serpentine imagery to underline his point but it is clearly possible to see even the Hamilton half of the novel as a continued exploration of its central biblical theme. As in Genesis, the victory over evil is never won once and for all: it has to be renewed and refought in every generation.

This, I would suggest, is central to Steinbeck's novel, the time frame of which stretches from the Civil War in which Adam's father fights (however briefly) to the First World War in which his son loses his life. Quinones argues that 'as the Civil War destroyed the agricultural and Edenic myth of an Adamic innocence, immigration and the emergence of America after World War II helped create the myth of a regenerate Cain'.[54] It is important that Lee, the servant who brings his 'oriental' wisdom to bear upon the ancient eastern story of Cain and Abel, is one of the founders of this modern America, protecting and encouraging Cal, the latter-day Cain, to overcome evil and to make the right choice.

How much Steinbeck himself was aware of the midrashic tradition, as I acknowledged at the beginning of this chapter, remains uncertain. The fact that he consulted Ginzberg, befriended Campbell and read Fromm is no proof that he read *The Legends of the Jews* or picked up the specific allusions in the last two writers to midrash. His reworking of Genesis chapter 4, however, as well as displaying 'midrashic' strategies, combining commentary on the biblical text with narrative augmentation of it, has been found to echo some of the details to be found in Ginzberg, in particular the rivalry of the twins over a woman. Steinbeck, as I recognised earlier, could have created this storyline from the Bible independently of the midrash. The biblical narrative, after all, demands *some* explanation of the murder of Abel (and midrash itself, as we have seen, is generated from gaps in the original text). Either way, however, whether Steinbeck is consciously or only unconsciously following midrash, the parallels between his creative interpretation of the story and that of the rabbis are worth noting.

---

54 Quinones, *Changes of Cain*, p.143.

Chapter 4

From the Flood to Babel: Jeanette Winterson

Bloom, Frye and Biblical Revision: *Boating for Beginners* and *Lighthousekeeping*

'The retellings of the Biblical story of the Flood' in Jeanette Winterson's *Boating for Beginners* of 1985 and Julian Barnes' *A History of the World in 10½ Chapters* of 1989 are cited by Steven Connor among a number of other novels which illustrate the way in which, 'in contemporary fiction, telling has become compulsorily belated, inextricably bound up with retelling', often as a form of pastiche.[1] He could have added to his list some other novels of the 1980s in which Noah cuts a somewhat comic figure, his tale being retold in the mode of parody. In Timothy Findley's *Not Wanted on the Voyage* (1984), for example, the ageing patriarch, now over six hundred, has to comfort and cajole his creator out of his depression with a series of magic tricks.[2] Sarah Maitland and Michelene Wandor produced an epistolary novel entitled *Arky Types* (1987) in which the correspondents include an Anglican vicar (Mrs Vicar) and an archetypal Jewish mother (Mrs Noah). Another Mrs Noah, a woman who fantasises that she is the wife of the patriarch, makes an eponymous appearance in Michèle Roberts' *The Book of Mrs Noah* (also of 1987), imagining the Ark hosting a creative writers' course in which a number of sybils at one point question 'the Gaffer' about all he left out of his work, the Book of Genesis. 'Why should you want to read what I left out, asks the Gaffer: why try to rewrite my story?'[3]

I have chosen to focus on Jeanette Winterson partly because she provides interesting answers to this question and partly because of the self-consciously allusive and intertextual manner of her writing, which engages productively not only with the Bible but with the work of literary critics of the Bible such as Harold Bloom and Northrop Frye. As she said at the Guardian Hay Festival in June 2004, 'One of

---

1   Steven Connor, *The English Novel in History 1950-1995* (London: Routledge, 1996), pp.166-7.
2   Timothy Findley, *Not Wanted on the Voyage* (Harmondsworth: Penguin, 1984), p.93.
3   Michèle Roberts, *The Book of Mrs Noah* (London: Minerva, [1987] 1993), p.70. Retelling the story of the Flood was not the prerogative of the 1980s, of course. Earlier attempts include H.G.Wells, *All Aboard for Ararat* (London: Secker and Warburg, 1940) and David Garnett, *Two by Two: A Story of Survival* (London: Longmans, 1963). More recent versions of the story include Geraldine McCaughrean, *Not the End of the World* (Oxford: Oxford University Press, 2004) and David Maine, *The Flood* (Edinburgh: Canongate, 2004).

the things I do is provide work for academics and I take that job very seriously'.[4] She repeatedly emphasises the importance of intertextuality, telling her partner Margaret Reynolds in an interview of 2002,

> All texts work off other texts. It's a continual rewriting and rereading of what has gone before, and you hope that you can add something new. There's interpretation as well as creation in everything that happens with books.[5]

To the question posed by Louise Tucker in an interview printed as a postscript to her most recent novel *Lighthousekeeping* (2004), 'Why is intertextuality so important to your writing?', Winterson replies, 'Books speak to other books; they are always in dialogue'.[6] Her character Jordan in *Sexing the Cherry* (1989) explains the process of grafting (one of Derrida's metaphors for intertextuality), which produces new fruits able to grow more fruitfully in new habitats.[7] 'In Bloomian terms,' Louise Humphries insists, she is a brilliant 'mispriser', taking texts such as the Bible and subjecting them to productive revision.[8] Feminist critics sometimes find it problematic that she should use 'a supremely patriarchal text to organize her own story'.[9] They cannot help noticing that her career was built upon the Bible: her autobiographical first book, *Oranges are Not the Only Fruit* (1985), takes its chapter titles from the first eight books of the Bible, her second, *Boating for Beginners* (also 1985), retells the story of the Flood, and her most recent, *Lighthousekeeping,* plays with the biblical account of the Tower of Babel. Even when not directly retelling the Book of Genesis, her writing, in Marian Eide's words, has 'consistently drawn on Biblical language and religious experience to produce her own exalted discourse of passion'.[10]

There are biographical reasons for this, of course, in her childhood immersion in the Bible, which for some time was the only book that she was allowed to read. Before discussing this childhood grounding in the Bible, however, and her later more critical but no less reverent attitude towards it, I want to consider her controversial career more broadly. Having burst onto the literary scene with her Whitbread Prize-winning first novel, for the equally successful television adaptation of which she

---

4   'Jeanette enthralls; Niall is stroppy', UK Newsquest Regional Press, 14/6/2004, accessed through www.lexis-nexis.com/professional 6/7/05.

5   Margaret Reynolds, 'Interview with Jeanette Winterson', 14/9/2002, in Margaret Reynolds and Jonathan Noakes, *Jeanette Winterson: The Essential Guide* (London: Vintage, 2003), pp.11-29 (p.18).

6   Jeanette Winterson, *Lighthousekeeping* (London: Harper Perennial, 2005 [2004]), 'P.S.', p.2.

7   Jeanette Winterson, *Sexing the Cherry* (London: Vintage, 2001 [1989]), p.78.

8   Louise Humphries, 'Listening for the Author's Voice: "Un-Sexing" the Wintersonian Oeuvre', in Helene Bengston, Marianne Borch and Cindie Maagaard, eds, *Sponsored by Demons: The Art of Jeanette Winterson* (Odense, Denmark: Scholar's Press, 1999), pp.3-16 (p.15).

9   Helena Grice and Tim Woods, 'Reading Jeanette Winterson Writing', in *'I'm Telling You Stories': Jeanette Winterson and the Politics of Reading* (Amsterdam: Rodopi, 1998), pp.1-11 (p.6).

10   Marian Eide, "Passionate Gods and Desiring Women: Jeanette Winterson, Faith, and Sexuality", *International Journal of Sexual and Gender Studies* 6 (2001) 279-91 (p.281).

wrote the screenplay, she quickly lost favour among the literary establishment in the 1990s, partly as a result of what was widely perceived as arrogance and pretension (which was not helped by her naming herself as 'greatest living novelist' and her tendency to doorstep unsympathetic critics). One victim of this tendency accused her of abandoning the telling of stories for 'the role of high priestess'.[11] Another critic suggested that she believed herself to be the heir not only to Virginia Woolf but to 'the author of the Epic of Gilgamesh'.[12] She seems genuinely to have been regarded by some or her readers 'as a prophet of the late twentieth century'.[13] Winterson herself, looking back at the vilification she received during this period, has recognised the extent to which she brought it upon herself.[14] The bitterness she manages to evoke in critics appears to be a response to her prophetic impulse, that evangelical streak in her temperament and upbringing which makes her not content simply to please her readers but to attempt to change them.

Winterson's childhood was certainly unusual. The sketch of her life on her official website records how she was 'adopted by Pentecostal parents' who disapproved of all reading outside the Bible. 'There were only six books in the house', she claims, 'including the Bible and Cruden's Concordance'.[15] Winterson describes her mother as 'a woman for whom the Bible was a living breathing thing. She lived inside it. She was Old Testament'.[16] An autobiographical essay collected in *Art Objects* (1995) captures the violence of her indoctrination, claiming that her 'body was tattooed with Bible stories' in these early years, when she 'was brought up to memorise very long Bible passages'.[17] Another set of 'Childhood Recollections' depicts her mother 'poking clothes into the seething…tub with one hand, and reading the Book

---

11 Nicci Gerrard, 'The Ultimate Self-Produced Woman', the *Observer* (5/6/94), Review Section, p.7. See also an earlier article by Gerrard entitled 'The Prophet', referring to Winterson's evangelical temperament and 'self-appointed task…to challenge the way people think', *New Statesman* (1/9/89), pp.12-13.

12 Philip Hensher, 'Sappho's Mate', the *Guardian* (5/7/94), p.T13.

13 Michèle Roberts, the *Independent* (19/6/94), Sunday Review, p.32. For two alternative ways of telling Winterson's story, see Libby Brooks, 'Power Surge', the *Guardian* (2/9/00): 'Once there was a girl with a gift.…She was proud. And worst of all, she loved her gift so intensely that she made the mistake of assuming that others would love it for its own sake. Instead they burned her'. Alternative version: 'Once there was a girl with an ego. She made a fuss about where she came from (this girl was working class). She believed her writing could save the world (this girl was a megalomaniac). In fact, it was pretentious and undisciplined (this girl called herself an artist). She was cruel, controlling and sexually manipulative (this girl was a lesbian). And as her work sagged with self-indulgence, the ego became more monstrous still, until she burnt out'.

14 Interview with Maya Jaggi, the *Guardian* (29/5/04), Saturday Page, p.20.

15 www.jeanettewinterson.com/pages/content/index.asp?PageID=207, last accessed 10/5/04. Her adoptive father John Winterson sheds doubt on this in an interview with Geoffrey Levy in the *Daily Mail* (28/11/94), p.32.

16 Quoted from Desert Island Discs, in an article by Geoffrey Levy in the *Daily Mail* (28/11/94), p.32. He also quotes John Winterson shedding doubt on this official version of his adopted daughter's life, recalling that his wife 'loved the fact that Jeanette read a lot'.

17 Jeanette Winterson, *Art Objects: Esssays on Ecstasy and Effrontery* (London: Vintage, 1996 [1995]), pp.155-6.

of Revelations with the other'.[18] This 'Mother from heaven' apparently stuck biblical texts on every available domestic surface:

> In the kitchen, on a loaf wrapper, my mother had written, 'Man Shall Not Live By Bread Alone'. In the outside toilet, those who stood up, read, 'Linger Not At The Lord's Business.' Those who sat down read, 'He Shall Melt Thy Bowels Like Wax.'[19]

The pile of paperbacks hidden by the young Winterson under the bed, like the biblical tower of which she would later come to write, was eventually brought tumbling to the ground by this formidable figure: 'dragging out a corner of D.H.Lawrence', Winterson records, she 'collapsed my wordy tower, and threw the books out of the window' into the back yard, where they were promptly burnt.[20]

As with much of Winterson's work, it is quite hard to separate the fact from the fiction in these childhood recollections. A short story called 'Psalms', for example, recalls a tortoise 'bought for me and named [Psalms] for me by my mother in an effort to remind me continually to praise the Lord'. Psalms, we are led to believe, was followed by some fish called Proverbs, Ecclesiastes the hen, Solomon the scotch terrier and two long-lived goats named Isaiah and Jeremiah.[21] Another fictional reworking of her childhood recounts a Christmas visit to an old people's home during which the daughter worries whether her mother will like 'the self-assembly kit of the Tower of Babel waiting for her under the tree at home'.[22] This continual reference of their own lives to the Bible, exaggerated in these stories for comic effect, seems nevertheless to have formed a central element in Winterson's upbringing.

That the Bible remains a primary source of inspiration to her long after her abandonment of a fundamentalist belief in the literal truth of its stories, is repeatedly acknowledged by Winterson herself. Asked in 1997 where her 'passion for language' comes from, she has little hesitation in saying,

> I suppose it comes from the Bible. I was raised on the Bible. I dare say I know it better than anybody else, certainly most modern people, and it is a wonderfully written book. It contains in its ways of speaking, parables and stories, fictions, which are very potent and very personal.[23]

In another interview of the same year she accepts that the Bible remains 'a foundational text' for her. Although it had been necessary to leave behind the fundamentalist approach encouraged by her upbringing, to rebel against it, she continues to regard

---

18 Jeanette Winterson, 'Childhood Recollections', *Harper's and Queen UK*, reproduced at www.jeanettewinterson.com/pages/content/index.asp?PageID=282, last accessed 28/4/05.

19 Jeanette Winterson, 'Mother From Heaven', *New Yorker*, reproduced at www.jeanettewinterson.com/pages/content/index.asp?PageID=110, last accessed 28/4/05.

20 Ibid.

21 Jeanette Winterson, 'Psalms', *New Statesman* (26/4/85), pp.27-9, reprinted in *The World and Other Places* (London: Vintage, 1999[1998]), pp.219-30.

22 Jeanette Winterson, 'Only the Best for the Lord', *New Statesman* (26/12/86) pp.46-7.

23 Eleanor Wachtel with Jeanette Winterson, 'Interview', *Malahat Review* 118 (Spring 1997), pp 61-73 (pp.63-4).

the Bible as a source of religious and literary inspiration: 'It helps me to think about things, it helps me to piece things together'.[24]

One of the writers who appears to have contributed to Winterson's more independent and critical attitude to the Bible is Harold Bloom, whose *Book of J* she reviewed in 1991. The review begins, after quoting Bloom himself on the way the Bible has been 'barricaded from us by normative moralists and theologians', by asking its readers to 'imagine a work of fiction...whose characters, because they stand for all of us, are soap opera as well as sublime'. This book, Winterson continues, deliberately defamiliarising its contents, is 'bawdy, undignified, painfully to the point and not at all the sort of thing to give to the vicar'. It is, of course, the Bible.[25] Winterson proceeds to explain Bloom's view of the Redactor of the Pentateuch (the Priestly Writer) as an 'arch-varnisher' and censor who succeeds to some extent in obscuring the 'blasphemous' nature of J's portrait of God. For to Bloom, as to Twain,

> J's Yahweh is volatile and violent and manifestly unfair. When we read J's story of the expulsion from the garden of Eden, we find no sense of sin or of a fall from grace. Rather we find two curious children to whom the rules have not been properly explained [whose] punishment is fantastically cruel and incommensurate with the offence.

Winterson joins Bloom in celebrating both J's literary craftsmanship (she is 'not a mediocre writer who needs to spell everything out, but one of enormous sophistication and literary cunning') and her lack of conventional prudery (she is not bothered by sexual misdemeanours, more concerned with the lack of hospitality among the Sodomites than with their predilections). Bloom's book, she concludes, is an important one, illustrating 'how little authority knows', how absurd it is for religious institutions to have employed this particular text above all others as a vehicle for repression and control.[26]

Harold Bloom, incidentally, re-appears in Winterson's novel *The PowerBook* (2000), when the narrator's lover proposes a toast to him 'for his translation of the Jewish blessing',[27] which suggests that for Winterson at least he is a latter-day patriarch (in a positive rather than a pejorative sense) handing down a transformed tradition to his literary heirs. The narrator of *The PowerBook* herself certainly seems to have gathered the main principle of midrash, since she later celebrates the way she can herself become 'part of the story, adding my version to the versions there. This Talmudic layering of story on story, map on map, multiplies possibilities but also warns me of the weight of accumulation'.[28] *Gut Symmetries* (1998) also contains a number of references to the Kabbalah, acknowledging at the outset a debt to 'my Jewish friends who taught me their love and mystery'. Theoretical physics and religious stories, it is suggested in the 'Prologue' to this novel, provide alternative

---

24 'Jeanette Winterson: The Art of Fiction', interview with Audrey Bilger, *Paris Review* 39 (Winter 1997/8), pp.68-112 (pp.80-1).
25 Jeanette Winterson, 'God the Sod', *New Statesman* (10/5/91), pp.37-8 (p.37).
26 *Ibid.*, pp.37-8.
27 Jeanette Winterson, *The Powerbook* (London: Vintage, 2001 [2000]), p.45.
28 *Ibid.*, p.54.

ways of imagining and describing not only 'the moment of Creation' but that universal sense of loss, of having been 'split off', expressed in the myth of having been 'forcibly removed' from Eden.[29] The Book of Genesis, in other words, retains a certain validity in the modern world so long as it is read not literally but literately.

One of the central characters of *Gut Symmetries*, named Sarah by her Jewish father 'after the wife of Abraham',[30] sees her own life very much in terms of scenes from the Book of Genesis. In a chapter entitled 'The Tower', for example, she looks back on her marriage as an equivalent within her own personal history of the famous tower of Genesis 11, a man-made construct providing a false sense of security:

> I think back to Nimrod, the mighty hunter of Genesis, who built the Tower of Babel that God destroyed. Babel. Even when ruined, a man could walk for three days and still be in its shadow. What did I build that has called down such wrath?[31]

Her father, she remembers, had always warned her, 'Never turn your back on the serpent'. But she had failed to see the problem lurking inside the walls of her marriage, forgetting that 'the enemy of Paradise is always already inside'.[32] Now she realises that she will have to remake herself 'as Jewish legend tells how God made the first man: by moulding a piece of dirt and breathing life into it'.[33] It is interesting that she makes no distinction between biblical 'Jewish legend' (such as the creation of man from dust) and extra-biblical midrashic detail, such as the extent of the ruined tower of Babel (not actually to be found in Genesis 11). What Winterson seems to like about Jewish legend in general and what links it to theoretical physics, is its indirect and provisional nature. 'The method of Kabbalah', to which Sarah's father turns from his own work with Heisenberg in Germany in the 1930s, 'is to free the individual from conceptual frameworks, which are all and always provisional'.[34] The central paradox of Judaism, experienced first by Moses at the burning bush, is that 'there is no life without God and yet to approach God means death'. The solution, for Sarah's father, at least, 'is to 'see as much as it was possible to see while inside the limitations of consciousness'.[35]

It is this recognition of the limits of all human constructs, especially language, that separates the prophet from the priest, to employ a distinction of which Winterson is particularly fond. Asked what would have happened if she had stayed with her mother and her church, the 'Jeanette' who is the heroine of *Oranges Are Not the Only Fruit* replies that she fears that she would, like Lot's wife, be similarly tempted to turn back to her past, have 'turned into a pillar of salt'. She would have become

> a priest instead of a prophet. The priest has a book with the words set out. Old words, known words, words of power. Words that are always on the surface. Words for every

---

29   Jeanette Winterson, *Gut Symmetries* (London: Granta Books, 1998), p.4.
30   *Ibid.*, p.92.
31   *Ibid.*, p.38.
32   *Ibid.*, pp.40-1.
33   *Ibid.*, p.45.
34   *Ibid.*, p.168.
35   *Ibid.*, p.178.

occasion....The prophet has no book. The prophet is a voice that cries in the wilderness, full of sounds that do not always set into meaning. The prophets cry out because they are troubled by demons.[36]

Handel, the defrocked priest in Winterson's highly experimental novel *Art and Lies* (1994), defrocked for slipping condoms into the Bibles given out free to the poor in Brazil, makes a similar distinction between the arts, which periodically 'break their own rules, to renew themselves and to invigorate themselves when the letter is killing and spirit is offering life', and the Church, which 'has not been either as brave or as wise': 'That is why I left the Church, not the teachings of Christ but the dogmas of Man'.[37] The excommunicated poet Sappho, one of the other narrative voices in this polyphonic novel, rails even more violently against 'the Church zombies....all mouthing platitudes, the language of the dead'.[38] She chooses instead 'the word that cracks the font', the voice of 'the ragged prophet in burning clothes'.[39] Winterson herself has clearly made a similar choice.

The 'calling of the artist', Winterson writes in *Art Objects*, her manifesto of Modernist principles, 'is to make it new'. This does not mean, she explains (following Eliot and Bloom on the nature of literary tradition), that 'the past is repudiated' but that it is 'reclaimed...re-stated and re-instated'.[40] She cites the story of creation in Genesis as a model of this refashioning of something new out of old material:

> Yahweh makes himself a clay model of man and breathes on it to give it life. It is this supreme confidence, this translation of forms, the capacity to recognise in one thing the potential of another...that is the stamp of creativity and the birthright that Yahweh gives to humans.[41]

Art pushes 'at the boundaries we thought were fixed', prising away 'old dead structures' and 'convenient lies'.[42] For Winterson therefore it is entirely appropriate to pick up on the wealth of stories, symbols and images she finds in the Bible and to develop them in her own work:

> The Bible is something that I know so well that it would be ridiculous for me to do without it...I don't accept the God myth of the church....But that doesn't mean that I don't accept the essential mystery of the Scriptures.[43]

Winterson can no longer sign up to official church doctrines but clearly continues to find the Bible of great value.

---

36 Jeanette Winterson, *Oranges Are Not the Only Fruit* (London: Vintage, 1996 [1985]), p.156.
37 Jeanette Winterson, *Art and Lies* (London: Vintage. 1995 [1994]), p.186.
38 *Ibid.*, p.64.
39 *Ibid.*, p.55.
40 Winterson, *Art Objects*, p.12.
41 *Ibid.*, p.142.
42 *Ibid.*, p.116.
43 Bilger, 'Jeanette Winterson', pp.79-80.

The remainder of this chapter will attempt to clarify what this 'value' entails, considering the ways in which three of Winterson's novels can be said creatively to remould elements from the Bible, especially the Book of Genesis (and within that the stories of the Flood and of Babel) not so much in the manner of midrash (though she is clearly aware of this tradition) as in the manner of a Modernist 'prophet', making something new of the old biblical material, breathing new artistic life into it. For the midrashist the biblical text itself remains of paramount importance, unchallenged in its authority over the present. The modernist, by contrast, self-consciously reworks the original text, which is recognised, in some respects at least, as in need of renewal.

Oranges Are Not the Only Fruit, as a number of critics have noted, expresses an ambivalence about the kind of religion in which 'Jeanette', its heroine, is brought up. The way in which Winterson's fictional reconstruction of her own life plays with the Bible, as Cindie Maagaard has observed, 'testifies both to her love for the Book which has shaped her and to the desire to wrest her own voice and story from it', transforming 'the priestly word into the prophetic cries of artistic text'.[44] The novel bears witness both to the positive aspects of her religious upbringing, the enabling qualities of the language and identity it gives her, while also noting the way 'it betrays and punishes her'.[45] On this negative side, Winterson herself has acknowledged that both the novel and its screen adaptation portray the church as 'an exercise of power' rather than 'a sacrament of love'.[46] For Jeanette is finally cast out of her fundamentalist church for daring to love someone of her own gender. This does not happen, however, before it has provided her with a language in which to tell her story.

That story, of course, as it appears in the novel, is structured by the Bible. The chapter titles are those of the first eight books of the Bible, which is partly 'comic parody' but also, as Tess Cosslett recognises, 'deeply serious appropriation'.[47] The opening chapter 'Genesis', for example, describes Jeanette's origins, her genealogy as an orphan adopted and formed for a special destiny as a missionary to the world. 'Exodus' describes the years of her exile from that world, wandering in the wilderness of exclusion from the ordinary life of her schoolfellows. 'Leviticus', 'Deuteronomy' and 'Numbers' detail the commandments, especially the laws regarding sexual activity, before in 'Joshua' Jeanette learns to blow her own trumpet, bringing down the walls fixing the boundaries of permissible behaviour. 'Ruth', the final chapter, brings about a kind of reconciliation with her adoptive mother and establishes the hope that alien women in a foreign land can bond together to form new lives.

---

44 Cindie Aaen Maagard, 'Jeanette Winterson: Postmodern Prophet of the Word', in Erik Borgman, Bart Philipsen and Lea Verstricht, eds, *Literary Canons and Religious Identity* (Aldershot: Ashgate, 2004), pp.151-61 (pp.158-9).

45 Marian Eide, 'Passionate Gods', p. 283.

46 Helen Barr, 'Face to Face: A Conversation Between Jeanette Winterson and Helen Barr', *English Review* 2:1 (1991) pp.30-33 (p.30).

47 Tess Cosslett, 'Intertextuality in *Oranges Are Not the Only Fruit*: The Bible, Malory, and *Jane Eyre*', in Grice and Woods, *'I'm Telling You Stories'*, pp.15-28 (p.16).

The tone of this biblically-structured narrative, however, is often that of pastiche, satirising evangelical bibliolatry. The young Jeanette, given 'some Fuzzy Felt to make biblical scenes', already displays a penchant for revisionary rewriting: 'I was just beginning to enjoy a rewrite of Daniel in the lions' den when Pastor Finch appeared' to remind her that the biblical figure had actually managed to escape.[48] She enjoys visiting Elsie Norris, one of the less orthodox members of the church, partly because 'she had a collage of Noah's Ark' which showed Mr and Mrs Noah leaning out of the ark while their offspring 'tried to catch one of the rabbits'. Again the young Jeanette invents 'all kinds of variations' on the biblical story, mostly involving 'a detachable chimpanzee, made out of a Brillo pad', which she 'usually...drowned'.[49] As the novel develops, Winterson clearly enjoys employing biblical references in similarly subversive fashion against the grain of their original meaning. When Jeanette falls in love with Melanie, for example, she celebrates the excitement of her first night of passion in words from the opening chapter of Genesis: 'And it was evening and it was morning; another day'.[50] Jeanette's discovery of lesbian sex is indeed a new dawn in her life but not quite in the way the Book of Genesis is normally understood.

The Book of Genesis also appears, albeit in disguise, in one of the many fairy-tales embedded in the novel, the account of the Fall being defamiliarised in a story about a secret walled garden on the banks of the Euphrates, at the heart of which lies an orange tree. To 'eat of the fruit' of this tree, in Winterson's reworking of Genesis chapters 2 and 3, 'means to leave the garden because the fruit speaks of other things, other longings'. It also means that you have to 'say goodbye to the place you love... knowing you can never return by the same way as this'.[51] There is an ambivalence about this version of the familiar story, however, since the recovery of paradise is not ruled out, even for lesbians. In the orange demon who from time to time visits Jeanette to keep her 'in one piece', there is a clear reversal of the usual biblical role assigned to its kind. Jeanette herself objects, 'In the Bible you [demons] keep getting driven out', but the orange demon replies, 'Don't believe all you read'.[52] The point of the whole novel, in fact, is that Jeanette needs to listen to her demons, to abandon the restrictions imposed upon her by the church in which she has been brought up in order to achieve personal 'wholeness'. Part of her identity continues irrevocably to be bound up in the Bible and its stories, but she has to reinterpret these in ways which can be fruitful if not exactly orthodox. This, of course, is the 'message' conveyed in the title of the novel, though there is a more literal reference to the only piece of fruit her mother ever buys.

Winterson's most sustained rewriting of a biblical text, the story of the Flood in Genesis 6 to 9, comes in *Boating for Beginners*. It's not a book of which Winterson is particularly proud, appearing in a category of its own, as a 'comic book', separate from her other 'fiction' in the list at the front of all Vintage editions of her work. On her official website she describes it even less grandly, though nevertheless accurately,

---

48   Winterson, *Oranges*, p.12.
49   *Ibid.*, p.24.
50   *Ibid.*, p.86.
51   *Ibid.*, p.120.
52   *Ibid.*, p.106.

as 'a comic book with pictures'. She denies having tried to persuade publishers to leave it out of print but accepts that she has been 'quiet about it'. It was 'written for money in 6 weeks', she explains, in embarrassed fashion, which may explain why it is 'full of silly things'. It is at times 'great fun' but ultimately 'doesn't matter'.[53] The biographical section prefaced to her interview with Audrey Bilger describes it in similarly disparaging fashion as 'a light revisionist romp through the book of Genesis'.[54] The apologetic nature of these comments may in part be a response to the novel's less than encouraging reception, many of the reviews criticising its 'wackier', whimsical elements.[55] 'Comic fantasy', complained Anne Barton in *The Sunday Times*, 'can develop a fatal affinity with whimsy and cuteness'.[56] Others labelled it a 'clanger' or a 'flop'.[57] In playing 'several different games with Noah's Ark' Winterson was seen to take on too wide a range of targets, from fundamentalism to the fashion and the food business.[58] Only David Lodge admitted actually to have enjoyed the novel, appreciating both its radical break with realism and 'extremely funny travesty of the Book of Genesis'. Acknowledging that 'the comedy is often blasphemous', he also saw that 'it is based on affection for as well as familiarity with the Bible'.[59]

The most obvious satirical target of the book is fundamentalism, the literal reading of the Bible mocked by Northrop Frye, who is referred to several times in the novel and even makes an appearance towards the end, emerging from a conference in a hotel which is one of the first victims of the Flood.[60] Gloria, the novel's heroine, is a great fan of Frye's, eagerly charting her own progress through his three stages of language: the metaphoric, the didactic and the prosaic (44). Her mother, she realises, is only at the first stage of language, highly poetic and concrete, making 'no distinction between thinking things and objects of thought' (48). The relevance of this theory, derived from Vico and outlined by Northrop Frye in *The Great Code: The Bible and Literature*, published three years before *Boating for Beginners*, is its application to religious texts. The first phase, according to Frye, involves the 'poetic' conception of language to be found in the 'pre-Biblical cultures of the Near East and in much of the Old Testament itself'. All words in this phase of language are concrete, containing a magical power when read in ritual, as when 'the Babylonian creation myth *Enuma Elish* was read at the New Year'.[61] In the first stage of language you have 'a plurality of gods', embodiments of natural objects

---

53 'Boating for Beginners', www.jeanettewinterson.com/pages/content/index.asp?PageID=19, last accessed 28/4/05.

54 Bilger, 'Jeanette Winterson', p.70.

55 Bill Greenwell, *New Statesman* (25/10/85), p.31.

56 Anne Barton, *Sunday Times* (12/1/86), p.45.

57 Natasha Walter, *Independent* (19/9/92), Weekend Arts Section, p.28; *Independent* (11/6/94), p.10.

58 Emma Fisher, *Times Literary Supplement* (1/11/85), p.1228.

59 David Lodge, *New York Review of Books* (29/9/88), pp.25-6.

60 Jeanette Winterson, *Boating for Beginners* (London: Minerva, 1990 [1985]), 153. All references in brackets in the text are to this edition.

61 Northrop Frye, *The Great Code: The Bible and Literature* (London: Ark Paperbacks, 1983 [1982]), pp.5-6.

and people. In the second stage (as in the work of the Priestly Writer) God becomes monotheistic, conceptual and abstract, 'a transcendent reality' behind all objects. In the third 'descriptive' phase, beginning with the onset of modernity in the sixteenth century, language is seen as pointing directly to things. The language of mythology is replaced by science and 'the word "God" becomes linguistically unfunctional'. For there is no 'object' to which it can be seen to point.[62] Frye's point is that it is only poetry (or literature) which can keep metaphorical language alive, referring like the Bible to God as a verb, a dynamic process, not a thing.[63]

People who read the Bible literally, Frye argues, misunderstand its use of language, applying third-phase thinking to first-phase writing. He recalls being asked, after 'the discovery of a large boat-shaped structure on Mount Ararat', if

> this alleged discovery 'sounded the death knell of liberal theology'. The first thing that occurred to me was that the Bible itself could not care less whether anyone ever finds an ark on Mount Ararat or not: such 'proofs' belong to a mentality quite different from any that could conceivably have produced the Book of Genesis.[64]

This, it would appear, is also the point of the epigraph to *Boating for Beginners*, taken from a report in the *Guardian* that 'bags of rocks and chunks of Ararat, Turkey, that Biblical archaeologists believe are relics of Noah's Ark have been taken to the US for laboratory analysis'. It also underlies the epilogue of the novel, which describes two archaeologists making similar 'discoveries' on Mount Ararat. This point is made explicit by a passage in the middle of the novel in which the narrator intervenes to explain both the dangers of literalism and the nature of biblical myth:

> Myths hook and bind the mind because at the same time they set the mind free: they explain the universe while allowing the universe to go on being unexplained; and we seem to need this even now, in our twentieth-century grandeur. The Bible writers didn't care that they were bunching together sequences some of which were historical, some preposterous, and some downright manipulative. Faithful recording was not their business. Faith was.(66).

After making further generalisations about the poetry of faith (and its potential for fanaticism) the narrator urges her readers to open the Bible and 'read it for its arrogance, its sleight of hand. It's very beautiful, and it's a pointer for living. The mistake is to use it as a handbook' (66-7). Understood as poetry, in Frye's sense, the Bible can still be fruitful; read literally, it can be dangerous.

Boating for Beginners can be said on one level to dramatise the layers of writing, of poetic (and not so poetic) invention in the Book of Genesis. It takes place supposedly as a daydream in Gloria's mind (perhaps inspired by her reading of Frye?) in which Noah, the director of a 'little pleasure boat company called Boating for Beginners', having received a direct call from Yahweh the Unpronounceable, announces to an astonished press conference that 'they were collaborating on a manuscript that would be a kind of global history from the beginnings of time'. Keen to make the book

---

62 *Ibid.*, pp.9 and 15.
63 *Ibid.*, pp.17 and 25.
64 *Ibid.*, p.44.

'dignified but popular', they 'had decided to issue it by instalments starting with *Genesis*, or *How I Did It*' (14). Both this and its sequel, *Exodus* or *Your Way Lies There*, sell well, enabling Noah and Yahweh to 'concentrate on something a bit more philosophical about the role of priests and things' (presumably Leviticus). They also plan a 'Good Food Guide' (Numbers and Deuteronomy), which will complete the Pentateuch (15-16).

God and Noah, encouraged by the success of these books, decide to dramatise the first two volumes as an epic, touring 'the heathen places of the world, like York and Wakefield'. To this end they enlist the romantic novelist Bunny Mix to add 'legitimate spice and romantic interest' (20). As well as referring to the dramatic power of the oldest stratum of the Book of Genesis, the descriptions of the 'original' version of the story (of which the two-volume epic is an adaptation) seem to refer to the *Enuma Elish*, described by Robert Graves (one of Winterson's favourite authors) as 'the Babylonian Creation Epic, in which the Creator is the Thunder-god Marduk who defeats Tiamat the Sea-Monster and cuts her in half'. Graves notes that 'the Deluge incident in *Genesis*' is been taken directly from the Babylonian Epic,[65] whose account of the defeat of 'the dragon-mother-goddess' has been seen as an example of the way women have been written out of the Bible.[66] In the novel there is mounting excitement 'amongst the privileged few who knew how Bunny Mix would interpret the characters of the overthrown goddesses' (21). Similarly, when Gloria thinks 'back to what she knew about the book of Genesis' later in the novel, she too appears to be remembering the *Enuma Elish*: 'There was an explanation on the pagan gods', she explains, 'then a blood scene where everyone went to war' (50). Doris, Noah's cleaner, unhappy with her 'bit-part as an unbelieving crone' in Bunny Mix's dramatised adaptation, also prefers the 'original' version as written by 'Noah and his cosmic friend' to the later version (69). The novel demonstrates a clear awareness on Winterson's part of the textual history of the Book of Genesis, its origins in a world full of dramatic epics about creation, all very much in Frye's first phase of language.

In *Boating for Beginners* Noah himself is caught up in the process of revisionary misprision, planning to 'rewrite *Genesis* and make it look like God did it all from the very beginning'. He is also very much aware of the problems surrounding the word 'God', discussing with Yahweh the unpronounceability of His name. 'It's not my fault', he argues, 'that we have to do this in Hebrew' without vowels, only for Yahweh to point out that 'it isn't always going to be Hebrew' (112). Noah finally resolves on a more easily translatable name, 'the Almighty'. It is Noah too who is responsible for the misogyny in the revised version of the book, resolving, 'when he sat down to re-draft *Genesis,* he would make sure everyone knew where the blame lay. Women; they're all the same...' (117). There is much discussion among the authors of the revised version of Genesis of the need to avoid anachronism (they can't let on that their ship is really built of fibre-glass so Noah has to plant pieces of gopher wood on Mount Ararat to corroborate their description). Bunny Mix meanwhile

---

[65] Robert Graves, *The White Goddess: A Historical Grammar of Poetic Myth* (London: Faber and Faber, 1952), p.458.

[66] Alicia Ostriker, *Feminist Revision and the Bible* (Oxford: Blackwell, 1993), p.34.

is unhappy about some elements in the original text, for instance God's apparent malice in destroying the whole world. The solution, she realises, is to 'explain how evil the world is, though myself I don't think it merits destruction' and to 'say how we eight were saved because we were the only worthwhile people' (137). It's Bunny Mix too who suggests the rainbow to round the story off. Noah agrees ('We can pretend we never had them before') but he wonders whether it's not 'too way-out for the reading public'. 'If they've swallowed it this far', Bunny replies, 'they'll love the rainbow' (139). In Winterson's novel there is a more accurate version of 'what really happened', the work of a group of women led by Gloria and Doris, who place it for safety in a bottle. In a final twist, however, the archaeologist who eventually discovers this parchment dismisses it as a 'cheap hoax' and throws it away (159).

The point of this elaborate dramatisation of the layers of rewriting involved in the production of the text of the Book of Genesis is not only historical (it is a parodic version of the complex textual history of the opening book of the Bible) but literary (these are the kinds of generic question, Winterson suggests, which lie behind the telling of any story). The Yahwist may not have been unduly concerned about the justice of Yahweh's decision to destroy his whole creation but the Priestly Writer attempts to present it as to some extent justified, making Noah 'a just man and perfect in his generations' in contrast with the rest of the earth, which 'was corrupt before God' (Gen. 6: 9-11). The scene of the rainbow is clearly not a 'historical' event, to be taken literally, but a symbolic representation of the covenant a just God makes never again 'to destroy the earth' (Gen. 9:11). *Boating for Beginners*, I suggest, succeeds in representing at least some of the theological, moral and literary questions involved in the original composition of the story of the flood.

The novel is more outrageous and perhaps less successful in its characterisation of the key figures in the story, Noah and God. Noah, 'a spherical man...around four feet tall' lacking both hair and teeth, is a parody of a revivalist preacher, addressing his crew as 'brothers' and promising that 'whatever you chew in his name will never make your belly ache' (50-1). Introducing Bunny Mix to the project, he assures his audience that she, like them, is 'on the Glory Trail' (51). Doris, however, is unimpressed, feeling it 'a pity that someone who had such a way with words should turn out to be such a lousy fascist bastard', should be so 'suspicious of women and totally committed to money as a medium for communication'. Noah, in the time-honoured fashion of evangelical preachers, plays upon the 'pain and disappointment' of his audience, painting a bright future for them if they come on board (literally) and damning them if they refuse to believe (69-70). He has some of the traits of his biblical original— he vows when he hits dry land to 'plant a vineyard and get roaring drunk and stay drunk for the rest of his life' (127)— but for the most part he remains a vehicle for Winterson's satire of evangelicals and their will to power.

The character of God in the novel is even more outrageous. In a pastiche of *Frankenstein* (and presumably a dramatisation of the idea that He is necessarily a projection of the human mind) He turns out to be the product of one of Noah's experiments involving 'a piece of gateau and a giant electric toaster' (85). He behaves, however, with all the arrogance of a chief executive. 'God is Love, Don't mess with me' is the message he emblazons in the sky in support of Noah's initial claims (14) while his first response to Noah's projected adaptation of Genesis is equally blunt:

'I want his ass!' (52). It is Yahweh who suggests actually flooding the world rather than simply writing about it. He positively gloats over the destruction He plans to unleash: 'I'll throw it down like there's no tomorrow. Hee hee, and this time there won't be' (114). The Yahweh of this novel is a monster of power, totally lacking in the qualities of compassion, justice and mercy ascribed to Yahweh in the Bible as a whole. But then the Yahweh of Genesis chapters 6 to 8, Winterson wants us to recognise, is hardly a model of nurturing fatherhood. *Boating for Beginners*, for all its playfulness, dramatises those elements in the biblical narrative which someone in Frye's third phase of language development is bound to find rather primitive. There is, in other words, a serious purpose to this 'comic book'. The jokes about this manifestly inadequate image of God should not be allowed completely to conceal an important point about the limits of religious language. Winterson's self-consciously playful revisiting of the story of the flood can also be found to shed some light upon those aspects of the biblical text which pose problems for modern readers, not the least of which is Yahweh's apparent indifference to the terrible fate of the majority of his creatures. The story, Winterson suggests, should be read with several pinches of salt.

The Book of Genesis also looms large in Winterson's most recent novel, *Lighthousekeeping*, whose protagonist is named Babel by his idealistic father 'after the first tower that ever was'.[67] As Winterson explains in the Postscript appended to the novel, '*Lighthousekeeping* is a story about telling stories', a 'net of stories about beginnings' (20-1). The Book of Genesis is perhaps the most important of the stories to which the novel refers, along with Darwin's *On the Origin of Species* and Wagner's *Tristan and Isolde*, both of which could also be called narratives 'about the beginnings of the world' (169). Robert Louis Stephenson's investigation into the origin of evil, *Dr Jekyll and Mr Hyde*, is another significant intertext; both Darwin and Stephenson meet the Reverend Babel Dark at various points in the novel to discuss their alternative accounts of human origins. But the Bible, and the Book of Genesis in particular, is the prime intertext in the telling not only of Babel's story but of Silver's, the girl who for a time helps the lighthousekeeper Pew to maintain the lighthouse built by Babel's father.

When Silver asks of Babel Dark, 'What was he like, Pew?', the latter, much to Silver's annoyance, replies with a question of his own: 'You know the Bible story of Samson?' 'Why can't you just tell me the story without starting with another story?', objects the girl, only to be told that 'there's no story that's the start of itself'. However far back you go, as Derrida repeatedly insisted, there is no final signified, no fixed point of origin. This, as we have seen, applies to the Book of Genesis itself, which draws on earlier accounts of the origins of the world in the ancient near east. Pew proceeds to narrate the story of Samson, 'the strongest man in the world' who was nevertheless 'brought...down' by a woman, as Babel himself will be torn between his wife and the love of his life, Molly. 'You could say Samson was two pillars of the community', Pew explains, after recounting his death tied to two pillars which

---

67 Jeanette Winterson, *Lighthousekeeping* (London: Harper Perennial, 2005 [2004]), p.15. All future references in brackets in the text will be to this edition.

he brought crashing down, 'because anyone who sets himself up is always brought down' (26-7).

The biblical story that means most to Babel himself and, as Pew later explains, the one he always reads in the pub, is 'his own story', that of 'the first Tower of Babel in the Book of Genesis'. Pew continues,

> That tower was built as high as the moon, so that the people who built it could climb up and be like God. When it came shattering down, the people were scattered to the ends of the earth, and they no more understood each other's language than they understood the language of fishes and birds. (64)

When Pew asks him why he always reads that story, he explains that it's because 'I have become a stranger in my own life' (64). Like Dr Jekyll, in fact, he has two lives, the respectable one as a minister to the small Scottish seaside community, and the passionate two months he enjoys every summer with his mistress Molly near Bristol. Babel Dark, with his theology degree from Cambridge, may appear to be a pillar of his community but his faith is undermined, in characteristic Victorian fashion, by a combination of geological discoveries about the origins of creation and of moral discoveries about his own nature. It is perhaps ironic that his first sermon is preached on a text from Isaiah 51:1, 'Remember the rock whence ye are hewn, and the pit whence ye are digged' (43), since it is his discovery of spectacular fossils in the cliffs which confirms his doubts about the literal truth of the biblical account of creation. It is also significant that on the one occasion that Molly attends his church, Dark preaches on Genesis 9:13: 'I have set my Covenant in the Heavens like a Bow'. Although the rainbow here is a symbol of God's side of the covenant, never again to destroy the earth, that covenant, as the Book of Exodus will confirm, also requires man to obey God's commandments. These, of course, include a prohibition of adultery.

As in the opening chapters of Genesis and in the story of Samson (in the Book of Judges chapters 13 to 16), it is a woman who tempts the man to disobey God's commandments. Again, however, Winterson retells the story so that Molly is seen to bring life rather than death to Adam, wakening him to new awareness, new life:

> Sometimes she opened her mouth to him, the way Adam must have felt God breathing first life into his sleeping body.

> But she was the one who slept. In the little death, he bent to kiss her and wake her, waking her with a kiss, so that her eyes opened sleepily and she smiled at him (68).

The whole biblical account of creation is placed in a new light by Dark's discovery of fossils in the cliffs near Salts. This section of the novel is entitled 'A Place Before the Flood', presumably because it sets Dark questioning the supposed origins of the world as described in the Book of Genesis:

> He had always clung to the unchanging nature of God, and the solid reliability of God's creation. Now he was faced with a maverick God who had made a world for the fun of seeing how it might develop. Hade he made Man in the same way?

> Perhaps there was no God at all. (120)

Dark's encounter with Darwin, one of the visitors who come to inspect the fossils for himself, suggests a different world from the 'stable-state system of creation and completion', a world of 'flux change, trial and error, maverick shifts, chance, fateful experiments, and lottery odds against success' (170). The sheer time scale of creation now appears to have been utterly different: 'It could no longer be imagined as a series of lifetimes, reeled off like a genealogy from the Book of Genesis' (171). 'I woke up in one world and I went to bed in another', Dark explains to Pew. 'You don't believe that the guid God made it in seven days then?', asks the lighthousekeeper. 'No, I do not', Dark replies (183).

A page of one of Babel's journals, entitled 'A place before the Flood' (with different capitalisation and different emphasis, dwelling on the change passion has brought to his life), asks similar questions:

> Was there ever such a place? The Bible story is simple; God destroyed the wicked world and only Noah and his family were saved. After forty days and forty nights the ark came to rest on Mount Ararat, and as the flood waters began to subside, it stayed there (127).

Dark now sees this as 'an impossible moment...absurd, grandiloquent, part miracle, part madness'. By giving up his belief in the biblical narrative and its commandments he can abandon himself to the tides of passion, the 'trail of shipwrecks and set-sails' brought by those tides (127). The last we hear of him (chronologically speaking) is that he quite literally abandons himself to the sea, attempting to 'swim back through time, to a place before the flood' (122), a place no longer under the control of the covenant and its demanding God. *Lighthousekeeping*, in other words, like *Boating for Beginners*, involves a severe critique of the story of the Flood, attempting to return to a place before and beyond the control of its destructive and controlling God.

All three of the novels on which I have focussed tell their stories intertextually, through repeated reworking of the Book of Genesis. In the process, they also retell that foundational book of the Bible, questioning and revising some of its assumptions about creation, about the God responsible for it, about the punishments He is supposed to have brought against his creatures for becoming so corrupt, punishments which include death, the Flood and the destruction of their greatest achievement, the Tower of Babel. Winterson continues to finds these stories powerful and suggestive while no longer able to accept the assumptions lying behind them (as these are to be found in the final form of the text, after the Priestly Writer had modified the Book of J). Her stories, as we have seen, often have their own origins in the Book of Genesis. By the time they have finished, however, they have assumed their own very different meanings, most of which run counter to those imposed on the 'original' stories as redacted by the Priestly Writer in the interests of an authoritarian male-dominated institution. Winterson's work, in the wake of Harold Bloom, not only attempts to let the genius of J out of the institutional bottles in which it has so long been confined, but to reconstitute her words in a manner which makes sense to modern (women) readers.

Chapter 5

The Sacrifice of Isaac: Jenny Diski

Diski's Journeys: Rediscovering Jewish Roots

It may seem strange, given the centrality of the Akedah to Judaism, Christianity and Islam, to select for its elucidation the work of another comic and often subversive contemporary novelist Jenny Diski. But her two recent novels, *Only Human* (2000) and *After These Things* (2004) provide interesting examples of precisely the kind of 'midrashic' rewriting of the Book of Genesis which this book is designed to explore. It is also significant that Diski herself, in the acknowledgements at the end of *After These Things*, admits that she 'benefited enormously' from the works of such biblical and midrashic scholars as Louis Ginzberg, Shalom Spiegel, Avivah Zornberg and Robert Alter.[1] The second section of this chapter will explore these intertexts between Genesis and Diski in some detail while the third will analyse the novels themselves. As in my treatment of earlier novelists, however, I will begin by considering where Diski comes from, both literally, in terms of her own family history, and intellectually, in terms of her beliefs and attitudes as these can be gleaned from her other writings, which include seven earlier novels, two collections of essays, a range of journalism, a number of interviews and two partly autobiographical travel-books: *Skating to Antarctica* (1997) and *Stranger on a Train* (2002).[2]

The first of these travel books, Diski's journey to 'the bottom of the world', also involves a probing of her own roots. She reveals early on that both her parents were 'the children of working-class Jewish immigrants'.[3] Their Jewishness, however, had become somewhat secular, so much so that two Zionist fellow-travellers on the boat call her 'a Jew who has lost her meaning'.[4] Diski recalls 'almost nothing in the way of religious practice in my family' apart from her mother sometimes lighting candles on Friday nights and her father taking her 'to the local synagogue on the last night of Yom Kippur [which is, in fact, a one-day festival] to hear the ram's horn being blown'. Neither she nor her parents may have understood much of Jewish liturgical practice but their 'Jewishness' in general 'was constantly reiterated...in their everyday conversation', which included 'bits of Yiddish from their East End immigrant families' and constant debates about whether 'famous people in the news were or were not Jewish'. 'Being Jewish', in other words, 'was in the air'.[5] It is

---

1   Jenny Diski, *After These Things: A Novel* (London: Little, Brown, 2004), p.217.
2   A third travel book, *On Trying to Keep Still* (London: Little, Brown, 2006), has just appeared.
3   Jenny Diski, *Skating to Antarctica* (London: Granta Books, 1997), p.14.
4   *Ibid.*, p.76.
5   *Ibid.*, p.104.

nevertheless portrayed as something of a shock when her father's birth certificate reveals that this sometimes loving and entertaining, at other times abusive, and finally absent father whom she had always known as James Simmonds had been born Israel Zimmerman, the son of a Polish immigrant whose own name is signed in what Diski thinks (but clearly does not know) 'must be Hebrew'.[6] Elsewhere she describes her family more prosaically as 'non-practising Jews'[7] and more cynically as 'a sorry mess, a ground zero of attempted suicides, mental institutions, dismal disappointments, destitution and love (or something called love) turned nasty'.[8] Her father, it seems, first left the house when she was six, finally abandoning her mother and herself five years later, when she was sent by social services to a progressive Quaker boarding school, which she was 'asked to leave' at the age 14.[9]

Diski's fiction, which often draws from her own experience, provides further insights into these early years. Miriam in *The Dream Mistress* (1999), for example, knows, though it has nothing to do with religion, 'that she was a Jew'. Like Diski, she recalls a childhood in which no attention was 'paid to religious observance— Passover passed them by and Friday evenings were just the beginning of the weekend— but to be Jewish was to be different'.[10] For postwar children such as Frances in *Like Mother* (1988), whose grandparents were also East European Jewish immigrants, the stories they hear about the war mingle almost inseparably with those of the Bible, since they too serve as 'creation myths', 'simple tales of good and evil, as uncomplicated as their narrators...coming from the distant times, like the stories of Genesis'.[11] A short story entitled 'Strictempo' sheds light on the atmosphere of the progressive boarding school to which Diski was sent, 'where self-government and rational discourse were the golden rule'. 'A dogged air of reason', she records, hung heavily about the place, founded upon the belief that children 'responded rationally to rational treatment'.[12] Diski herself did not, returning to live firstly with her father and his mistress and then for another brief spell with her mother before ending up, still aged 14, in a psychiatric hospital in Hove. From there she was rescued by Doris Lessing, the mother of one of her schoolfellows, who provided a home for the next four years.

Further years in psychiatric care were to follow, described intermittently in both of her travel-memoirs. At the Maudsley Psychiatric Hospital, for example, Diski sided with the 'bad girls' who rebelled against all forms of discipline, rather than the 'good girls' who 'wore knee-length pleated skirts and believed in God'.[13] She later trained as a teacher and taught for five years before studying anthropology

---

6   *Ibid.*, p.238.
7   Jenny Diski, *A View from the Bed* (London: Virago, 2003), p.39.
8   *Ibid.*, p.191.
9   'One Damn Thing After Another; Novelist Jenny Diski tells Michael Dibdin about her journey out of a nightmarish past', *Independent on Sunday,* 22/9/91, p.30
10   Jenny Diski, *The Dream Mistress* (London: Granta Books, 1999 [1996]), pp.39-30.
11   Jenny Diski, *Like Mother* (London: Granta Books, 1998 [1988]), p.38.
12   Jenny Diski, *The Vanishing Princess* (London: Phoenix, 1996 [1995]), pp.90 and 96.
13   Jenny Diski, *Stranger on a Train* (London: Virago, 2002), p.108.

as a mature student at University College London.[14] Now a full-time writer, Diski reluctantly accepts the label 'Hampstead intellectual', describing herself as 'a sort of liberal left wet human being who thinks things ought to be quite nice in the world'.[15] This self-mocking caricature, of course, masks a complex set of beliefs which I will attempt to tease out in more detail, paying particular attention to views which Diski has expressed about the Bible, about Judaism and about religion in general.

'I had absolutely no interest in the Bible as a child', Diski claims in an interview in 2004; 'I remember the stories from Ladybird books quite well because of the hideous pictures of people with towels on their heads'. But the stories 'only get good when you read them as an adult'. It's the narrative patterns, often a result of the editing, which now interest her. Asked if she feels 'any sense of guilt , as a non-believer, about messing with a sacred text', she responds by claiming her work as a form of midrash: 'If it's all right for the rabbis to reinterpret it, it's all right for me. Books are available for us to play with'. She clearly sees her project as a legitimate wresting of these texts from the control of narrower readings: 'I wanted to retrieve the Bible from stupidity', she claims, 'to take it back as an essentially human story' rather than one which belongs exclusively to any particular group.[16]

In another interview, published in 1999, which explores her fascination with faith of all kinds, Diski claims to be 'quite religious' about her disbelief. 'The more I read about Judaism', she argues,

> the less it seems to have anything to do with anything transcendental. I read the Bible recently, from beginning to end, and it terrified me. I don't know how they made a religion out of it...I can't see how you derive religion from the Old Testament. God is a monster made in our own image, but what wonderful stories![17]

She particularly admires the Book of Job, which 'has all the hallmarks of a classic Jewish joke'. Job, she argues, is not only 'the innocent victim of circumstance', caught in the crossfire between God and Satan, but 'also another kind of casualty, the sort we know well this century, the one who is implicated, through passivity, in the suffering of others'. One should never expect to find 'a satisfying answer' to Job's questions, Diski suggests. But it is important, 'even if no one and nothing is listening', that they are 'continually being asked'.[18]

The most important biblical figure for Diski has been Abraham, 'The Daddy of All Patriarchs', as she calls him in a review of a book by Carol Delaney, *Abraham on Trial*, a review which reveals a great deal about Diski's motivation in writing her two novels on the Akedah. Rejecting Delaney's pessimism about being 'lumbered' in Genesis with an irredeemably patriarchal text, as if we were 'helpless victims rather than interpreters of myth', Diski readily accepts that 'the Hebrew scriptures...do not

---

14 'One Damn Thing', p.30.

15 Ajay Close, 'Making a Solo Voyage' (Interview with Jenny Diski), *The Scotsman*, 12/8/02, p.2.

16 Helen Brown, 'A Writer's Life', *Telegraph*, 10/4/04, City Section, p.12.

17 Frederic Tuten, 'Jenny Diski', *Bomb* 66 (Winter 1999) pp.42-7 (p.46).

18 Jenny Diski, 'Hope is a Risky Business in a Cruel and Unjust World', *Guardian*, 20/8/93, p.18.

promote feminism'. 'You can point to the odd strong woman', she admits, 'but sit down and read the actual text and you soon discover that Yahweh can only be male, while the women are merely furthering the ambitions of sons and husbands'.[19] She understands that particular religious communities may wish to impose a particular reading of Abraham upon their followers which women may find problematic. If they reject the story entirely, however, as Delaney suggests, 'we lose the chance to read it again differently, more carefully, less reverentially' in ways that can subvert patriarchy.[20] Elsewhere Diski expresses anger at the exclusion of women from 'the central heartbeat of their culture: the study of the Torah', being 'exempted' from this duty in order to fulfil their domestic chores.[21]

The essays collected in *Don't* (1998) and *A View from the Bed* (2003) quite often address questions of religion, though not always in an entirely serious or even well-informed manner. A review of a new edition of Anne Frank's diary, for example, suggests (in apparent ignorance of the Hasidic tradition of the *tzaddik*) that she remains 'the only Jewish saint'. While Catholicism has a 'bevy of more approachable under-managers, each with their own speciality, willing and able to intercede with on high on behalf of the baffled individual', for the Jews, according to Diski, 'there is only a single very busy, self-important and fractious God'.[22] Diski's interest in Catholicism is evidenced by an account of visits to a Convent of the Poor Clares and a Carmelite monastery, though she characterises herself as something of a spiritual 'dilettante....It's precisely the *insoluble* nature of God that intrigues me'. She has some sympathy with Thomas Merton's 'deity beyond human imagining who exists in the emptiness of existential doubt' but less interest than she expects in Don Cupitt's postmodern theology, focused as it is upon language alone, without any sense of the reality to which it might point.[23]

One of the essays in *A View from the Bed* begins with the bold statement, 'I don't believe in God', before admitting, 'that's putting it too fervently. I don't think it's very likely'. It's best, she continues, retracting still further, 'never to entirely trust oneself when talking on the subject of God' and to accept that faith, 'real, honest-to-God, zonking faith...is a gift'.[24] She continues to employ theological words like 'grace' when she meets qualities she admires in other people.[25] She may have little time for fundamentalists such as the nineteen-year-old student in *Stranger on a Train* who insists, counter to all scientific evidence, that 'God made the world just as it says in the Bible', inserting fossils to make the world appear 'already old, with all its history already made'.[26] But she has little sympathy either for Richard Dawkins, 'such a fundamentalist in his atheism, so complacently contemptuous of thoughts that have kept better people than him up through sleepless nights'. For Dawkins, religion

---

19 Diski, *A View from the Bed*, pp.68-9.
20 *Ibid.*, p.73.
21 Jenny Diski, 'Book Review: *Off the Baricades, into the Kitchen; A Price below Rubies: Jewish Women as Rebels and Radicals*', *Independent on Sunday*, 19/9/93, p.38.
22 Jenny Diski, *Don't* (London: Granta Books, 1998), p.140.
23 *Ibid.*, pp.293-4.
24 Diski, *A View from the Bed*, p.24.
25 Diski, *Stranger on a Train*, p.122.
26 *Ibid.*, p.239.

is 'a virus; an infection in which ideas pass from brain to brain...a childish desire for hope and comfort'. For Diski, it may have been 'the excuse for a heap of trouble in the world. But it was also the excuse for Fauré's Requiem'.[27] Asked to nominate her favourite books and writers, she comes up with Montaigne, 'a hero of self-discovery' who 'allowed his judgments and beliefs to change over time and with experience';[28] Defoe, who has his character Robinson Crusoe 'proceed toward the spiritual (or, it may be, superstitious) life of humanity';[29] and Melville, whose novel *Moby Dick* explores the immensities of 'a universe at odds with itself'.[30] These writers clearly provide her with models for the exploration through literature of complexities which should not be reduced to simple straightforward statements.

Diski's own fiction prior to *Only Human* and *After These Things* displays a similar ambivalence towards religion, which is *both* an undeniable element of human experience *and* a 'scandal' to the modern world. Just as the heroine of her first novel *Nothing Natural* (1986) finds it hard to accommodate her strange pleasure in sado-masochism to her everyday self, so the scientific protagonist of her second, *Rainforest* (1987), a lecturer in anthropology, crumbles in the face of the 'fetid chaos' of her own sexual urges and of the jungle, a 'soaking, stench-filled labyrinth with no centre...gloomy, pointless, random'.[31] Utterly defeated in what Stephen Jay Gould (quoted in the epigraph to the novel) calls 'our desperate striving to make sense of a complex and confusing world', she retreats to a comfortable routine as a cleaner, attempting to impose at least an appearance of order on the houses in her charge. Diski's suspicion of the claims of scientific rationalism is also apparent in *Then Again* (1990), where the sensibly secular Esther, having been brought up by Jewish atheist humanists, teaches her own daughter Katya in turn to see all religions as 'monuments to humanity'. All 'creation stories', she insists, from 'Adam and Eve and the Garden of Eden to the Big Bang', demonstrate 'the curious, questioning, problem-solving nature of human beings'.[32] So when Katya at the age of fourteen experiences a moment of what she can only call 'grace', seeing 'God dancing in the particles of the universe' and hearing a voice calling her name,[33] her mother can only conclude that she is mad, a diagnosis which is shared not only by a psychotherapist but even by a priest.

Then Again is complicated by a parallel narrative from the fourteenth century, arising from Esther's research on Jewish persecution. This story involves an earlier Esther, the sole survivor of a massacre of Jews, who is brought up in a Christian family only to be raped by a priest. In spite of these events, the novel ends with her recalling the prayers said by her father, especially the Shema, with its injunction to teach these words and traditions '*diligently unto your children*'. Although Esther

---

27   Jenny Diski, 'Graven Images: Night and Day', *Mail on Sunday*, 29/1/95, p.30.
28   Jenny Diski, 'Heroes and Villains: Michel de Montaigne', *Independent*, 29/5/04, p.46.
29   Jenny Diski, 'Re-readings: Survival Instinct', *Guardian*, 17/7/04.
30   Jenny Diski, 'Book of a Lifetime: A Theme as Big as a Whale; *Moby Dick*, Herman Melville', *Independent*, 18/3/05, p.29.
31   Jenny Diski, *Rainforest* (Harmondsworth: Penguin, 1988 [1987]), p.177.
32   Jenny Diski, *Then Again* (London: Vintage, 1991 [1990]), p.109.
33   *Ibid.*, pp.111-4.

90   *The Genesis of Fiction*

realises that she won't have children and could not pass on an 'unquestioning faith' even if she did, she also recognises

> a great truth in the second part of the prayer. That *something* should be passed on: what is known, what is understood; what is not understood and cannot be, but can be asked...If the questions went on being asked, a universe of possible answers was available...Perhaps it would even be possible to return to faith eventually, a faith that rose out of questions; a possible faith that arose from the possibility of questioning.[34]

This most tentative suggestion is probably about as positive about faith as Diski will allow any of her characters to become.

Most of Diski's novels treat the question of religion in subversively comic or parodic mode. The 'God' who appears in *Happily Ever After* (1991), for example, engaging in prolonged dialogues in the mind of an ageing novelist named Daphne Drummond, likes nothing better than to 'brood darkly over the face of the waters'. He explains to her that 'the Creation had never been intended to be a major project. He was just diddling about'. Pressed by her about the alleged events that followed creation, he insists it was 'nothing to do with Him'. 'What about the Fall?', asks Daphne, 'Adam and Eve and the Garden of Eden and all that stuff?' 'Nothing to do with Me', God repeats. He also complains like a grumpy old man of 'constantly being disturbed by exhortations and exaltations and praise and prayers; sung to, implored, adored, abhorred, revered and reviled...when all he wanted to do was to be left alone to get on with a bit of brooding'.[35]

Belief, or the loss of belief, is central to Diski's next novel *Monkey's Uncle* (1994), which narrates parallel stories of deconversion, firstly on the part of the evangelical Robert FitzRoy, Captain of the Beagle, the boat on which Darwin travelled to collect evidence in support of his theory of evolution, and secondly on the part of Charlotte FitzRoy, who sees in the fall of the Berlin Wall the triumph of materialism, the end of her socialist belief 'in the innate goodness and perfectibility of humanity'.[36] Robert FitzRoy, in dialogue with Darwin, presents the fundamentalist argument that the Book of Genesis must either be taken literally or reduced to 'a charming fable about moral and social behaviour'. Utterly incapable of accommodating his beliefs to the evidence with which he is confronted, he is depicted holding a copy of the Bible above his head and bellowing 'The Book' at the supporters of Darwin who are themselves chanting 'Monkeys' at the famous meeting of the British Association in 1860. In a parallel development (albeit travelling in the opposite direction) the rationalist Charlotte grows increasingly dissatisfied with her three prophets of modernity, Darwin, Marx and Freud, who argue incessantly in her mind. All of them, she tells her therapist, have been shown to be inadequate, leaving us 'with no real, serious structures to think with'.[37]

The Dream Mistress (1996) displays a similar ambivalence, its heroine Bella abandoning the Judaism in which has been brought up for the more systematic

---

34   *Ibid.*, pp.214-5.
35   Jenny Diski, *Happily Ever After* (Harmondsworth: Penguin, 1992 [1991]), pp.58-9.
36   Jenny Diski, *Monkey's Uncle* (London: Phoenix, 1994), p.61.
37   *Ibid.*, p.64.

'structures of Catholicism'.[38] Like her author, Bella joins the Poor Clares for a while but finds herself unable to share 'the simplicity and delight of their belief, their utter conviction'. Hers is a negative theology, founded upon 'the blackness and unknowability of an unpicturable, unpraisable, infinite, infinitely strange God...a negation, and then a negation of a negation'.[39] In a development reminiscent of Graham Greene, Diski complicates matters still further by making Bella the source of an inexplicable miracle, the healing of a neighbour's child, an event which turns Bella briefly into a local saint.[40] She soon loses their sympathy, however, by refusing to repeat or explain this apparent moment of grace.

Diski's journey as a writer towards her two novels on the Akedah can thus be seen to display an ambivalence towards religion, a dissatisfaction with any of the answers traditionally accorded to metaphysical questions. Her relationship towards Judaism is also strangely ambiguous, combining a fascination with a lack of knowledge about it explicable only by her extraordinary personal history. In some ways, it could be argued, Diski's alienation from her own roots gives her the advantage as an interpreter of the Book of Genesis that she comes to it perfectly 'fresh', unconditioned by childhood indoctrination. This enables her to 'take on' the Akedah in ways which no member of a believing community would dare to do. This, one could say, is how the story appears to an intelligent modern woman unconditioned to accept its difficulties, responding simply to the story as it stands. It would be wrong, of course, to suggest that Diski is altogether uncontaminated by knowledge. She can be seen to have made up for lost childhood time by devoting herself to recent research on the Akedah by a range of Jewish biblical and midrashic scholars. And it is to this research that I now want to turn before considering (in the final section of this chapter) its impact upon her own treatment of the subject in *Only Human* and *After These Things*.

Midrashic Intertexts: Ginzberg, Spiegel, Zornberg, Alter

The scholars on whom Diski was most reliant for her two novels on the Akedah, as we have seen, are listed in her acknowledgements at the back of *After These Things*:

> Robert Alter— his literary criticism of the Hebrew Bible, and his translation and commentary of *Genesis* (Norton, 1996); Avivah Gottlieb Zornberg's book of meditations, *The Beginnings of Desire—Reflections on Genesis* (Doubleday, 1996); Shalom Spiegel's *The Last Trial* (Jewish Lights, 1993); Louis Ginzberg's *The Legends of the Jews* (Johns Hopkins University Press, 1998), and the collection of essays edited by Robert Alter and Frank Kermode, *The Literary Guide to the Bible* (Fontana, 1997).[41]

---

38 Diski, *The Dream Mistress*, pp.75-6.
39 *Ibid.*, pp.82-3.
40 *Ibid.*, p.144.
41 Diski, *After These Things*, p.217.

Of these, Robert Alter's book on *The Art of Biblical Narrative* and the volume he co-edited with Kermode are discussed in my opening chapter. I will focus here therefore on the three studies of midrash, by Ginzberg, Spiegel and Zornberg, along with Alter's translation and commentary on Genesis, which also discusses a range of midrashic material. All four of these studies, as I hope to demonstrate, feed significantly into Diski's two novels on the Akedah. The dates Diski gives for these books, it should be noted, are those of the editions she consulted. The first volume of Ginzberg's *Legends,* however, appeared as early as 1909 while Spiegel's thesis was first published in 1950; only Zornberg's and Alter's works are actually the product of the 1990s. Since the later studies necessarily build on the earlier volumes, I will consider them here in chronological order of their first publication.

Ginzberg's account of *The Legends of the Jews*, also discussed in chapter 3 as one of the possible intertexts for Steinbeck's *East of Eden*, was designed to introduce general readers to the riches of rabbinic literature. The first four volumes themselves read like a novel, synthesising the whole range of Haggadah on the Bible. Ginzberg explains in the notes (which occupy volumes five and six, volume seven comprising an index) that these first four volumes, 'containing the Bible as mirrored by Jewish imagination and phantasy, are intended for the general reader and not for the scholar', arranged as they are 'to offer a readable story and narrate an interesting tale'.[42] The notes unpick the different sources on which he has drawn, highlighting particular areas of scholarly interest. Only the first volume, *From the Creation to Jacob,* and the relevant notes in volume five, relate to the lives of Abraham, Isaac and Jacob, which are the subject of Diski's two novels so it is on these volumes that I will concentrate.

Ginzberg begins his chapter on 'Abraham' earlier than Diski, with the boy's miraculous infancy: left by his mother alone (apart from the angel Gabriel) in a cave, he has learnt to talk after twenty days and is soon denouncing the idolatry of his contemporaries. At twenty years, asked by his father Terah to look after some of King Nimrod's religious statues, 'he struck the king's idols from their thrones, and began to belabor them with an axe', hacking off their feet and heads (I 197). Later, in a section entitled 'The Iconoclast', he prepares meat for his father's idols, mocks them for not being able to eat and again takes a hatchet to them. He and his brother Haran are consequently placed for three days in a furnace, which Abraham (but not his brother) miraculously survives. Diski, as we shall see, chooses to omit all the miraculous elements from her novels, whose focus, as her title suggests, is only human. In her version of the story, for example, Haran commits suicide.

Abraham, in Ginzberg's synthesis of midrashic material about him, following the tradition begun in the Book of Jubilees, is subjected to ten trials, the first of which is departure from his native land and the second famine, as a consequence of which he and his entourage travel to Egypt. It is there that Sarah, who is so beautiful that she makes all other women look 'like apes', causes Pharaoh to be 'bewitched...by her charms' (I 222). Pharaoh, however, is prevented from consummating his desire by 'an

---

42 Louis Ginzberg, *The Legends of the Jews*, trans. Henrietta Szold (Baltimore: Johns Hopkins University Press, 1998), 7 vols, V vii. Subsequent references in brackets in the text are to this edition.

angel...armed with a stick', who smacks his hand every time he attempts to remove any item of her clothing, finally infecting him with leprosy (I 224). Again, Diski will have a more naturalistic explanation for Pharaoh's refusal to take advantage of the opportunity Abraham allows him, mocking God's claim to have been responsible for this. But the midrashic tradition summarised by Ginzberg can nevertheless be seen to have contributed to the way *Only Human* treats this episode, which occupies only a few verses of Genesis 12.

The command to sacrifice Isaac, in Ginzberg's summary of the midrashic tradition, is the last of Abraham's ten trials, for which the rabbis make Satan directly responsible. Turning up at the feast which Abraham arranges to celebrate the weaning of Isaac ('he always appears at a feast at which no poor people participate'), Satan complains to God that Abraham is lacking in gratitude. God, as in the Book of Job, boasts to Satan of his servant's virtues before agreeing to allow Abraham to be tested by the ultimate demand, to sacrifice his own son. Even Satan is surprised by this, questioning whether God would do any man 'such evil, to command him, Go and slaughter thy son' (I 272-7). He suggests to Isaac that Abraham must have gone mad but Isaac too passes the test, yielding himself to the knife 'with joy and cheerfulness of heart' (I 279). God is thus able to boast to the angels about human obedience, contributing to the jealousy they already feel about His most recent creation (a rivalry which Thomas Mann will explore more fully). In Ginzberg's summary of the midrash, the angels intervene to prevent Abraham from actually slaughtering his son. Isaac's soul nevertheless leaves his body 'from terror', proceeding to spend three years in paradise. This leads Sarah to believe that he is really dead; in one version she dies from grief at this and in another from joy at discovering that he is not really dead (I 285-7). Although far from realistic (from a modern perspective), the rabbinic narratives summarised by Ginzberg can be seen to have encouraged Diski to explore the human consequences of the Akedah, in particular the reaction of Sarah.

The rabbis themselves can be seen to explore some of the psychological consequences for Isaac both of the Akedah and of his mother's death. That his wife Rebekah 'comforted him after his mother's death' is part of the original biblical narrative (Gen. 24:67), to which the rabbis add the telling detail that 'she was the counterpart of Sarah in person and in spirit' (I 297). Isaac is similarly depicted as 'the counterpart of his father in body and soul. He resembled him in every particular' (I 311). These are regarded by the rabbis as commendable attributes though Diski will consider the oedipal issues so obviously raised for modern readers by a man who mimics his father even to the extent of marrying a woman exactly like his mother. For the rabbis, Rebekah is as pious as Isaac, praying with him for their marriage to be blessed by children. She first sees him in 'the posture of praying' and notes his 'unusual beauty' (I 296), a very different and much less critical stance than that of Diski's character. Diski will pick up, however, on a detail recorded in Ginzberg: Isaac's 'longing for tidbits', his delight in 'particularly palatable morsels' (I 330). This, of course, paves the way for Jacob's capture of his father's blessing, for which the rabbis exonerate him from all blame. In a just-plausible reading of the biblical Hebrew, they have Isaac reply to Jacob's question, 'Who art thou my son?' (Gen. 27:18), separating the pronoun from the rest of the sentence: 'It is I, thy first-born son is Esau' (I 333). The AV, by contrast, has him answer with a brazen lie: 'I am

Esau thy firstborn' (Gen. 27: 19). But, as Ginzberg comments in a note on this verse, 'The Haggadah would not admit that Jacob uttered an unqualified untruth' (V 283). For the rabbis Jacob is a model not only of rectitude but of devotion, spending every night of his twenty years at Laban's reciting the psalms (I 350).

The rabbis make explicit the irony only implicit in the biblical account of Jacob's deception by Leah that she has learned from him how to be economical with the truth. When Jacob rebukes her for pretending to be Rachel, the midrash has her reply, 'Is there a teacher without a pupil...I but profited by thy instruction. When they father called thee Esau, didst thou not say, Here am I?' (I 361). 'Jacob's aversion to Leah', Ginzberg records, 'began the very morning after their wedding, when his wife taunted him with not being wholly free from cunning and craft herself' (I 361-2). Jacob is generally idealised in the midrash and Esau correspondingly demonised, turned into a serial adulterer, who 'made a practice of violating the wives of other men' (I 358). Dinah too is made at least partly responsible for what Ginzberg calls 'The Outrage at Shechem':

> While Jacob and his sons were sitting in the house of learning, occupied with the study of Torah, Dinah went abroad to see the dancing and singing women, whom Shechem had hired to dance and play in the streets in order to entice her forth. Had she remained at home, nothing would have happened to her. But she was a woman, and all women like to show themselves in the street.(I 395).

Diski is unlikely to have been impressed with the misogyny evident in such rabbinic judgments but they may well have provoked her into probing the story still further in terms of her own very different understanding of human behaviour.

The second study of midrash acknowledged by Diski, Shalom Spiegel's *The Last Trial: On the Legends and Lore of the Command to Offer Isaac as a Sacrifice*, first appeared in Hebrew in 1950. It is an extended introduction to a twelfth-century poem by Rabbi Ephraim of Bonn, entitled 'The Akedah', in which Isaac is actually slaughtered not only once but twice. In order to illustrate that this is not particularly unusual in the context of midrash, Spiegel demonstrates how creative and divergent rabbinic handling of the topic could be. Whereas Ginzberg, by synthesising this material into a coherent narrative, could be said (in spite of his scholarly notes) to have given a misleading impression of the homogeneity of the midrashic tradition and to have failed to make clear that the main point of midrash is to interpret the Bible, Spiegel begins by demonstrating that the rabbis started from a textual problem, a question raised by the biblical text. Genesis 22:19, for example, which records that 'Abraham returned unto his young men, and they rose up and went together to Beersheba', makes no mention of Isaac. So the rabbis ask, 'Where was Isaac?', coming up with a range of possible answers: that he had been sent home by Abraham, that he was sent away to study Torah with Shem ben Noah, that he remained for three years upon Mount Moriah, that he lagged behind out of shock, that he was sent home by another route to tell Sarah what had happened, or (as in Ginzberg) that he spent three years in paradise.[43] The rabbis are also intrigued by the fact that Rebekah falls from

---

43 Shalom Spiegel, *The Last Trial*, trans. Judah Goldin (Woodstock, Vermont: Jewish Lights, 1993 [1950]), pp.3-5. Subsequent references in brackets in the text are to this edition.

her camel on first seeing him (Gen. 25:64). One suggestion, reported by Spiegel, is that 'what she perceived was Isaac coming down from Paradise, and he walked the way the dead walk, head down and feet up' (6). That would clearly disturb anyone's sense of balance.

Diski, as we shall see, spurns such supernatural explanations but she too makes much of Rebekah's first encounter with Isaac, whom she sees as metaphorically dead. The difference is highly significant but again the midrash appears to have directed Diski to this important moment in the biblical narrative. She also pays close attention to something Spiegel highlights in his study of the midrash surrounding the Akedah, the fear from which Isaac continues to suffer as a result of this traumatic moment. The rabbis wonder why Isaac 'trembled very exceedingly' on discovering that he has been deceived by Jacob in Genesis 27:33, Midrash Tanhuma attributing it to

> the fact that before the present terror there had already been one...on Mount Moriah. When his father bound him, and took the knife to slay him, the Holy One, blessed be He, revealed himself to the angels and opened up the heavens. Now Isaac lifted his eyes...*and beheld the Holy One blessed be He*...and was seized with trembling (31).

Diski's explanation is less pious, more psychoanalytic, but she presumably noted Spiegel's fascination with rabbinic explanations not only of this episode but of the reference Jacob makes to the 'God of Abraham, and the fear of Isaac' being with him during his twenty years at the house of Laban (Gen.31:42). Spiegel refers to a number of rabbinic sources which relate this to Isaac's 'fear as he lay bound on top of the altar, and his soul flew out of him' (32). Spiegel also explores the rabbinic interest in Sarah's reaction to the events, their relation of Sarah's sobs to the blasts of the shofar on Rosh ha-Shanah, the first of the ten days of penitence in the Jewish Calendar, 'a day of sobs— the purpose being that the Holy One, blessed be He, shall remember for our sake the wailings of *Mother Sarah,* and forgive us'(75). Diski, as we shall see, has a more naturalistic, less liturgical interest in these sobs, which do not, of course, appear in the biblical narrative.

The most important of these studies of midrash for Diski's own treatment of the Akedah is probably Avivah Gottlieb Zornberg's book *The Beginning of Desire: Reflections on Genesis.* Based on ten years' experience of teaching Bible classes in Jerusalem, these essays, first published in 1995, comprise 'personal meditations' upon the weekly Parasha, 'a weaving of biblical, midrashic, and literary sources' upon the biblical text.[44] Each Parasha, of course, is named after the key Hebrew words of the text, so the first of relevance to Abraham is *Lekh Lekha,* God's call to the patriarch in Genesis 12:1. Literally translated 'Go to yourself' (AV 'Get thee'), these words are glossed by Zornberg, 'Go forth to find your authentic self, to learn who you are meant to be'.[45] Zornberg is more altogether sympathetic than Diski

---

44 Avivah Gottlieb Zornberg, *The Beginnings of Desire: Reflections on Genesis* (New York: Doubleday, 1996 [1995]), p.xi. Subsequent references in brackets in the text are to this edition.

45 *Etz Hayim: Torah and Commentary*, ed. David L.Lieber (New York: Rabbinical Assembly/Jewish Publication Society, 2001), p.70.

towards Abraham's existential wanderings, referring to the twelfth-century rabbinic commentaries by Ramban (Nahmanides) and Rambam (Maimonides), both of whom marvel at Abraham's faith and courage at setting out on a journey whose destination lies entirely in God's hands: 'a land that I will shew thee' (Gen. 12:1). He therefore has to wander 'aimlessly' (Ramban's adverb), subject to 'mocking voices that weave through Abraham's consciousness as he travels'. These are given dramatic expression in the midrash: 'Look at this old man! Travelling through the country, looking like a madman!' (75-6). Diski, who presumably discovered these suggestions of madness in Zornberg's work, will be developing them even further in her own.

To challenge received wisdom in this way, however, as Zornberg acknowledges, is to run the risk of at least appearing to be mad. She cites Rambam on Abraham's having

> had no teacher or source of knowledge but he was sunk among senseless idol worshippers in Ur of the Chaldeans; his parents and the whole people worshipped idols and he worshipped with them. But *his mind roamed* in search of understanding till he achieved the true way and understood out of his own natural intelligence....He knew that the whole world was in error and that the cause of their error was that they worshipped idols and images (80).

This 'inner process', Zornberg emphasises, 'alienates him...from his entire world' (81). She again quotes Rambam (who himself follows midrashic accounts of Abraham's iconoclasm) on the way Abraham breaks with the family tradition of manufacturing and selling idols:

> He would take a hammer and batter the head of each idol, saying 'Is it this one you want? Or this one?' And when the buyer saw this, he would give up his intention and go away. And Abraham would *roam in his mind*, thinking, 'How long shall we bow down to the work of our own hands?' (83).

Diski, as we shall see, also highlights Abraham's mental wanderings, his dramatic shattering of the family idols and his obsession with the One God, but leaves it open to her readers whether or not to diagnose genuine madness.

Zornberg, like Spiegel, notes that it is Satan in the midrash who provokes the Akedah, forcing God to test Abraham's faithfulness. She also quotes the Babylonian Talmud (*Sanhedrin*) interpreting the phrase from the opening verse of Genesis 22, 'After these things', which supplies the title of Diski's second biblical novel. For this tractate it is after Satan's complaint that Abraham held 'a great feast' to celebrate Isaac's weaning without sacrificing 'a single turtle dove' that God boasts, 'If I were to say to him, "Sacrifice your son to Me," he would immediately obey' (97). The phrase 'after these things', of course, will take on additional meaning in Diski, referring to the psychological consequences of the Akedah. But Zornberg may well have brought the biblical phrase to her attention. Other details in Zornberg which appear to have fed into Diski's two novels on the Akedah include the debate among the rabbis about the precise meaning of the *eshel* which Abraham plants in Beer-sheba in Genesis 21:33. The Authorised Version calls it a 'grove'. Zornberg quotes the Babylonian Talmud (*Sotah*) in which 'R.Yehudah said that this *eshel* was an orchard, while R.Nehemiah said it was a hotel' (102). Diski resolves the dispute by having Abraham set up a tent in the shade of an orchard and calling it 'the Orchard Hotel...the first purpose-built traveller's inn'.[46]

Diski also resolves a more serious ambiguity noted by Zornberg in Sarah's laughter at the news that she will, at her great age, give birth. Zornberg sees ambiguity even in her celebration after Isaac's birth, when she puns on the literal meaning of his name ('Laughter'), 'God hath made me to laugh, so that all that hear will laugh with me' (Gen. 21:6):

> Sarah internalises the tension set up by laughter as joy at enlarged possibilities, on the one hand, and the laughter that (bitterly?, cruelly?) denies any possibility but the quotidian reality. To laugh is to confront the pressures of necessity on one's individual destiny.... The reaction, the explosion of laughter, may run a long gamut (from mockery to joy, as Ramban puts it) but the very fact of laughter places man firmly, absurdly, at the center of his world (99-100).

For Diski too, as we shall see, Sarah's laughter, like all laughter, is a distinctly human characteristic, a complex way of coping with what is beyond our control and our understanding, which God (one of her narrators) finds hard to understand.

Diski also appears to follow Zornberg in the 'complex midrashic tradition' summarised by Rashi which sees Sarah as 'the true victim of the Akedah, her death...its unexplicated, inexplicable cost' (123). Zornberg's subtitle for the Parasha beginning with the opening words of Genesis Chapter 23, *Hayyei Sarah* (AV 'And Sarah was', JPS 'Sarah's Lifetime'), is 'The Residue of the Akedah'. She quotes the *Pirkei de Rabbi Eliezer* on Sarah's reaction to Satan's account of what happened on Mount Moriah:

> He [Satan] said, 'Your old husband has taken the boy Isaac and sacrificed him as a burnt offering, while the boy cried and wailed in his helplessness [lit., for he could not be saved]. Immediately, she began to cry and wail. She cried three sobs, corresponding to the three *Teki'ah* notes of the Shofar, and she wailed (*Yelalot*) three times, corresponding to the *Yevavah,* staccato notes of the Shofar. Then she gave up the ghost and died (124).

Only Human too, as we shall see, begins and ends with Sarah weeping, emitting 'three long, languishing notes' in a 'howl of loss'.[47]

Other midrashic accounts of Sarah's response to the news of the Akedah cited by Zornberg include that of *Midrash Tanhuma*, in which Satan appears to Sarah '*in the guise of Isaac*' to give a graphic account of what his father has done. Zornberg also cites *Va-yikra Rabbah,* which has the real Isaac reporting the event. In both cases the news proves fatal (125-6). Zornberg points to several midrashic accounts of the anxieties both Abraham and Isaac have about Sarah's suicidal potential. Isaac, for example, implores his father not to tell her 'when she is standing at the edge of a pit or on a roof, lest she throw herself down and die' (133). There is for the whole family, in other words, 'a tragic residue of the Akedah' of which 'the darkening of Sarah's light is one manifestation' (140).

---

46   Jenni Diski, *Only Human* (London: Virago, 2000), pp.189-90).
47   *Ibid.*, p.214.

The tragic residue of the Akedah is also the subject of the Parasha entitled *Toledot* (generations) from the second word of Genesis 25:19 (AV: 'And these are the generations of Isaac, Abraham's son: Abraham begot Isaac'). It might appear, as Rashi observes, that the last part of this sentence is redundant but God himself reputedly 'formed Isaac's facial features like Abraham's' in order to silence any doubts on that score. One of Rashi's midrashic sources claims that this occurred on the day of the weaning feast. If this had been the case, Zornberg notes, it would have made Isaac 'the wearer of a life-long mask', undermining his sense of separate identity (151). 'Everything in Isaac's life-experience', however, 'is shaped by the Akedah'. The biblical narrative may make no explicit reference to it after chapter 22 but the rabbis do not fail to make connections with later events. Rashi, for example, following *Genesis Rabbah*, attributes Isaac's blindness 'when he was old, and his eyes were dim, so that he could not see' (Gen. 27:1) to the fact that some tears of the watching angels fell into his eyes. Zornberg herself turns to modern trauma theory to explain what she sees as 'a delayed reaction to the Akedah...a response to trauma that is delayed, repressed, and that emerges in psychosomatic dysfunction' (157). The 'awareness of death', Zornberg suggests, drawing on his repeated references to death in the opening verses of Genesis chapter 27, fills every moment of his life. She also quotes *Midrash Tanhuma* on the way 'one who is blinded is *like the dead*' (157-8).

Isaac's inner struggles, according to Zornberg, are apparent to Rebekah on their first meeting when Isaac 'went out to meditate in the field at the eventide' (Gen. 24:63). Zornberg cites *Midrash Rabbah* on Rebekah's initial response as one of shock, causing her not only to fall from her camel but to be 'dumbfounded in his presence'. But the Hebrew translated 'dumbfounded' (*toheh*), according to Zornberg,

> recalls one dimension of that other moment of confusion, doubt, suspense. What Rebecca sees in Isaac is the vital anguish at the heart of his prayers, a remoteness from the sunlit world...that she inhabits. Too abruptly, perhaps, she receives the shock of his world (142).

Rebekah herself is changed by this, Zornberg argues: there is a 'fatal seepage of Isaac's ashen being' into hers, making her question the value of her life. 'I am weary of my life', she tells her husband, the biblical narrative supplying a particular reason: 'because of the daughters of Heth' (Gen. 27:46). Earlier, battered by the struggle of the twins within her womb, she asks the ultimate existential question, 'Why do I exist? (*Lama zeh anokhi*, literally, 'Why this I am?' (159, Gen. 25:22). Zornberg provides an entirely human, psychological explanation of Rebekah's feelings, one which displays more sympathy towards the religious dimension of the biblical narrative than Diski but one on which the novelist can build her own interpretation.

Another member of the biblical family to suffer from the after-shocks of Isaac's trauma, of course, is Jacob, whose 'Quest for Wholeness' is the subject of Zornberg's meditations on the Parasha entitled *Va-Yishlah* (And he sent) from the opening words of Genesis 32:4 (AV 'And Jacob sent messengers before him to Esau...'). She quotes the strange, apparently conditional vow Jacob makes after his vision of the heavenly ladder at Beth-el (using the Jewish Publication Society translation of the *Tanakh*):

'If God remains with me...and if I return safe [*be-shalom*] to my father's house—the Lord shall be my God' (Gen. 28:20-1). Rashi, she notes, interprets *be-shalom* as 'intact, uncontaminated by sin', uncorrupted by Laban's wicked world. She concludes therefore that Jacob 'desires a wholeness and a closing of the circle', to be achieved by 'his reabsorption into his father's house' (216-7). Jacob certainly seems to suffer from the 'fear of Isaac' by which he swears (Gen. 31:53). He makes no great effort to return to his father after arriving 'safe [*shalem*, lit., whole] in the city of Shekhem' (33:18, JPS). The rabbis, as Zornberg records, are highly critical of this delay in returning to his father, interpreting his sufferings after arriving in Shechem as a punishment for it: first Dinah is raped, then there is the scandalous massacre of the inhabitants by his sons, then there are further deaths (those of Deborah and Rachel) and then Reuben sleeps with Jacob's concubine Bilhah. All these events, for Zornberg, contribute to Jacob's ongoing anxieties.

Jacob displays his fear most obviously on the eve of his first encounter with Esau after falsely gaining their father's blessing. The biblical narrative reports that he 'was greatly afraid and distressed' (Gen. 32:7). *Genesis Rabbah* glosses this, 'He was afraid of being killed. And he was anxious at the idea of killing' (229). The mysterious being with whom he subsequently wrestles, identified by the rabbis as Esau's guardian angel, does accede to his demand for a blessing but also cripples him. Zornberg relates this injury to the earlier maiming of his father Isaac:

> This is Jacob's dilemma. At the core, what 'cripples' him is his sense of his father's crippling. Isaac, in the branding moment of his life, was bound hand and foot; and Jacob, in spite of all his movements of hands and feet, in spite of the freedom and energy he expresses in love and work during the years away from his father's house, remains profoundly absorbed by his father's trauma (238).

Just as Isaac worried about his worthiness to receive the blessing— he tells his mother, 'I shall seem to him as a deceiver' (Gen. 27:12)—Jacob also confesses to God on the eve of his encounter with his brother, 'I am not worthy of the least of all the mercies, and all the truth, which thou hast shewed unto thy servant' (Gen 32:11). It is this sense of unworthiness on their part, of Bloomian belatedness, of crippling inadequacy, which Diski will explore further in *After These Things*.

The final acknowledged intertext between the biblical narrative and Diski's novels on which I want to focus is Robert Alter's *Genesis: Translation and Commentary*, published in 1996. In a lengthy introduction to the volume Alter comments firstly on the linguistic properties of the Hebrew, its love of 'profound and haunting enigmas', ambiguities which resist 'neat resolution' and should not be 'explained away by translation'. He also emphasises its 'earthiness', its tendency towards concrete metaphors 'often rooted in the human body', the most famous of which is 'seed', which retains a sense of semen even when referring to distant progeny.[48] He proceeds to discuss "Genesis as a Book", insisting that 'the edited version of Genesis...has powerful coherence as a literary work' since 'the redactors had a strong sense of the nature and narrative purpose in the way they wove together the inherited literary

---

48 Robert Alter, *Genesis: Translation and Commentary* (New York: Norton, 1966), pp.xi-xiii. Subsequent references in brackets in the text are to this edition.

strands'. The final product is thus a 'collage' of earlier material, a work of 'composite artistry' (xlii). Although the introduction focuses mainly on the literary qualities of the final biblical text, Alter's commentary refers to a wide range of midrashic material which continues the interpretive process begun by the redactors.

There are a number of occasions when Alter's comments on the biblical text can almost be read as instructions to a later novelist. For example, discussing the first 'sister-wife...type-scene', when Abraham in Genesis chapter 12 tells Pharaoh that Sarah is his sister (which, of course, she is), Alter comments,

> One might imagine a tense exchange between Pharaoh and Sarai ending in a confession by Sarai of her status as Abraham's wife. In the laconic narrative art of the Hebrew writer, this is left as a gap for us to fill in by an indeterminate compound of careful deduction and imaginative reconstruction (53).

This, as we shall see, is precisely what Diski provides. Alter may even have contributed to the title *Only Human*, since his commentary often focuses on the human element in the biblical narrative. He notes, for example, that Abraham's first speech to God at the beginning of chapter 15 'reveals a hitherto unglimpsed human dimension of Abraham'. Previously limited to 'silent obedience', Abraham now shows that he is beginning to be sceptical about God's promises: 'What can You give me when I am going to my end childless' (63, quoting Alter's own translation of Gen. 15:2). Sarah's 'first reported speech' at the beginning of chapter 16, Alter notes, 'like that of Rachel later in the cycle, is a complaint about her childlessness', leading to the 'first domestic squabble' (67). Abraham's initial response to the announcement that Sarah will indeed bear him a child, 'And Abraham flung himself on his face, and he laughed' (Gen. 17:17), indicates for Alter that he is 'living within a human horizon'. In 'subsequent chapters', Alter continues, 'the narrative will ring the changes on this Hebrew verb [*yitshaq*], the meanings of which will include joyous laughter, bitter laughter, mockery, and sexual dalliance' (75). All human emotion, in other words, can be expressed by laughter, a response Diski's God will find hard to understand.

Alter also finds particular interest in the two variations on the 'betrothal typescene' to be found in Genesis. The one involving Rebekah and Abraham's servant in chapter 24 is 'the only version in which the bridegroom himself is not present', also the only one in which 'the young woman, not the man, draws the water'. This, Alter suggests, serves as an 'intimation...of the subsequent course of the marriage', in which he proves 'the most passive of all the patriarchs, she forceful and enterprising' (115). This is something Diski will develop in her novels, in some respects going beyond Alter, who finds nothing disturbing in Isaac's being 'comforted' by Rebekah at the end of this chapter: 'Rebekah fills the emotional gap left by Sarah's death.... It is thus exactly right that Isaac should bring her into his mother's tent' (123). Diski finds this altogether more problematic.

Alter does appear, however, to have contributed some details to Diski's understanding of Isaac's passive, traumatised character. Chapter 26, he observes, is the only one in which Isaac figures as an active protagonist. Before, he was a bound victim; after, he will be seen as a bamboozled blind old man....He remains the pale and schematic patriarch among the three forefathers, preceeded by the exemplary founder, followed by the vivid struggler (131).

When he is seen by Abimelech 'laugh-playing' with Rebekah in a suggestive manner (Gen. 26:8), Alter finds 'some suggestion' (which Diski will develop) that 'Isaac is a man of strong physical appetites', compensating for his lack of heroic attributes with a delight in food and sex (133).

Alter also notices 'only human' elements in Jacob too, pointing for instance to his conditional promise to God in Genesis 28:20: he 'remains the suspicious bargainer—a "wrestler" with words and conditions' (150). Rachel by contrast displays an 'impetuousness' evident in her first direct speech (Gen. 30:1), translated by Alter, 'Give me sons, for if you don't, I'm a dead woman!' (158). The verb Leah uses at 30:16 (translated by Alter, 'With me you will come to bed'), a word 'ordinarily used for intercourse with a woman the man has not previously enjoyed', suggests for Alter 'that Jacob has been sexually boycotting Leah' in revenge for being tricked into marriage (160). Diski will explore in more detail the ramifications of Jacob's complicated marriages, the sexual tensions implicit in the biblical narrative. The point is that she doesn't entirely invent them: they are there in the original, as Alter seems to have helped her to recognise.

Alter may also have developed Diski's interest in the fear passed down from Isaac to his son, who swears in Alter's translation of Genesis 31:54, 'by the Terror of his father Isaac'. Alter is more reverent than Diski, suggesting that Jacob 'senses something numinous, awesome, frightening' in the God he has inherited from his father (176). He interprets Jacob's wrestling with the mysterious antagonist in chapter 32 in terms more open to the numinous than Diski while still perhaps contributing to her own 'only human', psychoanalytic reading of the event. For Alter it is Jacob's 'dark night of the soul', the antagonist being 'an externalisation of all that Jacob has to wrestle with within himself' but ultimately resisting identification (181). 'Of all the patriarchs', Alter comments,'Jacob is the one whose life is entangled in moral ambiguities' (182). Alter worries about his silence when confronted with the appalling events of chapter 34, although he notes that there is a real ambiguity about whether or not Dinah is raped (an ambiguity deepened rather than resolved by Diski). Jacob's 'disastrous inaction', Alter sees, encourages the indefensible vengeance of his sons (195) while Reuben's violation of his father's concubine in 35:22 represents yet another challenge to Jacob's authority. Alter presents these human weaknesses in the overall context of a biblical narrative clearly designed to celebrate the divine favour or 'blessing' enjoyed by the patriarchs. Diski, as we shall see, builds an alternative narrative in which these weaknesses, while 'only human', undermine the credibility of the claim of divine support.

All four of these midrashic scholars acknowledged at the end of *After These Things* appear to have directed Diski towards psychoanalytic elements implicit in the biblical narrative and developed more fully by the rabbis. In each case, as we shall see, she plays down the supernatural elements evident in all stages of the rabbinic tradition. She will be much less reverent towards the biblical text and its characters than they are. But these scholars provide significant intertexts between the Bible and its midrashic interpretations and Diski's novels. Whether her scepticism places her outside the midrashic tradition altogether is a question which a closer study of the novels must attempt to resolve.

'The Residue of the Akedah': *Only Human* and *After These Things*

Diski's re-telling of the story of the Akedah and its 'residue', for all its debts to the midrashic tradition, is undoubtedly her own. None of the scholars listed in her acknowledgements, she accepts, 'should be held responsible for the final outcome of my imaginings'.[49] *Only Human*, to begin with, is subtitled 'A Comedy', displaying much less reverence for the biblical narrative on which it is based than all of the commentaries analysed above. Even its 'God', who appears as a joint narrator of the story, interspersing His comments with those of another technically 'omniscient' but third-person narrator, is presented as a somewhat comic figure, puzzling over the strange behaviour of his most sophisticated creatures. The other narrator provides an example of this human complexity, engaging in much self-conscious discussion of the process of telling stories. The opening chapter, for example, is entitled 'Endings', the second 'Beginnings'. It soon becomes very clear that it is *how* the story is told, *how* the original material is 'edited' (to use one of Diski's recurrent metaphors), which determines its ultimate meaning.

Only Human begins and ends with the dying Sarah (as in the biblical narrative, she and her husband have their original names Sarai and Abram changed after God appears in person to announce the birth of their son in Genesis 17). But she herself can make little sense of her existence; when those surrounding her press her at the end of her life to comment on its meaning, she cannot muster any kind of 'conclusion', offering only a shrug of the shoulder.[50] At the beginning of the novel the narrator plays self-consciously with the opening line of Genesis, 'In the beginning there was love', which she then modifies: 'In the beginning...there was life itself', only for God to interrupt, 'Who dares to speak of the beginning?' (5). The two narrators are clearly not going to agree on the meaning of this story, leaving the reader to decide between their very competing interpretations.

Each chapter, apart from the first, begins with an epigraph from the biblical narrative, cited in the Authorised Version, which, in midrashic fashion, provides the basis for the narrative development that follows. The first epigraph, for example, is from Genesis 11:27-8, establishing Abram's origins in Ur as the son of Terah. God, however, takes the story right back to 'before the beginning', when only 'I was...And nothing had its say. And it was good' (6). In making God employ the language of Genesis chapter 1, spoken *after* the creation, to refer nostalgically to a time *before* He was disturbed by his creatures, Diski clearly signals her subversive

---

[49] Jenny Diski, *After These Things* (London: Little, Brown, 2004), p.217. All future references in brackets in the text are to this edition.

[50] Jenny Diski, *Only Human* (London: Virago, 2000), p.4. All future references in brackets in the text are to this edition.

intent, giving notice that her God-the-Narrator will diverge significantly from more orthodox characterisations of Him.

The rival narrator focuses on the human side of the story, dramatising the coming to consciousness of Adam and Eve. Just as Zornberg follows Rashi (himself drawing on earlier midrash) in highlighting the importance of relationship, celebrating 'Adam's free perception and desire' for a partner,[51] so Diski's human narrator recognises that it is only through the perception of their 'otherness' from the rest of creation and 'from each other' that the possibility of relationship 'entered the beginning of the world, and with it, desire' (8). Zornberg sees this as part of 'God's original intention'.[52] But for Diski's God this is His 'great error. I made sentience. I made self-consciousness. I made *I am*. Whatever anyone might say, I did not know what the consequences' of splitting the 'human singleton' into 'a doublet of self-awareness' would be (12). The 'anyone' He refers to here is presumably the redactor of the text of Genesis itself, especially chapter 1, the work of the Priestly Writer, who presents a God very much in control of creation. Diski's God, by contrast, proceeds to trace the unforeseen consequences of his instruction, 'Be fruitful and multiply', deploring 'the way these humans made more of reproduction than I had intended', glorifying 'the sticky insult that I had condemned them to' (25). Sex was never supposed to be so important (or so much fun).

Far from omniscient, Diski's God is constantly surprised by the complexities of human behaviour, resulting in consequences He hadn't envisaged. No sooner do His creatures invent 'responsibility to one another' than they proceed to shrug it off, causing their puzzled Creator to ponder the significance of Cain's question:

> Am I my brother's keeper? I just wanted to know where the lad was. The scent of roasted sheep meat pleased me. It was a new sensation in the world I had made. And it had stopped. It was an innocent enough question. But suddenly, there was a family. And suddenly, there was death (41).

Like the anthropomorphic deity of the Yahwist, Diski's God enjoys simple things such as the smell of meat (cf. Gen. 8:21) and dislikes the way in which His creatures complicate and pervert all His gifts. He gives them 'the Word', for example, and they re-arrange it, inventing 'lies'; He devises a system of reproduction and they discover 'the pleasures of the flesh' (56). Even when He invents 'goodness' to counteract their evil, endowing the 'dull and unimaginative' Noah with this quality, the first thing this supposedly righteous man does on returning to dry land is to get drunk (66-7).

God's puzzlement at the complexity of human emotions, in particular their romanticising of love, is counteracted by the rival narrator's more sympathetic account of Sarai's emotional development, beginning with her idealisation of her older brother Abram as she watches him engaged in the 'family business', carving and moulding figures of the gods. As in the midrash, Abram himself is no idolator, explaining to Sarai that the figures he makes 'are just the images of what we worship. They aren't the actual gods themselves' (36). When their father Terah suggests that Abram marry his sister Sarai, both initially struggle with the transition from

---

51 Zornberg, *The Beginning of Desire*, p.16.
52 *Ibid.*

brotherly to conjugal love but they learn gradually to recognise desire and enjoy their sexuality. Only Sarai's continuing failure to produce children leads Terah to insist that Abram take a concubine, causing Sarai to experience the complex emotions of rage and jealousy.

God dismisses all these emotions as 'irrationality', which He views in the same light as Dawkins sees religion, as 'a rogue tendency that arrived like a virus out of nowhere', an 'unintended corollary perhaps to the great big brains I had bestowed on them to think with' (94). God's plan is to find 'a solitary, needful one whose history I could develop and control' (Abram) in order 'to infiltrate humanity with my kind of human being' (95). It is not only Sarai, however, who develops out of her dissatisfaction an 'interior world' full of questions. Abram too begins to question 'what it [life] is for' (98), leading him to invent (or discover) religion. As in the midrash, Abram is depicted openly challenging his customers. 'We do not sell gods', he bellows at one of them, 'We sell lumps of stone' (99-100).

Diski again provides rival explanations of God's first call to Abram in Genesis 12:1-3, the translation of which she supplies in full. Firstly God-the-Narrator congratulates himself on having 'got the tone of the first calling just right', having known all along that 'walking away from everything he knew, everything he had, and throwing himself and his fortunes on the mercy of a voice in his head', would be 'irresistible' to Abram (112-3). The human narrator, however, focuses on Sarai, for whom 'religion did not go very deep'. She sees the whole event very differently, immediately suspecting Abram's sanity (116). When Abram disappears for three days, returning filthy and dishevelled to smash 'every remaining statue in the workshop' (118), she can only hope that 'the anguish that had caused the voice inside Abram's head would ease' (125). She also becomes savagely jealous of this 'phantom voice', this 'spectral voice engendered by despair' (128).

Diski's characterisation of Sarai, of course, is very different from any that would be sanctioned by Judaism, within which she plays a key role. *Etz Hayim*, for example, the authorised text, translation and commentary on the Torah within Conservative Judaism, explains of Genesis 12:5, in which 'Abram took his wife Sarai…and the persons that they had acquired in Haran; and they set out for the land of Canaan',

> The Midrash understands this anachronistically as referring to converts whom they had led to belief in the one true God (Gen.R. 39:14). For that reason, when converts to Judaism are given a Hebrew name they are called son or daughter 'of Abram and Sarah.' …Although the women of Genesis seem to play a minor role in what are presented as patriarchal narratives, we find the Midrash pointing to the larger role they undoubtedly played. Sarah was every bit the pioneer and 'soul-maker' that Abram was.[53]

This is clearly not the case in Diski's novel, in which Sarai opposes Abram's religion at every turn, displaying a response which is 'only human' in two senses: she herself insists on seeing everything in entirely human terms while Diski's human narrator presents her behaviour sympathetically as an understandable human response to these events.

---

53 *Etz Hayim*, p.71.

When Abram first announces, 'The Lord has spoken to me', for example, 'Sarai's heart sank' (114). When he tells her, after they have camped outside the village of Shechem, 'We have arrived....This is where my seed will develop into a nation', she has to suppress her initial scepticism: 'so far his seed had failed to develop into a single baby' (131). Once Abram starts to lead the life of 'a holy man', building altars all over the place and preaching sermons, she has 'no doubt' that they are 'following the wayward steps of a man who had lost his reason' (134). When he tells her that they must travel to Egypt to escape the famine afflicting their own land, however, Sarai to some extent envies him both 'his passionate vision and his belief in it' since her own 'acid disbelief' is 'all she had to sustain her in the chaos of her life' (140). Her response to all these developments, one could argue, is entirely human in the second of the two senses outlined above, completely understandable in the circumstances.

It is in Egypt, in the latter part of Genesis chapter 12, that Sarai's beauty is brought to Pharaoh's attention, Abram having persuaded her that 'it will go better for us' if they say they are brother and sister (Gen. 12: 13). Diski's God rages against such deception, which puts at risk the whole enterprise involving Abram's seed. But He also realises for the first time that He too has emotional 'needs':

> And now I loved, as if I had caught it like a virus, as if I were their creation, as if I were a mere emotional being like them. I who drifted with eternity, solitary needing nothing, I, it seemed, had fallen—oh how appropriate the metaphor— in love (146).

In Diski's narrative, then, even God suffers a fall, though, as in Twain, it is hard to decide whether he falls up or down. He certainly finds it impossible to abandon Abram, to take revenge for such betrayal, but is forced to intervene to rescue him in order to keep his grand plan on course.

The dual narrative works particularly well in providing two alternative versions of the scene in which the rabbis took such great interest, when Pharaoh is only just prevented from consummating his love for Sarai. Diski's human narrator tells the story from Sarai's perspective, recounting her growing excitement as Pharaoh, whose hands 'were soft and supple as the finest gloves made from the silky underbelly of day-old kid', caresses her body, providing her with 'a masterclass on love'. He has 'pushed her thighs apart' and is about to enter her, when he makes the mistake of whispering, 'I will commend your brother to the gods for giving you to me'. At this, Sarai feels obliged to correct his misapprehension, causing Pharaoh's sexual excitement immediately to 'wither'. Indignant at the deception, he offers to kill Abram and take her to his harem but Sarai pleads for her husband's life, explaining in comically banal terms that 'he has been under great mental pressure' (147-51). Pharaoh accordingly relents, making a version of the speech recorded in Genesis 12:19:

> What have you done?...Why did you tell me she was your sister?...Why did you not tell me she was your wife? Do you think I need to steal other men's wives? I have not touched her? Take her, and get out (152).

It is in his commentary on this passage of his translation that Alter makes the suggestion cited above that 'one might imagine a tense exchange between Pharaoh and Sarah'.[54] And this is precisely what Diski provides, dramatising the episode in convincing 'human' terms. But she also provides God's version of this episode, developing Genesis 12:17 (using Alter's translation): 'And the Lord afflicted Pharaoh with terrible plagues'. In his commentary on this verse, Alter cites Rashi, who 'infers a genital disorder'.[55] Ginzberg, as we have seen, has angels armed with sticks to keep Pharaoh down. Diski has her divine narrator claim that it was He who caused Pharaoh's failure to consummate: 'He withered at my command, not her words' (153). Again, readers of the novel are given a choice which of the two versions to accept, the human or the divine.

What is clear in both narratives is that from this point onwards the rivalry between God and Sarai for Abram's affections is of a deadly intensity, to be fought literally to the death. Sarai herself becomes catatonically depressed, 'an empty shell', so lacking in confidence that the human narrator opines, 'if he [who is not here accorded an initial capital] had spoken to her, she would even have heard Abram's lord' (154-5). God too recognises, with a somewhat callous triumphalism,

> She was ripe for the taking. But I decided I did not want her….I left her to herself to know the paltriness, the mere contingency of life on earth without the gift of my voice and the introduction of my purpose. I rejoiced in her lovelessness (157).

He is surprised, however, on appearing again to renew His promises to Abram, that His chosen one makes no response, withholding himself, and sulking. 'I am your shield', God coaxes him, only for Abram to complain that he is still childless (as in Gen.15:1-2). To ratify the renewed covenant (as in Gen. 15:9) God demands a sacrifice of three three-year-old animals, though His tone in Diski's novel is somewhat less serious both about what He calls 'the old three times three trick' and His 'hocus-pocus with a flaming torch' (166-7). God's flippancy about these rituals belies the fact that He now recognises His own vulnerability in craving love.

Sarai, seeing that Abram's God, whether real or invented, was her 'greatest rival', continues to be 'quietly suicidal'. In an effort to undermine Abram's faith and trust in God, she tells him some of the stories that the women tell each other in their tents about the Garden of Eden, the Flood, and Babel, which portray Him as 'capricious, dealing life and death, bestowing misery and hope, enticing and withdrawing like any flirtatious girl' (171). The fact that God paradoxically 'promises you a destiny, and stops up my womb', Sarai insists, confirms His perverseness and unreliability (174-5). She succeeds once again in weaning Abram away from his Lord, persuading him to turn to Hagar to supply them with a child.

Only Human at this point follows the biblical narrative about Hagar, the birth of Ishmael and their banishment fairly closely, embellishing only its consequences for God, who learns pity for the outcast, and even has some sympathy for Sarai's jealousy —'she was only human' (183). Diski departs from the biblical story, however, or develops it in unorthodox ways, when it comes to God's announcement that Sarai,

---

54 Alter, *Genesis*, p.53.
55 *Ibid.*

even at her advanced age, will bear a son. Both she and Abram, as in the biblical narrative (Gen. 17:17 and 18:12), respond to the news with laughter, though God at first misreads the now-renamed Abraham's behaviour as a Kierkegaardian 'fear and trembling'. Once He works out that it is laughter, He resolves to discipline his unruly servant, to 'have him trembling again in his uncertain world' (191-3). This, in Diski's novel, is the motivation for the Akedah.

It is God's fear of abandonment, His anxiety that Abram, as a final 'irony' (202), might learn, like Richard Rorty, 'to be content with contingency'(203), which Diski sees as the key to the Akedah. She appears here to be drawing on some ideas in Rorty's book *Contingency, Irony and Solidarity*, the first three chapters of which appeared in the same paper as much of Diski's journalism, *The London Review of Books*. Rorty takes the term 'ironist' to refer to someone 'who faces up to the contingency of his or her own most central beliefs and desires', unlike 'a theologian or metaphysician', who believes in 'an order beyond time and chance'. In a 'postreligious culture', he argues, people can turn to novelists and poets to generate a sense of continuity and solidarity, for 'narratives which connect the present with the past' and provide an imaginative sense of what the future might be.[56] This, I suggest, is what motivates Diski's depiction of the Akedah, though she may be less confident than Rorty that postmodern society can do without religion, can remain altogether content with contingency.

At the climax of *Only Human*, in fact, Diski appears to resist Rorty's suggestion. Her God-narrator rails against the 'happy, human family' which Abraham and Sarah think they can achieve (206), resolving on the Akedah as a way of separating them and of reinforcing their vulnerability to time and chance. Both He and Abraham appear 'implacable' in their resolve to go through with the terrible demand. It is God, in Diski's account, who buckles, who fails the 'test', unable to sacrifice the hope of reciprocated love. God calls out at the last minute to prevent Abraham from completing the sacrifice. Abraham's reply, however, 'Here I am', turns out to be his final one, 'the last words he ever spoke to me' (213). God therefore loses his leading prophet and the novel ends on a completely human level with Isaac, 'a wraith, a pale, shivering ghost', reporting the events to his mother and her emitting the 'three long languishing notes', the 'howl of loss' recorded in the midrash, before taking to her deathbed (214-5).

The account of the Akedah in *Only Human* is ultimately ambivalent, with neither of the narrators completely vindicated. The human narrator is left to lament the break-up and disintegration of Abraham's family, for whom the contingencies of time and chance bring only tragedy. But God-the-Narrator too is left with a silent and resentful Abraham, who is no longer prepared even to speak to him. This God, of course, is not that of Jewish or any other orthodoxy. He is a creature of Diski's own imagining developed in response to the biblical text as she reads it, highlighting some of its absurdities and contradictions. He is a God in whom she cannot (and would not want to) believe. He will play a much smaller role in *After These Things*. But in *Only Human*, as in some of her other writing, Diski appears to understand and to

---

56 See Richard Rorty, *Contingency, Irony, Solidarity* (Cambridge: Cambridge University Press, 1989), pp.xv-xvi.

some extent sympathise with that dissatisfaction with contingency, the vulnerability to time and chance (the downside of being 'only human') which drives people to religion in the first place. 'Only human' solutions to these problems do not appear to be entirely satisfactory.

After These Things, Diski's sequel to *Only Human*, could be said in some ways to celebrate God's defeat over the Akedah and His retreat from direct involvement in human affairs. It begins with a very self-conscious meditation on the part of the only (and only human) narrator of this novel on the way 'humankind beat the Lord at the story game', causing Him to 'sulk' in defeated and resentful silence: 'He did not walk and eat and dicker with them for the lives of the Sodomites, as He had with Abraham; He only ever came in dreams to them'.[57] God's relegation to an off-stage role, of course, is apparent in the second half of the Book of Genesis itself, about which there is some self-conscious reflection in the opening pages of the novel. Once they had made up 'the cracking tale of creation', the narrator suggests, people 'told it over and over…trying to get it straight, or just idling the time away. Version after version; story without end' (2). Editors come along to 'patch and refit the various stories', creating new meanings by restructuring earlier stories. The narrator even sees herself (assuming that she is feminine) as just another of 'us editors', although this particular version of the story, she insists, 'is certainly mine'. Even that claim she is forced to qualify, however, given the amount of inherited material, from the Bible itself and from the midrash, that she employs: 'Mine as much as anyone's' (4-5).

Although there is only one narrator of *After These Things*, Diski's exploration of the consequences of the Akedah for Isaac and his family, there is a constant change of perspective, a switching from one focaliser (the character through whose eyes the events are supposedly seen) to another. The novel opens, for instance, with the elderly Isaac, 'blind and bedridden', aware as he has been since the Akedah itself 'how close death was', characteristically trembling as he waits to bestow the blessing on his favourite son (7-8). His memories and reflections alternate with those of Rebekah, seated outside her husband's tent, aware that he is fading. Isaac relives the momentous events on Mount Moriah in his mind, recalling how he 'had walked on, step by step towards death without protest. A stupefied boy. A stupid boy' (10). Diski takes him once more through the whole event, remaining very close to the text of Genesis chapter 22 from the saddling of the donkey through the cutting and carrying of wood to their silent walking together. Even the dialogue she invents is in keeping with the terseness of the narrative as analysed by Auerbach: 'We must go', Abraham tells him while Isaac himself, as Zornberg had noted, 'shrivelled with fear' (11-12).

Isaac's memories, in Diski's retelling of the story, are interrupted by Rebekah's recalling of her betrothal scene, the dialogue in the novel again following that of Genesis very closely (Gen. 24: 22-7). But she quickly returns to Isaac, who recalls the question he put to his father, where the 'sheep for the sacrifice' was, and his father's ominous reply, 'The Lord will see to the sheep for the sacrifice, my son'

---

57 Jenny Diski, *After These Things* (London: Little, Brown, 2004), p.1. All subsequent references in brackets in the text are to this edition.

(Gen. 22:7-8). Isaac can identify the menacing tone in his father's words but sees it as directed against God more than himself, part of a silent battle between them. Isaac also remembers his inability even to scream as his father prepared to kill him, Diski providing an entirely human explanation for his later blindness (in contrast to the somewhat extravagant claims of the rabbis):

> Isaac stared up at the aching blue sky above him directly into the scorching sun and his eyes began to overflow, drenched with something more caustic than tears, something that burned and stung and then seared with a pain of sharpened sticks being twisted in his eyeballs. These acid tears clouded the blue of Isaac's pupils with a pale, milky scarring, like the cataracts of old, blinding him... (21).

Like Zornberg, in other words, Diski sees Isaac's blinding as psychosomatic, a particularly severe symptom of the trauma he undergoes.

That Isaac had been irretrievably damaged by this trauma is also evident in Rebekah's recollection of her first encounter with him. Again, Diski draws on rabbinic interpretations of the last five verses of Genesis chapter 24, which themselves oscillate between Isaac's perspective ('and he lifted up his eyes, and saw, and, behold the camels were coming') and hers ('And Rebekah lifted up her eyes, and when she saw Isaac, she lighted off the camel'). That he is praying, as the rabbis argued, remains a possibility even in Diski's account of Isaac (as Rebekah sees him) wandering 'alone, with his head bowed, his hands limp at his sides'. Rebekah herself cannot decide whether he is 'meditating, or praying, or pondering a problem deeply, or just pacing blindly through the open country without a thought in his head' (25). What she does realise for certain is that he is 'a man already defeated' (26), a judgment confirmed by Isaac's own sense that 'He had been killed that day', that the sight of his father preparing to execute him had 'sucked the soul and spirit out of him, leeched him of all substance, bled him to death' (27). He recalls returning to his mother, as in some of the rabbinic versions of the story, standing in front of her like 'a wraith, a pale shivering ghost', unable initially to speak. Only after she had 'soothed his trembling body' and allowed him a night's sleep, could he tell her what had happened, his broken narrative in turn producing the same midrashic 'howl of loss', the 'terrible cries' with which *Only Human* ended (29-30).

Continuing to intercalate Isaac's memories of his mother's death with Rebekah's recollection of their first encounter, Diski, as might be expected from her perennial interest in human sexuality, makes much of the biblical account of Isaac bringing Rebekah 'into his mother Sarah's tent' and being 'comforted after his mother's death' (Gen. 24:67). 'This was where my mother died', he tells her in a less than convincing opening gambit, before proceeding to clutch needily at her body. His 'ignorant hands' then explore her body 'clumsily', leading to a hasty and unreciprocated climax. Rebekah quickly recognises that her future husband, who is 'blind to everything except the pursuit of his own relief', combines a 'wraith and a rapist in the one person', a 'ghost-beast' who consoles himself for his inner deadness with physical pleasures (40-3). Isaac himself recalls feeling momentarily 'alive' after their lovemaking, gratified at last to have 'a woman, a wife', who 'would make him food, and provide him with sexual pleasure whenever he wanted' (48). In this respect, he is as patriarchal (in the modern feminist sense of the word) as his father.

Diski's Rebekah, as in Zornberg's reading of her, becomes understandably depressed, disgusted by 'the way he [Isaac] gorged on food and drink, the way he snatched at her unwilling flesh' (50). Her bitter complaints culminate in the claim, 'I hate my life' (53, cf. Gen. 27:46). She shouts at her husband that his Lord, or rather his 'father's Lord', is nothing but a 'trickster': 'It's not enough he demanded your blood, and turned you into a quivering old man before your time, now he prevents you having children' (55). Isaac meanwhile receives 'not a word, not a whisper', from this Lord (56). He 'waited and listened, but heard nothing' (65). Eventually he claims that the Lord has indeed spoken to him in his sleep, Diski here taking liberties with Genesis 26:2-4, where God's appearance is not qualified by any reference to Isaac being asleep. Throughout chapter 26, however, as Zornberg notes, 'Isaac…finds himself reliving many of the events of his father's life', travelling south, passing off his wife as his sister, coming into conflict with his neighbours and even re-opening the wells first dug by Abraham.[58] So it is not unreasonable for Diski to infer an insecurity on Isaac's part about living up to the standards of his father. 'I am the patriarch', she has him shout at Rebekah when she asks him, 'Will you ever be anything more than the shadow of your father' (68).

What is particularly galling for Isaac in *After These Things* is that his sons appear to repeat the pattern that he has established, struggling in turn to live up to his expectations. Esau, for example, marries Ishmael's daughter in a misguided attempt to appease his father. The narrator clearly finds the repetition in these biblical narratives somewhat wearisome: 'And so on. And so forth. Round and round and on and on. How early in the telling of the story of the family the pattern emerges' (83). As the 'editor' or 'redactor' of this particular story, however, she can impose her own coherence upon it and 'have the last word' (84). So she fast-forwards at this point to Jacob lamenting over the bloody clothes of his favourite son and suffering the 'barely suppressed terror that there was no God, no meaning for him' of the kind that had supported not only Abraham but 'his tremulous father, Isaac' (85). All Isaac appears to have passed on to his son is a disposition to anxiety.

The second half of the novel supplies an account of Jacob's early life from the deceptive gaining of the blessing through the wooing of Rachel to the reconciliation with Esau and delayed return to Canaan, a delay, as we have seen, punished by the awful events of Genesis chapter 34. These events are interspersed in Diski's narrative with the repeated image of the older Jacob holding his son's bloody coat in his arms, a moment in which everything he has ever believed about the family destiny appears to have been undermined. The young Jacob, as in the midrash discussed by Zornberg, fashions himself in direct opposition to his active brother, as a passive, lifeless scholar, 'absorbed in the worlds of his father and his grandfather'.[59] In the novel we are told, 'Jacob sat in tents and learned' while 'Esau roamed the wilderness and hunted' (87). It is scarcely surprising therefore that he should dream of 'a voice, or a sort of voice' making the same promises that had been made to his father and

---

58   Zornberg, *The Beginning of Desire*, p.149.
59   *Ibid.*, p.166.

grandfather. It may be a 'dreamed promise' and not 'the face-to-face covenant that the Lord and Abraham had made', but it was 'a voice and a promise nevertheless that placed him in the direct line' (90). Diski notes that his own vowed response, as at the end of Genesis 29, is only 'conditional...on things going well' (91).

That all is not well with Jacob's psyche, however, is apparent in his weeping after kissing Rachel at the well, as in Genesis 29:11. Diski makes much of this moment, of the way

> hot tears spilled from his eyes and streamed down his face....Tears of he-did-not-know what....As if he were being shaken by some interior mechanism, his whole body convulsed with the deep sobs that had been released by the touch of Rachel's lips on his (101).

Diski also dwells (perhaps predictably) on his night of passion with Leah in the guise of Rachel. As in the midrash cited by Zornberg, Leah's words are made to echo his own: 'Yes, I am, I am your Rachel', she murmurs, in direct imitation of his words to Isaac (122-4). As in *Only Human*, however, Diski departs from that earlier 'editor', the Priestly Writer, in portraying Jacob as a man who suffers, like his father, from a lack of the strong sense of religious purpose that Abraham seems to have enjoyed: 'There was not the slightest sense that anything or anyone was "with him" or he with them' (141). The narrator wonders whether there was or had ever been 'such a Lord, except in Abraham, Isaac and now Jacob's wishful imagination' (142). Perfunctory, even cruel, in fulfilling his marital obligations to Leah, Diski's Jacob is made to reflect cynically on the 'perversity' of events, that their dutiful and unenthusiastic conjugal embraces always appear to produce children while Rachel, to whom he makes frequent and passionate love, remains barren. It is almost, he opines, as if there were 'a scheming, playful, vengeful God somewhere at the back of it. Or a malicious editor' (147).

Jacob continues to live with his inherited 'dread', described in terms which recall the Akedah as 'a knife paring away his insides', and with a sense of 'incommensurateness with his grandfather', who 'was given or invented for himself a purpose out of the nothingness, the blankness, the mere contingency of life'. Abraham's faith, Jacob realises, may have been merely 'a leap of imagination'. But it was all the greater, all the more heroically human for that' (171-2). Jacob himself appears to have no heroic attributes, trembling with anxiety, as in the biblical account, at the prospect of meeting Esau again so many years after robbing him of his birthright. Diski, like Zornberg, treats his wrestling with the angel immediately prior to this encounter as a psychomachia, an inner struggle with inherited demons, ghosts of the past which 'reared up and fought for their meaning against Jacob's emptying, terrified and exalting soul' (190). Tempted to run away, to abandon all these claims, he finally resolves to remain with his family. But he looks back on his night on the banks of the Jabbok with at best conditional faith: 'Perhaps, after all, the Lord had come to him that night....Perhaps this was how the voice of the Lord...now was heard' (191). When he finally does come face to face with his brother, instead of them both weeping, as in the biblical account (Gen. 33:4), Diski has Jacob return Esau's genuine emotion with calculated and self-interested generosity. His 'terror' continues to outweigh any genuine sense of contrition (192).

The novel narrates the awful events of Genesis chapter 34 as yet further symptoms of the dysfunctional family now ineffectively led by Jacob. The violent response of Leah's sons to their sister's supposed rape is seen to be motivated in part by the anger they are unable to direct at their father for his 'continuing insult to their mother' (203). As they decide how to respond to Shechem's offer of marriage, the brothers are seen to replace Jacob as the real leaders of the family: 'In just those few moments Jacob had become an old man, fearful, dithering, no longer the head of the household'. This, the narrator records, fast-forwarding once again to the scene of Jacob holding the bloody coat of his favourite son, 'was the birth of the enfeebled old man who now wept inconsolably over the loss of his beloved son Joseph' (206). Jacob's feeble objections to the slaughter of the inhabitants of Shechem, and the disdain with which his sons now look at him, remind him of the way he had regarded his own 'whining, fearful father' (209). The death of Rachel in childbirth, in another echo of the Akedah, twists another 'knife in his heart' (212), while Reuben confirms the transfer of power within the family by sleeping with his concubine Bilhah. Finally, news comes of Isaac's death, leaving Jacob with only 'sadness, fear and death (214). The novel ends with yet another portrait of Jacob confronted by Reuben 'with a bloody rag in his hand'. The tears he is made to shed once again have their roots, the narrator confirms, in the Akedah: 'At last, there was only terror. The terror of Abraham, Isaac and Jacob' (216).

Diski's is a bleak retelling of the biblical narrative, a modern redaction which edits out the Priestly Writer's confident belief in a guiding, providential hand behind the events narrated in Genesis. She dwells continually on the human elements in the original story, the only elements which she finds entirely credible, exploring ways in which they fit into our contemporary psychoanalytic understanding of human behaviour. She remains in some respects sympathetic to the search for religious meaning in Abraham and his descendants but she provides an entirely human account of them, one which does not require (though it does not altogether deny) the supernatural explanation of the ancient redactor of Genesis. To this extent, of course, her rewriting of the Akedah and its residue, while drawing creatively upon the midrashic material cited in her intertexts, goes well beyond the limits one would normally expect of midrash.

Chapter 6

Rachel and Her Sisters: Anita Diamant

***The Red Tent*: A Publishing Phenomenon and its Liberal Jewish Context**

In the 'Prologue' to Anita Diamant's first novel, *The Red Tent* (1997), Dinah, the first-person narrator, refers to her story as a biblical 'footnote', 'a brief detour between the well-known history of my father, Jacob, and the celebrated chronicle of Joseph, my brother'. In the biblical account of her supposed rape at the beginning of Genesis chapter 34, Dinah notes, she is treated as no more than 'a voiceless cipher'. Her 'four mothers', by which she means not only her biological mother Leah but also her three 'mother-aunties' (Rachel, Zilpah, and Bilhah), can also be seen as victims of the same 'great silence that swallowed me'. Her own narrative aims to rescue them all from oblivion, to fill the lacuna in the biblical account, to provide an act of 'remembering' which is 'holy'.[1]

The first hardback edition of the novel, Diamant recalls in the 'Preface' to her second novel, *Good Harbor* (2001), was met with a 'thunderous silence' apart from a few reviews in some small newspapers.[2] The paperback edition of *The Red Tent*, however, as Diamant records on her website, quickly became 'a publishing phenomenon'. Partly through 'word-of-mouth', partly through the support of independent booksellers and through the recommendation of rabbis but most of all through the influence of informal reading groups, the novel went on to sell nearly two million copies in 19 different languages.[3] Some astute marketing also contributed to this process: when the original publishers (St. Martin's) were about to remainder the unsold copies of the hardback edition prior to the appearance of the Picador paperback, Diamant suggested they use them instead for promotional purposes. Copies were sent first to all the female rabbis in Reform Judaism, then to all the Reconstructionist rabbis, who recommended it to their congregations. *Reform Judaism*, a magazine with a readership of some 400,000 households, made it one of the four significant Jewish books that all Reform Jews in the United States are recommended to read every year. Picador also mailed copies to all female Christian clergy and to the leaders of independent reading groups. Diamant herself was assiduous in responding to invitations to discuss the book.

The phenomenal success of *The Red Tent* may therefore have had more to do with the interests of this identifiable readership than with the intrinsic merits of the book, though Diamant is perhaps unduly defensive in describing herself as 'not a literary writer', not having attended 'whatever school it is…you need to get reviewed in the

---

1   Anita Diamant, *The Red Tent* (London: Pan Books, [1997] 2002), pp. 1-4.
2   Anita Diamant, *Good Harbor* (London: Pan Books, [2001] 2003), p.x.
3   www.anitadiamant.com/theredtent.htm, accessed 26/9/2005.

New York Times'.[4] She has now published three novels and several handbooks about Judaism. She may belong to a different (non-Ivy) league to some of the 'major' authors studied elsewhere in this book. But she writes for and is read by a whole group of people (women) previously disenfranchised by religious institutions. It is also important in relation to a key strand of this book that she is a self-conscious exponent of midrash. In this section therefore I will first consider some of the views she has expressed on the subject of midrash before exploring the nature of the 'liberal Judaism' she espouses. Among the significant intertexts for *The Red Tent* to be studied in the second section of this chapter is the work of Rabbi Lawrence Kushner, her own rabbi at the time of writing the novel. I will also explore texts by two Jewish feminists (Susannah Heschel and Susan Schneider), by the historian of ancient goddess-worship, Tikva Frymer-Kensky, and by the novelist and practitioner of new Jewish rituals, E.M. Broner. I will then return in the final section to *The Red Tent* itself.

It is to the example of midrash that Diamant turns, defending herself in an interview of 2002 in the *Guardian* against the charge of being 'sacrilegious' in her reworking of the Bible. Midrash, she suggests, provides a model for 'such imaginative wrestling with Biblical texts…a kind of creative, interactive reading that attempts to explore the Bible's mysteries and lacunae':

> 'You are supposed to bring every element of your intellect, your emotions, and your imagination to this sort of study,' she says, because the Bible is by its nature incomplete and, on occasion, contradictory. 'It's up to us to figure out what it means, it's incumbent upon us to make sense of it'.[5]

Asked after a lecture on the novel, 'How did you have the audacity to do this to the Bible?', she replies, 'It is my birthright. My audacity is the Jewish approach to Scripture. I approach the Bible as the heir to this tradition of Midrash'.[6] A similar reference to 'the ancient but still vital literary form' of midrash appears on her page on the Barnes and Noble website, 'Meet the Writers', where she explains that 'the rabbis used this highly imaginative form of story telling to make sense of the elliptical nature of the Bible— to explain, for example why Cain killed Abel'. She proceeds to liken the 'compressed stories and images of the Bible' to photographs. They may give us a moment of insight but 'don't tell us everything we want or need to know. Midrash is the story about what happened before and after the photographic flash'.[7]

In representing *The Red Tent* as a modern development of the ancient rabbinic art of midrash Diamant may have been influenced in part by some early reviewers and commentators. Rabbi Laurie Katz Braun, for example, providing an online

---

4   Faith L.Justice, 'An Interview with Anita Diamant', www.copperfieldreview.com/interviews/diamant.html, accessed 26/9/2005.

5   Alex Clark, 'A Life in Writing: Rewriting the Good Book', *Guardian* 30/3/2002, Saturday Pages, p.11.

6   Joan Gross, 'Jacob's Daughter Hits the Bigtime in 2002', www.jewishsf.com/content/2-0/module/display/story, accessed 26/9/2005.

7   'Meet the Writers: Anita Diamant', www.barnesandnoble.com/writersdetails.asp, accessed 26/9/2005.

'study guide' for the novel, describes it as a form of 'Modern Midrash'.[8] Bonnie Fetterman too, in her review of the novel, discusses the way 'many contemporary women writers have turned to the art of midrash-making to cast new light on figures such as Lilith, Miriam... and now Dinah'.[9] In an article entitled 'Midrash— or Not', however, reprinted in *Pitching My Tent* (2005), Diamant appears ambivalent about the term. In writing *The Red Tent*, she claims, 'I thought I was writing historical fiction', researching food, clothing and funeral customs of the ancient Near East in great detail. 'But from the moment *The Red Tent* was published, Jewish readers and writers labelled it "midrash"', a term she sees as having expanded almost indefinitely to include almost any intertextual piece of writing.[10] She also questions Rabbi Braun's category, 'modern midrash', wondering a little disingenuously whether this is 'a whole new food group, or just watered-down soup'.[11] In an interview for *Jewish News* she again insists that she did not set out to write a Biblical midrash: 'I looked at the commentary and turned away'. The biblical text was clearly the starting point but 'after that, she let her imagination take over'.[12] In a reply to a question of my own about the role of midrash in the writing of *The Red Tent* she uses the word 'permission' for the encouragement midrash gave her 'to play with biblical texts and to fully own the stories in the Torah'. She acknowledges Ginzberg and other commentators on midrash but insists that she set aside all such material 'VERY early in my process and closed the Bible soon after, to keep myself from being "faithful" to the text or prior readings'.[13]

Diamant's interest in the Jewish tradition, like that of Diski, developed relatively late in her career. Her parents, she acknowledges at the beginning of *Pitching My Tent*,

> were not religiously observant at home and we didn't belong to a synagogue until I was in junior high school, so I had little formal religious education. But my parents survived the Holocaust in Europe, and Yiddish was one of the languages spoken at my house. I never had any doubts about my ethnic or religious identity; still, it was only when I fell in love with a lapsed Presbyterian and began to think of us as a family-to-be that I realized how important it was to me that any child of mine know that she was Jewish.[14]

It was with that in mind that she began what she refers to as her 'remedial religious education' within Reform Judaism, a process which gathered pace when her partner decided to convert to Judaism.[15] Like her character Joyce in *Good Harbor*, she graduated from being a 'lox-and-bagel Jew', whose observance was limited to

---

8   Rabbi Laurie Katz Braun, '*The Red Tent: A Study Guide*', http://urj.org/Articles/index.cfm, accessed 26/9/2005.
9   Http://reformjudaismmag.net/599bf.html, accessed 26/9/2005.
10 Anita Diamant, *Pitching My Tent* (New York: Macmillan, 2005), pp.207-8.
11 *Ibid.*, pp.209-10.
12 Vicki Cabot, 'Woman's Voice: "Red Tent" tells other side of the story', www.jewishaz.com/jewishnews/000114/tent.shtml, accessed 26/9/2005.
13 Anita Diamant, email to myself of 28/9/05.
14 Diamant, *Pitching My Tent*, p.6.
15 *Ibid.*; see also Anita Diamant, *Choosing a Jewish Life* (New York: Schocken Books, 1997), p.xviii.

lighting a menorah for Hanukkah and eating at the Passover seder of friends,[16] to one intent on discovering as much as possible about the tradition. Having settled as a freelance journalist in the Boston area in 1975, she started writing about contemporary Jewish practice ten years later.[17] A series of handbooks on various aspects of Jewish life would follow, of which the most important are *Living a Jewish Life* (1991), *Choosing a Jewish Life* (1997) and *Pitching My Tent* (2005). A brief consideration of these will illustrate the decidedly liberal understanding of Judaism which Diamant offers.

'Liberal Judaism', as Diamant explains in *Living a Jewish Life*, aims at a 'synthesis of tradition and modernity'. The goal of reconstructing traditional practice to reflect the 'powerful insights of the present', she continues, is one to which the Reform, Conservative and Reconstructionist movements in America all aspire.[18] All three movements ordain women as rabbis since feminism 'has transformed the ways Jewish men and women conceive of themselves in relation to each other and in relation to the Holy'.[19] Jewish public life had previously been 'an all-male arena', with women concealed in the synagogue behind a curtain or in the balcony. Now, however, women take a much more active role in the synagogue.[20]

'It is tempting to imagine a counter-history, a counter-practice of Judaism known only to the women', Diamant admits, proceeding to detail some of the ways in which Jewish feminists have adapted traditional ceremonies. Rosh Hodesh, for example, initially conceived as a celebration coinciding with the appearance of the new moon of God's rewarding women for refusing to contribute their jewellery to the golden calf, has been reconceived in the modern era as an opportunity for raising 'feminist consciousness', to 'talk about what it means to be a Jewish woman'. *Mikveh* too, Diamant explains, which was traditionally a requirement of ritual cleansing after menstruation, has been 'reclaimed as a ritual of spiritual renewal for women and men at special times of life'.[21] *Living a Jewish Life* also recommends the practice of midrash as a means of making traditional texts relevant to the present.[22] In *Shavuot*, for example, the seven weeks after Passover, Diamant recommends 'writing modern *midrashim* or imaginative commentaries on a biblical passage'.[23]

Choosing a Jewish Life, which appeared in the same year as *The Red Tent*, presents a similar picture of Judaism as a dynamic evolving religion. A personal 'Preface' again explains how it arose from her own decision about the 'kind of Judaism' Diamant wanted to pass on to her daughter, not a 'purely ethnic or historical kind of Jewishness' such as she had inherited, but one in harmony with contemporary ideas.[24] 'Faith, belief and creed', Diamant explains in the 'Introduction', have always been

---

16 Diamant, *Good Harbor*, p.13.
17 'About Anita Diamant', www.anitadiamant.com/about anita.htm, accessed 26/9/2005.
18 Anita Diamant with Howard Cooper, *Living a Jewish Life*, pp.7-9.
19 *Ibid.*, p.278.
20 *Ibid.*, p. 283.
21 *Ibid.*, pp.283-5.
22 *Ibid.*, pp.83.
23 *Ibid.*, pp.173 and 236.
24 Diamant, *Choosing a Jewish Life*, p.xvii.

'of secondary importance in Judaism', which is not a 'belief system' so much as a way of life.[25] Liberal Jews, she continues,

> share the basic assumption that Judaism evolves over time, and that Jews in every generation struggle to reconcile ancient ways with modern challenges. For liberal Jews, *halacha* (Jewish law) is a historical collection of human responses to the divine and thus is open to interpretation and change.[26]

Diamant again portrays midrash as part of this evolving process, an activity which can be both 'personal and collective, academic and creative, hard work and great fun'.[27] Torah study, she insists, does not have to be 'deferential or worshipful'; it can involve 'arguing, wrestling, imagining, and interjecting contemporary dilemmas into ancient settings'. Midrash, she explains, begins with two assumptions:

> first, that the biblical text is sacred and has something of ultimate importance to say to everyone— not just rabbis and scholars; and second, that the Torah's message is not obvious but hidden, so that people have to work at it, play in it, seek it out....*Midrash aggadah*— the search for stories— is how Jews have filled in the blank spaces in the biblical narrative. An entire rabbinical literature of such stories, collectively called 'the Midrash,' takes remarkable liberties with the text, imagining whole scenes and conversations that seem 'missing' from the text.[28]

After illustrating some of the ways in which the ancient rabbis attempted to fill these gaps in the biblical text, Diamant argues that in more recent times fiction has provided a similarly open means of attempting to treat 'unspeakable' events such as the holocaust within the framework of Jewish faith.[29]

A similar view of Judaism as a religion rapidly evolving to meet the needs of a quickly-changing society emerges in some of Diamant's more specialised handbooks such as *Saying Kaddish* and *The New Jewish Wedding*. In the latter, for example, she insists that Judaism is 'a living tradition because it has been examined, debated, and reinvented, generation after generation'.[30] This claim is repeated throughout *Pitching My Tent*, a collection of articles from Diamant's recent contributions to a range of journals. Among the new practices she observes within contemporary Judaism is 'The Orange on the Seder Plate', an innovation to the traditional symbolism of Passover introduced by the teacher and writer Susannah Heschel as 'a symbol of inclusion for lesbian and gay Jews, and in following years for all those who have been marginalized in the Jewish community'. Diamant is clearly proud of this development, which 'represents the creative piety of liberal Jews, who honor tradition by adding new elements to the old'. She likens it to 'the presence of another new ritual item, the Miriam's Cup, which acknowledges the role of Moses' sister,

---

25 *Ibid.*, pp.5 and 17.
26 *Ibid.*, pp.5-6.
27 *Ibid.*, p.77.
28 *Ibid.*, pp.220-1.
29 *Ibid.*, pp.77 and 79.
30 Anita Diamant, *The New Jewish Wedding* (New York: Fireside, 2001), p.31.

the singer-songwriter-prophet, in the story'.[31] She also writes about 'Living Waters' (*Mayyim Hayyim*), the traditional term for the purifying waters of a *mikveh* but also the name of the Community Mikveh and Education Center she helped to establish in Boston. The article with this title in *Pitching My Tent* expresses the hope that 'women will find new ways to celebrate all the unheralded passages of their bodies as they see fit' and thereby learn to 'sacralize their sexuality'.[32]

Diamant's books on contemporary Judaism give a clear indication of her theological position, very much on the liberal end of the Jewish spectrum of belief. The following section of this chapter will consider some of the intertexts which have contributed to this position (and to elements in *The Red Tent*), looking firstly at the work of the rabbi who introduced her to midrash, Lawrence Kushner, secondly at a number of Jewish feminist writers, and finally at some examples of traditional midrash about Dinah, often misogynistic in nature, which may serve to explain her desire to produce a rather different mode of midrash in her own creative reworking of the Book of Genesis.

Kushner, Midrash and Feminism: *In the Wake of the Goddesses*

Throughout her work, Anita Diamant makes frequent acknowledgements of the debt she owes to Rabbi Lawrence Kushner, who is thanked at the end of *The Red Tent* for introducing her to midrash.[33] *Living a Jewish Life* credits him with having 'had the most profound influence' both on her and her husband,[34] while *Choosing a Jewish Life* is dedicated to him.[35] Kushner, she says at the beginning of *Pitching My Tent*, 'remains our teacher and dear friend', having served as rabbi for 28 years at the Beth El Congregation at Sudbury, Massachusetts, where she and her husband worship. Rabbi Kushner is credited later in the volume with teaching her that 'liberal Jewish piety' is not a contradiction in terms, and with introducing her not only to midrash but to 'many other wonderful teachers'.[36] Kushner's books, which may be taken to represent his teaching at Beth El, celebrates the Jewish spiritual tradition in a broad and inclusive manner. *Honey from the Rock* (1977), for example, explains that religions can easily become 'ossified', 'hopelessly encrusted by centuries of mindless repetition'.[37] They can also become too cerebral, codified in law and doctrine. 'Entrances to holiness are everywhere', he insists, not only in officially sanctioned places. Jacob, for example, was on the run from his brother in the wilderness when he experienced the mystical vision of the ladder between heaven and earth.[38] *Honey*

---

31   Diamant, *Pitching My Tent*, p.149
32   *Ibid.*, p.214.
33   Diamant, *The Red Tent*, p.385.
34   Diamant, *Living a Jewish Life*, p.xvii.
35   Diamant, *Choosing a Jewish Life*, p.vii.
36   Diamant, *Pitching My Tent*, pp.6 and 198.
37   Lawrence Kushner, *Honey from the Rock* (San Francisco: Harper and Row, 1977), p.15.
38   *Ibid.*, p.48.

from the Rock has several references to midrash, including *Genesis Rabbah*, although its main source is the *Zohar* and other kabbalistic works.

The book by Kushner that Diamant herself recommends in *Living a Jewish Life* as 'a modern introduction to midrashic thinking' is *The River of Light* (1990).[39] 'Like midrashic literature in general', Kushner explains in the introduction, *The River of Light* is its own 'contemporary American fantasy-commentary on seven verses from the book of Genesis',[40] the first seven verses of chapter 18, in which Abraham provides hospitality for his three divine visitors. Kushner quotes a number of midrashic explorations of the 'river of light' which Abraham is said to have observed between running to his herd and taking a calf in verse 7. Midrash, according to Kushner, is 'a literature which appears in the spaces in between' the biblical text itself.[41] Midrashic reading, he continues, like deconstruction (unsurprisingly, as argued in chapter 1, given their shared roots in rabbinic thinking), pays 'special attention to the seemingly trivial details' of a text, asking for example why there are *three* visitors. Kushner quotes a talmudic answer: 'One to bring the "good news" to Sarah. One to overthrow Sodom. One to heal Abraham'.[42] After citing several classic collections of midrash, he ends the book with a few midrashic developments of his own about the lunch Abraham served to his visitors.

The book by Kushner that is probably of most relevance to *The Red Tent* is *God was in this Place and I, i did not know* [*sic*], an extended meditation on these words from Genesis 28:16, Jacob's own exclamation after waking from his dream. The acknowledgements at the front of the book explicitly thank 'the members of congregation BETH EL of the Sudbury River Valley', which would have included Diamant herself, 'for permitting me to "field test" so many of the following ideas on them in sermons, classes, and at meetings'.[43] Kushner calls the book 'one long midrash', which he glosses as 'fiction concealed beneath the apparent text of the biblical narrative', an attempt

> to 'imagine' how the apparently discordant 'words' of the text might be woven into a larger coherent whole. Such an approach is more than literary criticism. Only when the words of the text are holy, or, like a love letter, are read with a diligence of attention bordering on reverence, can midrash occur.[44]

What Kushner does in this book, in fact, is to expand upon seven Jewish commentators upon this passage in Genesis, drawing upon his own imagination to flesh out the personality of each commentator. The first of these is Rashi, whose work itself drew heavily upon midrash. Kushner himself frequently uses quotations from Genesis Rabbah, from the Pirkei de Rabbi Eliezer and other midrashic collections, interspersed

---

39   Diamant, *Living a Jewish Life*, p.89.
40   Lawrence Kushner, *The River of Light: Spirituality, Judaism, Consciousness* (Woodstock, Vermont: Jewish Lights, [1981] 1995), p.xviii.
41   *Ibid.*, p.29.
42   *Ibid.*, p.18.
43   Lawrence Kushner, *God was in this Place and I, i did not know* (Woodstock, Vermont: Jewish Lights, 1991), p.[5].
44   *Ibid.*, p.15.

with more recent works such as Harold Bloom's *Kabbalah and Criticism*, with its demand that 'strong poetry' receive 'an intensely personal response'.[45] Other commentators he explores include a nineteenth-century Polish woman, Hannah Rachel Werbermacher, Hasidic Masters such as Dov Baer, the Maggid of Mezritch, the Spanish Moses de Shem Tov de León and the fourth-century Palestinian Shmuel bar Nachmani. What is significant, however, is not the details of these commentaries but the fact that Kushner refers so extensively to English translations of midrashic collections, the publishing details he gives in the margins. His readers are thus enabled (and indeed encouraged) to follow up some these references themselves.

One of the aspects of Kushner's approach to traditional Jewish spirituality which Diamant would no doubt have welcomed is his preparedness to modify its 'sexist God language'.[46] He envisages the deity, for example, announcing himself to Jacob as 'the God of Abraham and Sarah, Isaac and Rebecca'.[47] Such inclusiveness of gender in traditional blessings and other parts of the liturgy were the result of a generation of Jewish feminist activity in the United States in which Anita Diamant herself was much involved. *Living a Jewish Life* recommends two books in particular as illustrating the 'impact of feminism on Judaism': *On Being a Jewish Feminist*, by Susannah Heschel, and *Jewish and Female* by Susan Weidman Schneider.[48] Both shed light on the context out of which *The Red Tent* arose, illustrating the kinds of questions Jewish feminists were asking of their tradition in the 1980s, when Diamant first became interested in it.

All of the essays in the volume *On Being a Jewish Feminist* deplore the restricted role women have hitherto been allocated in their religion, in which, as Heschel explains in her introduction,

> older, biblical, rabbinic, and medieval images [of women] continue to thrive even in secularized contexts. These images reveal not who women really are, but how women are made to appear and function from a male-dominated perspective....In their struggle with contemporary discrimination, feminists are actually wrestling with these unspoken, hidden images which often keep the community from making changes even when no rules forbid them.[49]

Lilith, for example, the mythical first wife of Adam, can be found to lurk behind the fear and mistrust of women that delayed their ordination even in Reform synagogues until the 1970s.

There are also, however, as Heschel argues in the introduction to the first part of the volume, 'many positive teachings and legends about women in Jewish tradition' which can be recovered by modern feminists.[50] It may not be enough, Rachel Adler

---

45 *Ibid.*, p.24.
46 *Ibid.*, p.19.
47 *Ibid.*, p.181.
48 Diamant, *Living a Jewish Life*, pp.89-90.
49 Susannah Heschel, ed., *On Being a Jewish Feminist* (New York: Schocken Books, 1983), p.xxxi.
50 *Ibid.*, p.3.

argues, merely 'to make lyrical exegeses on selected *midrashim* and *aggadot*'.[51] Nevertheless, it is worth considering the portrait of women in Jewish fiction, as Erika Duncan does in another essay in the volume. There, alongside the stereotypical male portrait of the hungry Jewish mother swamping her children with tenderness and chicken soup, new images can be found in writers such as E.M.Broner, whose novel *Her Mothers* interweaves stories of mothers from ancient and modern times. Among Broner's 'Foremothers' is the 'First Matriarch', Sarah, who is seen to have suffered appallingly at the hands of Abraham on their journey to Egypt. Broner augments the text of Genesis chapter 12 for comic effect, having Avram (as she transliterates his name) offer 'her strong body to the passing soldiers' in return for sustenance. Later he gives her 'to Pharaoh, who had her while Avram sat outside of the Great House counting his newly gained sheep, oxen, asses'.[52] The passivity of the wives of the patriarchs, their willingness to suffer such humiliation, drives Broner's narrator to despair. 'What do I learn from my mothers?', she asks: 'Sara! Rivka! Lea! Rahel! You have taught your daughters that women fight for the penis of a man'.[53] The women in what Broner irreverently labels 'the Old Testicle' appear to be valued solely for their fertility. Leah accordingly gives thanks as she dangles 'every year another son' while Rachel is punished by God for her 'pretty face' with 'spontaneous abortions'.[54] Broner clearly provides Jewish feminists with a strong model for the subversive rewriting of the scriptures.

Another essay in Heschel's volume cites a scene in *A Weave of Women* (1978), another novel by Broner, in which a group of women in Jerusalem are portrayed performing 'a hymenotomy', a female equivalent to circumcision, which involves the 'devirginization' of an infant girl by piercing her hymen. 'May all orifices be opened', pronounces her godmother. 'May she not be delivered intact to her bridegroom or judged by her hymen but by the energies of her life'.[55] This ritual, of course, is imaginary but Broner has developed a whole range of rituals designed actually to be performed by women, details of which can be found in *Bringing Home the Light: A Jewish Woman's Handbook of Rituals*. A section in this book is devoted to 'Moon Rituals/Rituals of the Body', including one for the onset of menses. In one of the rituals of shelter based on the traditional *Sukkot*, Leah bewails her daughter's barrenness: 'From Dinah, nothing comes, no tribe, no posterity. And her name becomes synonymous with rape, shame, vengeance. And she is not to be heard from again'.[56] So when *The Red Tent* not only gives Dinah both offspring and a voice but imagines an ancient ritual combining a hymenotomy with a celebration of the onset

---

51   *Ibid.*, pp.12-13.

52   *Ibid.*, p.34, citing E.M.Broner, *Her Mothers* (New York: Holt, Rinehart, and Winston, 1975), pp.149-51.

53   *Ibid.*, p.191 citing Broner, *Her Mothers*, pp.164-8.

54   *Ibid.*, pp.165-6.

55   *Ibid.*, p.25, citing E.M.Broner, *A Weave of Women* (New York: Holt Rinehart, and Winston, 1978), pp.25-6. I have quoted slightly more of the original novel than Claire Sadoff does in her essay in Heschel's volume.

56   E.M.Broner, *Bringing Home the Light* (San Francisco: Council Oak Books, 1999), p. 33. The book postdates *The Red Tent* but many of the ceremonies it describes, including the 'Sukka in the Sky', performed on top of the Grace Building in New York in October 1986,

of menstruation Diamant can be seen to be drawing on a flourishing tradition of recent Jewish practice.[57]

Part Two of Heschel's volume, 'Forging New Identities', contains much discussion of midrash. Cynthia Ozick, for example, as well as drawing on feminine imagery to be found in kabbalistic writing, refers to the *Tsena Urena*, a Yiddish translation of the Torah, including a homiletic commentary drawn from midrashic and later traditional sources, composed for women around 1600. 'We may think of it as the first Yiddish novel', she writes, 'the first *Jewish* novel', sharing the same lowly literary status as that genre at that time.[58] Ozick is also cited later in the volume calling for a new midrash for our own age, a new brand of imaginative literature helping to preserve Torah by augmenting it.[59] She has since, of course, incorporated midrashic elements in her own creative writing, in particular *The Shawl*, with its cross-references to the Akedah.

Midrash, as Heschel claims in the introduction to Part Three of the book, 'Creating a Feminist Theology of Judaism', is seen to offer women a persuasive method of changing Jewish attitudes, all the more acceptable because it is recognised as a traditional Jewish genre. Other writers advocate importing elements from other religions but most contributors prefer to find their inspiration from Jewish sources. Arthur Waskow, for example, adds his voice to the call for the adaptation of traditional rituals such as Rosh Hodesh. 'Is it possible', he asks, 'that the household *terafim* that Rachel took from Lavan's household...were sacred moon-symbols?' If this were the case, he continues, it would make it highly appropriate that she should conceal them from her father 'by explaining she was in the time of her menstrual flow'.[60] These and other suggestions in Heschel's volume provide a contemporary context of feminist Jewish thought in which *The Red Tent* should be placed.

Another significant intertext between the Book of Genesis and Diamant's novel is Susan Schneider's *Jewish and Female: A Guide and Sourcebook for Today's Jewish Woman* (1984), recommended by Diamant herself in *Living a Jewish Life* as 'a kaleidoscopic view of the issues facing Jewish women today'.[61] Schneider too charts some of the developments in Jewish rituals in the United States in the 1970s and 80s. One obvious way of going 'Beyond the Patriarchal Premise' (the title of Part One), she argues, is to modify traditional prayers, blessing in the name of 'the God of our mothers and fathers', the 'God of Sarah, Rebecca, Rachel and Leah' as well as 'of Abraham, Isaac, and Jacob'.[62] Schneider specifically recommends the prayer book produced by 'lay people' at Diamant's synagogue in which 'God is referred

---

predate Diamant's novel. Diamant would almost certainly have been aware of the kind of ceremony Broner was famous (at least in Jewish feminist circles) for performing.

57 For similar developments within Judaism in Britain, see Sylvia Rothschild and Sybil Sheridan, *Taking up the Timbrel: The Challenge of Creating Ritual for Jewish Women Today* (London: SCM Press, 2000).

58 Heschel, ed., *On Being a Jewish Feminist*, pp.130-1.

59 *Ibid.*, p.203.

60 *Ibid.*, pp.263-8.

61 Diamant, *Living a Jewish Life*, pp.89-90.

62 Susan Weidman Schneider, *Jewish and Female* (New York: Simon and Schuster, 1984), pp.80-1.

to without gender references or else androgynously'.[63] She also devotes a section of the book to '*Rosh Chodesh*: Rediscovering Ceremonies for Welcoming the New Month'. Talmudic versions of the story of Creation, Schneider explains, 'say that the moon, now smaller than the sun, will some day be restored to equality with it'. Since women's menstrual cycles are said to renew them just as the moon is renewed each month, feminists can 'draw parallels between the moon's future equality with the sun and the equality for women that is to come'.[64] Schneider also includes a ritual for the onset of puberty, complete with a special 'moontree' necklace, and points to 'alternative, or feminist haggadot' that have been written for Passover.[65]

As well as devising new rituals, Schneider recommends the writing of new midrash. In San Diego, she notes, the Jewish Women's Network have produced their own volume of Haggadah. Rabbi Lynn Gottlieb too performs a range of feminist midrash including one in which Leah,

> described in the original tale with the phrase '*rakot eynahim*' (weak-eyed— that is, unattractive), becomes a mystic, a seer, whose children will become the people of Israel. Gottlieb translates *rakot eynahim* as 'inward-seeing,' a metaphor for the woman's visionary quality.

She is thus no longer 'an object of pity who gets married off through a stratagem of her father's', as in the biblical narrative, but 'a strong individual with unique powers'. Such exercises in 'midrash-writing', Schneider reports, 'are immensely popular, as are the reconstructions and expansions on stories only suggested in the Bible'.[66] It is clear from this that Diamant's expansion of Dinah's story should be seen as part of a widespread re-reading of the Bible with its roots in the feminist movement of the previous two decades.

Schneider also has a section of her book devoted to 'The Mikveh Revival' exploring how Jewish feminists have returned to the rituals surrounding traditional laws of impurity in such a way as to celebrate rather than denigrate their bodies. They may still be divided about the extent to which this ritual was initially the product of 'a primitive blood taboo', reflecting 'male fear and loathing of women' but can unite over the manner in which it may be reclaimed as 'a symbolic rebirth'.[67] *The Red Tent*, as we shall see, combines both views, mocking the patriarchs for their fear of women's bodily functions while portraying the red tent itself as a domain exclusive to women in which they can develop rituals and ceremonies to support and encourage each other.

A final acknowledged intertext between Genesis and *The Red Tent* by a scholar who classifies herself as 'a late-twentieth-century postmodern American feminist

---

63 *Ibid.*, p.83.
64 *Ibid.*, pp.94-5.
65 *Ibid.*, pp.131 and 108-9.
66 *Ibid.*, pp 188-9.
67 *Ibid.*, pp. 204-7.

Jew',[68] is Tikva Frymer-Kensky's *In the Wake of the Goddesses*.[69] Frymer-Kensky accepts that her motivation to explore the goddesses worshipped in the ancient Near East prior to the gradual triumph of monotheism was 'a desire to remedy the results of millennia of misogyny' through historical scholarship.[70] What she discovered from recently-unearthed tablets written in Sumerian and Akkadian from the early third millennium was a rich vein of goddess-worship, the vestiges of which survive in the earliest strands of the Bible before being completely obliterated in the official monotheism which developed in exile. Many of these goddesses, as we shall see, reappear in the pages of *The Red Tent*.

The most important goddess in ancient Sumerian religion (as in Diamant's novel) is Inanna (though she becomes Innana in the novel). Celebrated in the poems of Enheduanna, priestess of the moon-god Nanna in the ancient city of Ur, Inanna, known in Semitic languages as Ishtar, was the goddess of desire and fertility, although she remained herself free of children and of other domestic duties, such as spinning and weaving, thereby increasing both her seductiveness and her availability.[71] Surviving poems about her, such as the frankly-titled fragment 'Plow my Vulva', involve an unashamed celebration of her sexuality. Several hymns celebrate Inanna's courtship by the god Dumuzi, a role played in ritual by the kings of Sumeria.[72]

The Goddesses of Sumeria, however, became increasingly marginalised, especially in Babylonian literature of the second millennium. In the *Enuma Elish*, for example, Tiamat, as we have seen, has to be defeated in order for Marduk to become King of the Gods. Ishtar offers to marry Gilgamesh but he refuses. This eclipse of the older goddesses is seen by Frymer-Kensky to reflect a decline in the public role of women in society, a process accelerated in Israel in the first millennium BCE. Part Two of her book traces this process in the pages of the Bible itself, whose oldest strands, she claims, display vestiges of these older goddesses. Jacob's blessing of his sons in Genesis chapter 49, for example, refers to the 'blessings of the breast and of the wombs' (Gen. 49:25). In Genesis generally, however, Yahweh takes over responsibility for fertility, shutting and opening the wombs of the women as He sees fit. Deuteronomy demands that the Israelites destroy the altars and 'sacred poles [asherahs]', the images and pillars of other cults (Deut. 16:20), while the prophets continually denounce the tendency of the people to follow after strange gods.[73]

Perhaps the most important chapter of Frymer-Kensky, at least in terms of its influence upon *The Red Tent*, is that on Asherah, a Canaanite goddess of the ocean, linked to Yahweh in a number of eighth-century inscriptions, possibly as a consort. An asherah was also the name given to a stylised tree-image, made out of wood, standing next to the altar but since there are no capital letters in Hebrew it is difficult sometimes

---

68   Tikva Frymer-Kensky, *In the Wake of the Goddesses: Women, Culture, and the Biblical Transformation of Pagan Myth* (New York: Free Press, 1992), p.ix.
69   Anita Diamant, emails to myself of 28 and 30/9/05.
70   Frymer-Kensky, *In the Wake of the Goddesses*, p.viii.
71   *Ibid.*, pp.25-9.
72   *Ibid.*, pp.47-57.
73   *Ibid.*, pp.83-99. See also Monica Sjoo and Barbara Mor, *The Great Cosmic Mother: Rediscovering the Religion of the Earth* (San Francisco: Harper and Row, 1975), pp.269-70 for a description of the Asherah and of rituals involving menstrual blood.

to know whether the word refers to the goddess or to the symbol. Frymer-Kensky speculates that Asherah was tolerated as a goddess until the eighth century when the official religion banned her (though 'the people' persisted in worshipping in the old style, much to the annoyance of the prophets). A number of female figurines from this period survive, rounded figures with a pillar base, breasts and molded heads, often found in domestic settings.[74] What they were and how they were used remains a matter of speculation but they provide sufficient historical basis for Diamant to make a plausible connection between them and the teraphim or household gods which Rachel conceals from her father in Genesis 31, and to imagine a domestic cult involving similar figurines.

The most eye-catching chapter of Frymer-Kensky's book, 'Sex in the Bible', explores the disappearance of sexuality as an aspect of the divine. There are references in the Bible to Yahweh's hand and arm, even to His tears, but He is not, of course, 'imagined below the waist...the sexual and divine realms have nothing to do with each other'. Whereas in ancient Sumeria the sacred rites associated with Inanna provided a religious sanction for sexual desire, in Israel, according to Frymer-Kensky, a 'desacralization of sexuality' took place, evident in the impurity laws, requiring all evidence of sexual activity to be removed before approaching the Temple.[75] Other laws attempted to control or regulate sexuality, outlawing adultery, homosexuality, bestiality and any other imaginable sexual activity outside the family structure. The so-called 'rape' of Dinah would therefore have been objectionable to the house of Jacob not because it involved a forcing of her against her will but because of the impropriety of failing to obtain parental permission for sexual intercourse.[76] In this particular detail, as in her general thesis about the existence of some vestige of the worship of goddesses in the early biblical period, Frymer-Kensky's book seems also to have proved fruitful for Diamant's novel, providing historical suggestions upon which her imagination could build.

Another aspect of Frymer-Kensky's study which is significant for *The Red Tent* is the distinction she makes between the Bible, which is reasonably sympathetic towards women, and the midrashim, which were influenced by Hellenistic scorn for women. The Bible presents men and women as having similar inherent characteristics, celebrating the trickery of heroines such as Rebecca, Tamar and Leah as much as that of the patriarchs. Midrashic retelling of the same stories, however, simultaneously debases and eroticises these women.[77] This is particularly evident in the treatment of Dinah in *Genesis Rabbah*, one of the many collections of midrash to which Diamant makes reference in her books on Jewish tradition. Ginzberg's summary of the midrash of 'The Outrage at Shechem' in *The Legends of the Jews*, which Diamant acknowledges studying before writing *The Red Tent*,[78] places much of the blame on Dinah herself, whose ostentatious exhibition of herself contrasts with the sober piety of her father and brothers:

---

74 *Ibid.*, pp.154-9.
75 *Ibid.*, pp.187-9.
76 *Ibid.*, p.194.
77 *Ibid.*, pp.120, 137 and 206-10.
78 Anita Diamant, email to myself of 28/9/05.

While Jacob and his sons were sitting in the house of learning, occupied with the study of the Torah, Dinah went abroad to see the dancing and singing women, whom Shechem had hired to dance and play in the streets in order to entice her forth. Had she remained at home, nothing would have happened to her. But she was a woman, and all women like to show themselves in the street.[79]

Genesis Rabbah presents this episode as the culmination of the wicked behaviour illustrated by all the women in Genesis. Even Leah is condemned as a whore because she 'went out to meet him [Jacob]' (Gen. 30:16), while Rabbi Joshua of Sikhnin rehearses the faults attributed to women which made the Creator ponder the decision where to begin his creation of Eve before settling on the rib (quoted in chapter 1). The women of Genesis who realise all His fears include Dinah, the 'gadabout' who 'went out' (Gen. 34:2).[80] *Genesis Rabbah* displays a prurient interest in what actually happened, interpreting 'seized her and lay with her' as vaginal intercourse and 'humbled her' (Gen. 34:2) as 'sexual relations through the anus'.[81]

It should not therefore be surprising that Anita Diamant, while taking midrash as a model for the creative reworking of scripture, should adopt little specific material from the rabbinic midrash about Dinah and her mothers/aunts. She follows *Genesis Rabbah* and the *Pirkei de Rabbi Eliezer* (also referred to in her handbooks on Judaism) in making both Bilhah and Zilhah, the handmaids given to Jacob, Laban's daughters (and therefore Dinah's aunts). But she departs from *Genesis Rabbah* and *Jubilees* over Leah's eyes, Rachel's motives for stealing the *terafim* and the provenance of Asenath, to cite just a few significant examples. *Genesis Rabbah* explains Leah's 'weak eyes' (Gen. 29:17) as a result of her weeping at the prospect of marrying Esau,[82] while *Jubilees* compares the two sisters very much to the elder's disadvantage: 'Jacob loved Rachel more than Leah, for Leah's eyes had no sparkle, despite her shapely figure, whereas Rachel had attractive eyes as well as an attractive and very shapely figure.'[83] According to Ginzberg, Rachel steals her father's household gods so that they can't tell him about their flight,[84] while Rabbi Eliezer sees it as a protest against the worship of idols.[85] *Joseph and Aseneth* is just one of many legends 'circulating in Jewish circles in the first centuries of the Christian era' suggesting that Potiphar's daughter, given to Joseph in marriage, was 'in fact the daughter of Dinah, born after the rape by Shechem and spirited

---

79 Louis Ginzberg, *The Legends of the Jews* (Baltimore: Johns Hopkins University Press, 1998), 9 volumes, I, 395. Diamant would not, of course, have read this edition but one referred to in p.52, n.8.

80 Jacob Neusner, trans, *Genesis Rabbah* (Atlanta, Georgia: Scholar's Press, 1985), 3 vols, III, 146-9.

81 *Ibid.*, III, 149.

82 *Ibid.*, III, 39.

83 H.F.D.Sparks, ed., *The Apocryphal Old Testament* (Oxford: Oxford University Press, 1984), p.88.

84 Ginzberg, *Legends of the Jews*, I, 371.

85 Gerald Friedlander, trans., *Pirkei de Rabbi Eliezer* (New York: Hermon Press, [1916] 1970), p.273.

away to Egypt by an angel'.[86] Such miracles would clearly be out of place in a realistic novel so Asenath is made genuinely Egyptian in *The Red Tent*. Joseph, as we shall see, cuts an altogether less sympathetic a figure in Diamant's novel than in the ancient romance. It is clear, in other words, that Anita Diamant was aware not only of the existence of ancient midrashic stories surrounding Dinah and her mothers but also of its misogynistic nature. When she came to write her own 'midrashic' novel therefore she reserved the right to interpret the biblical tale in a manner much more sympathetic to the women characters at its heart.

The Red Tent: Recovering a Sacred Space for Women

All the events narrated in *The Red Tent* are seen from the perspective of the women protagonists. Dinah, as we have seen, is the primary narrator, which means that the first part of the novel has to be filtered through the memories of Rachel, Leah, Bilhah and Zilpah, 'who told me endless stories about themselves'.[87] In these Leah is characterised far more positively in the novel than in the Bible or in the rabbinic midrash. Far from having weak eyes, ruined 'according to one of the more ridiculous fables embroidered around my family's history...by crying a river of tears over the prospect of marrying my uncle Esau', Leah's eyes, in Dinah's account, are so penetrating that they 'made others weak': 'few could stand to look her straight in the eye' (12-13). Jacob is one of these 'few', attracted also by her smell, a combination of the yeast used in brewing and baking 'and— it seemed to Jacob— of sex' (14).

Leah is described in *The Red Tent* as 'the lewdest of her sisters', claiming to know from the sensual manner in which Jacob devours her stew and her bread 'how to please the rest of him' (21). She is also the most practical, so that it is to her that Jacob turns with questions about pasturing or brewing. Dinah reports Zilpah noticing the obvious chemistry between them: '"It was like being near rutting he-goats," she said. "And they were so polite. They almost bent over not to see each other, lest they fall on top of each other like dogs in heat"' (34). This strong sexual attraction explains a significant departure from the biblical narrative in the plot of the novel: Zilpah tells Dinah that Jacob was perfectly willing for Leah to be substituted for Rachel on their wedding night, a plot in which Rachel herself colluded, having been driven to panic at the idea of sexual initiation:

> She had no expectation of pleasure— only of pain....Zilpah told her sister that the shepherds spoke of Jacob's sex as a freak of nature. 'Twice the size of that of any normal man,' she whispered, demonstrating an impossible length between hands. Zilpah took Rachel up to the highest pasture and showed her the boys having their way with the ewes, who bleated pitifully and bled (35).

Diamant's graphic account of the sexual habits of this ancient agrarian community may appear prurient but her concern with anatomical details was shared by the

---

86 Sparks, *Apocryphal Old Testament*, p.468.
87 Diamant, *The Red Tent*, p.3. All subsequent references in brackets within the text are to the paperback edition (details of which can be found in footnote 1 above).

rabbis; the Book of Enoch, as D.H.Lawrence discovered to his delight, has similar accounts of the prodigious size of the members of the Sons of God who came into the daughters of men.[88]

The Red Tent devotes considerable space to the sexual acrobatics of Jacob and Leah. Dinah somewhat improbably reports what she could only have heard from her mother, that Leah enjoyed flexing 'her legs and her sex with a kind of strength that surprised her and delighted him'. In explanation of what the Book of Genesis records, however, the two lovers decide that Jacob should emerge from their 'golden week' in the nuptial tent 'feigning anger' (40). Again, while recognising that having to share Jacob's love caused some initial jealousy between Rachel and Leah, Dinah reports that the sisters were soon reconciled after Rachel's first miscarriage. Women are thus seen to be more sensible than the (male) biblical narrative suggests. It is also the astute 'husbandry of the women', we are told, rather than any divine favour, which is responsible for Jacob's prodigious accumulation of wealth (54).

Another significant addition to the biblical narrative, built upon the reference there to the household gods or *terafim* which Rachel takes with her when they leave Laban's house (Gen. 31:19), is *The Red Tent's* account of the religion practised by its women. From the moment of his arrival, it is clear that Jacob's severe monotheism is very different from their rich polytheism. Zilpah tells Dinah that Jacob spoke of El, 'the god of thunder, high places and awful sacrifice', a god who could 'demand that a father cut off his son— cast him out into the desert, or slaughter him outright' (references, of course, to Abraham's treatment of Ishmael and Isaac). Zilpah finds such a conception of God 'alien and cold', though she can recognise in Him 'a consort powerful enough for the Queen of Heaven', Ninhursag, the great mother goddess of Sumerian religion (15).[89]

All the women of Laban's household appear to partake of this goddess-worship, handed down from the Sumerians. Rachel, for example, desperate for children, takes herself to 'the asherah', the acacia tree 'sacred to Innana', and prostrates herself before 'the wide-mouthed grinning goddess'. It is to her that she whispers her biblical line, 'Give me children or I will die' (66, cf. Gen. 30:2). The teraphim which Rachel takes with her are clearly part of these religious rites. In the Book of Genesis it is when Laban comes in search of them that she sits on them, telling him that she can't get up since 'the custom of women' is upon her (Gen. 31:34-5). In the novel she provokes him even further, declaring that the teraphim 'now bathe in my monthly blood', which means (for him at least) that they are 'polluted beyond redemption' (141).

Details about the religious practices of the women of Jacob's household only emerge gradually in the course of the novel, as Dinah herself matures. When she encounters her grandmother Rebecca, who enjoys a strong reputation as 'a diviner, healer, and prophet', playing a dignified if rather aloof host to the large numbers of pilgrims who visit her tent at Mamre, she hears of the tradition of female religious leaders beginning with 'Sarai the Prophet' (176-81). Diamant thus constructs an

---

[88] D.H.Lawrence, *Apocalypse and the Writings on Revelation*, ed. Mara Kalnins (Cambridge: Cambridge University Press, 1980), p.101.

[89] Frymer-Kensky, *In the Wake of the Goddesses*, p.223.

alternative lineage of powerful prophetesses who are far more than simply the wives of the patriarchs. Their mode of worship too is very different. Rebecca at one point recites 'a short poem about the great Asherah, consort of El and goddess of the sea' (183-4). She is portrayed as angry with the women of Canaan because they fail to maintain the proper worship of 'the great mother whom we call Innana', who is 'the center of pleasure, the one who makes women and men turn to one another in the night'. It is Innana, Leah explains to Dinah, who bequeathed to women 'the secret of blood. The flow at the dark of the moon, the healing blood of the moon's birth' (187). This secret, unknown to the narrators of the Book of Genesis (or censored by them), is the focus of their worship, which the women of Canaan have abandoned:

> They do not celebrate the first blood of those who will bear life, nor do they return it to the earth. They have set aside the Opening, which is the sacred business of women, and permit men to display their daughters' bloody sheets, as though even the pettiest baal would require such a degradation (188).

What Leah is referring to here, of course, is the male expectation of virginity on the part of their brides, the importance to them of the undisturbed hymen, to which the expected bloody sheets bear gruesome witness. And what 'the Opening' entails, as we discover when Dinah experiences her first period, is a ceremony combining hymenotomy (as suggested by E.M.Broner, only in Diamant's novel it is performed on an adolescent rather than an infant girl) with a celebration of the onset of puberty (as recommended by Schneider). In the novel Dinah describes her own initiation in vivid detail:

> Rachel brought out the teraphim, and everyone fell silent....I remembered them like old friends: the pregnant mother, the goddess wearing snakes in her hair, the one that was both male and female, the stern little ram. Rachel laid them out carefully and chose the goddess wearing the shape of a grinning frog....

Dinah is then undressed and taken outside, surrounded by her mothers and aunts, who place her face down on the soil 'to embrace the earth' and 'to give the first blood back to the land'. Rachel then implores 'Innana, Queen of the Night' to accept 'the blood offering of her daughter'. The triangular-shaped obsidian figure of the little frog-goddess, which has been rubbed with oil, is then inserted into Dinah, who imagines that 'the Queen herself was lying on top of me, with Dumuzi her consort beneath me' (205-6). These rituals, however, the vestiges of Sumerian religion, are brought to the attention of Jacob, who orders Rachel to bring him 'the household gods she had taken from Laban' and shatters them 'one by one, with a rock' (207-8). The whole episode presents a vivid dramatisation of the narrative to be found in Frymer-Kensky of the gradual supplanting in Israel of Sumerian goddess-worship by the new monotheistic religion of the biblical patriarchs.

Dinah's own story develops rapidly towards the gory climax recorded in Genesis 34. Unlike the rabbis, however, Diamant does not present Dinah's curiosity about the city and palace of Shechem as something to be deplored. Rather, she has Dinah narrate the onset of her love for the prince (whose name is changed from Shechem to Shalem presumably to avoid confusion with the city) in terms which all readers of romantic fiction are likely to recognise. Encouraged by the Queen Re-nefer, Shalem and Dinah are left alone in the palace to discover the joys of sex: 'Our coupling was exquisitely slow', Dinah records. 'We made love again and again....We kissed each other everywhere' (226-7). In a further departure from the biblical narrative, Dinah's 'mothers' are portrayed as generally supportive of the match. Leah is a little concerned that Dinah will abandon her own family to live with foreign women but Rachel and Bilhah rejoice in her new-found happiness (232-3). Only the men are offended, Simon and Levi seizing the opportunity to vent their bitterness at being supplanted by Reuben in Jacob's affection and at the failure of a recent slave-trading venture. When Joseph as a joke suggests insisting on the circumcision of the men of Shechem as a condition of the marriage, they take the proposal seriously, seeing in it an opportunity to enact the slaughter that follows (as in Gen. 34:25-6).

Again unlike the rabbis, Diamant makes no attempt to excuse the outrage at Shechem, presenting the event in all its gory horror as the turning point in the family's history. After this, in her account of the fortunes of the house of Jacob, everything disintegrates. As in the Bible, Rachel dies and Reuben is discovered in bed with his father's concubine Bilhah. Jacob changes his name to Israel, not as in the Bible at the instructions of Yahweh but because his own name has become 'another word for "liar"' (247). Diamant adds to the biblical narrative the disappearance of Bilhah, the death of Zilpah and the paralysis of Leah. It is a sombre end to what the Book of Genesis presents as a triumph on Jacob's part.

Part Three of the novel, which has little basis either in the Bible or in midrash, depicts Dinah's life in Egypt, where she is taken by Queen Re-nefer and her bodyguard Nehesis, the sole male survivor of the massacre at Shechem. At the queen's insistence, the child resulting from Dinah's union with Shalem, who is renamed Re-mose, is trained to be a scribe. Dinah herself continues to practise as a midwife, returning to the paganism of her upbringing, although now it is a statue of Isis which she sets over her bed. The only biblical element in this part of the novel is the appearance of Joseph under his Egyptian name Zafenat Paneh-ah (cf. Gen. 41:45). But the portrait Diamant gives of the young hero is far from sympathetic. He is 'an arrogant son of a bitch', Dinah is told by an attendant, who 'likes to talk of his lowly beginnings' (341). Having been sold to Po-ti-far, who 'used him for his own pleasure', he is discovered in bed with the lovely Nebetper, Po-ti-far's wife, before being sent to prison from which he escapes through his skill at interpreting dreams (this much at least in accordance with the biblical narrative). It is Joseph, in Diamant's reworking of the biblical narrative, who persuades Dinah to return to Canaan, where she is shocked to discover that her father appears to have forgotten her altogether.

It is central to Diamant's purpose, however, that Dinah does not remain entirely forgotten. Benjamin's daughter Gera, thinking her to be the nurse of the vizier's sons, rehearses the history of their family as it has been handed down to her (the official version of Genesis itself). When Dinah asks, somewhat disingenuously, what became of the girl, 'the one who was loved of the prince', she is comforted to hear that her name is still remembered, if only because it 'was too terrible to be forgotten' (379). The novel ends as positively as it possibly can, with Dinah dying peacefully, having been reconciled to her brother Joseph and been given the ring Jacob had initially given to Rachel, which she in turn had passed on to Leah. Not for the first time in the novel it is suggested that there is a female tradition to be passed on. Dinah ends her narrative pronouncing a blessing upon all her readers, once more appropriating to herself a role normally reserved for the patriarchs.

Part of the point of these repeated retellings of Dinah's story within the novel, of course, is that it emphasises the point that it is *how* a story is told that determines its meaning. The biblical narrative, clearly told from a male perspective, takes no account whatsoever of the experience of Dinah herself. Even the stories involving Dinah's 'mothers' reduce them to jealous siblings, squabbling with each other over their 'man', apparently incapable of solidarity or compassion. It is true that they share with Jacob a tendency towards subterfuge and cunning, which are presented as admirable qualities (in their mother Rebecca at least, helping Jacob to deceive his father, in Tamar too, making a fool of Judah, and perhaps also in Rachel deceiving her father over the theft of his household gods). But the main purpose of the Book of Genesis in its final redacted form is clearly to celebrate the piety, courage and ingenuity of the patriarchs.

Diamant's novel overturns this, retelling the story in such a way as to make the men appear foolish and the women heroic. Utilising the evidence supplied by historians such as Frymer-Kensky and pursuing a similar agenda to the Jewish feminist writers considered earlier in this chapter, she provides an alternative account of the supposed 'events' narrated in so androcentric a manner in the Bible. The fact that *The Red Tent* became such a publishing phenomenon demonstrates how much of a demand there is for such imaginative 'herstory', recovering from a patriarchal tradition elements with which women can identify. It is undoubtedly a *Tendenzroman*, a novel with a purpose, which male readers may well resist, resenting the depiction of theirs as so obviously the weaker sex. But Diamant in turn can respond to such resistance by reminding them that they are simply learning what generations of women-readers have experienced in the male-centred narrative of the Book of Genesis. *The Red Tent* is no masterpiece but it is a highly significant work of fiction performing a similar function for its modern feminist audience as the misogynistic midrash of the ancient rabbis. That function, of course, is to make sense of the biblical text in its new context.

Chapter 7

Joseph and His Brothers: Thomas Mann

Mann's Spiritual Journey: From the Bourgeois to the Fully Human

To write of Mann's *spiritual* journey (even allowing for the broad sense of the German word *Geist*) may cause some surprise. But then it surprised Mann himself, working on *Joseph and His Brothers* in the 1930s (his own late 50s) that he could devote so much time and energy to reworking the Bible: 'I never imagined that religious history and theology could gain such a hold over me'.[1] He confided to Karl Kereny in 1934 his 'growing interest in myth and religious history', which had meant a gradual turn in subject-matter 'from bourgeois individuality to what is typically and generally human'.[2] His essay on 'Freud and the Future' (1936) makes a similar observation about the development in his subject matter 'from the bourgeois and individual to the mythical and typical'.[3] What Mann means here by the bourgeois (*burgerlich*) is not entirely pejorative; in his autobiographical *Reflections of a Non-Political Man* (1918) he devotes a whole chapter to his own 'Burgherly Nature'. It is 'my burgherly love for what is human, alive, and ordinary', he claims, which gives his work its 'warmth' and 'humour'.[4] But he insists at the end of the book that 'the human question is never, never, to be solved politically, but only spiritually-morally'.[5]

There was, I want to suggest, a development in Mann's attitude to religion which I will attempt briefly to outline in this section. The second section will explore his relation to the three thinkers who contributed most to the perspective he brought to *Joseph and His Brothers*: Nietzsche, Schopenhauer and Freud. In the third section I will focus on his encounter with midrash in the mid-1920s, when he began working on the Joseph tetralogy (not finished until 1942). It is important to recognise how significant a role the midrashic material from bin Gorion's anthologies play in the textual montage of the novel. Although the midrashim are often reproduced almost verbatim, Mann's subtle and significant changes, as I hope to demonstrate, reveal a great deal about his motivation. Finally, in the fourth section, I will consider Mann's independent contribution to the Joseph-tradition, his exploration of what he called 'the depths beneath'.

---

1 Richard and Clara Winston, ed. and trans., *Letters of Thomas Mann, 1889-1955* (London: Secker and Warburg, 1970) 2 vols , I 183.

2 *Ibid.*, I 213.

3 Thomas Mann, *Essays of Three Decades*, trans. H.T.Lowe-Porter (London: Secker and Warburg, n.d.), p.422.

4 Thomas Mann, *Reflections of a Non-Political man*, trans. Walter D.Morris (New York: Frederick Ungar, 1983), p.400.

5 *Ibid.*, p.434.

There is considerable critical disagreement over Mann's attitude to religion. Some critics insist that he remained resolutely secular, seeing the satirical treatment of religion in early works such as *Buddenbrooks* (1901) echoed in late works such as *The Tables of the Law* (1944), which presents Moses in a far from reverent light. God, Hatfield claims, both in this work and in the *Joseph* tetralogy is presented as merely a projection of the human mind.[6] For others, however, a development can be found, culminating in the *Joseph* novels, which 'represent the high point of Mann's lifelong involvement with religion'. His early work up to and including *Buddenbrooks* is highly critical of the bourgeois Protestantism in which he was brought up while even *The Magic Mountain* of 1924 remains ambivalent about the competing positions it represents. But 'the late Mann' of *Joseph*, *Doctor Faustus* and *The Holy Sinner* can be seen to go beyond the detached secularism of his early work 'and makes literature the vehicle for theological speculation'.[7] He would remain almost inscrutably ironic throughout his career, of course, these last three novels filtering their narratives through unreliable narrators ranging from angels (for some of *Joseph*) through the Catholic humanist Zeitblom in *Doctor Faustus* to the Irish Benedictine monk responsible for narrating *The Holy Sinner*. It is never easy to work out precisely where Mann himself stands. I will attempt, however, to track these developments, focusing on three distinct phases in Mann's career: the early hostility to Christianity leading to a period of ambivalence followed by a period from the 1930s to his death in 1955 in which Mann saw religion (albeit of a non-metaphysical or doctrinal cast) as the only hope for man's future. In exploring each phase I will attempt to combine material from recently published biographies, letters, diaries and essays with his fiction, placing *Joseph and His Brothers* in the context of Mann's whole life and work.

Both Donald Prater and Hermann Kurzke, the two most recent biographers of Mann, make much of the autobiographical elements to be found in *Buddenbrooks*, in particular its satire of the bourgeois Protestantism encapsulated in the family motto, "*Dominus providebit*", inscribed on the portal over the family house. Both biographers compare the account of Thomas Buddenbrooks' death in the novel with Mann's description of his own father's death, the 'energetic "Amen!"' of the dying man being designed to cut short the 'pious nonsense' of the Lutheran pastor.[8] 'That Amen', Mann continues, 'rings in my ear whenever I am asked about my

---

[6] Henry Hatfield, 'Myth versus Secularism: Religion in Thomas Mann's *Joseph*', in Inta M.Ezergalis, ed., *Critical Essays on Thomas Mann* (Boston: G.K.Hall, 1988), pp.115-23. See also Werner Frizen, 'Thomas Mann und das Christentum', in Helmut Koopman, ed., *Thomas-Mann-Handbuch* (Stuttgart: Alfred Kröner, 1990), pp.307-26. Frizen provides an extensive bibliography of earlier German criticism on the topic. Susan von Ruhr Scaff takes issue with this whole view of the anti-Christian Thomas Mann in 'The Religious Base of Thomas Mann's World View: Mythic Theology and the Problem of the Demonic', *Christianity and Literature* 43 (1993) 75-93.

[7] Wolf-Daniel Hartwich, trans. Ritchie Robertson, 'Religion and Culture: *Joseph and His Brothers*', in Richie Robertson, ed., *The Cambridge Companion to Thomas Mann* (Cambridge: Cambridge University Press, 2002, pp.151-67 (p.152).

[8] Hermann Kurzke, *Thomas Mann: A Biography*, trans. Leslie Willson, (London: Allen Lane, 2002), p.84.

attitude to religion',[9] exposing as it does the impossibility of speaking accurately and authoritatively on religious questions. In the novel it is Antoinette's loud singing of a pious hymn over her father's deathbed which causes everyone to 'shiver with embarrassment'. The sanctimonious Pastor Pringsheim is mercilessly satirised throughout the novel while the narrator's own scepticism emerges clearly in his description of the way Thomas Buddenbrook the younger, having briefly been illuminated by reading Schopenhauer and death, sinks 'weakly back to the images and conceptions of his childhood', striving 'to subscribe to the whole confused unconvincing story, which required no intelligence, only obedient credulity'.[10]

Mann would never be an admirer of such blind piety. He called himself 'a Christian' in a letter to his brother of 1904, but Kurzke is probably right to characterise his position at this stage of his life as summed up in Renan's phrase, the title of a planned novella of Mann's, 'Pietà sans la foi'. He was never an adult churchgoer, as Kurzke points out; he didn't even marry in church although his Jewish wife had been baptised and brought up a Protestant. All the children were baptised and confirmed as Lutherans but Mann never felt that he belonged to any church. In his own words, he preferred 'to look the sphinx in the eye alone'.[11] It was the Great War, in particular his own initial enthusiasm for it and later disillusionment with its outcome, which forced on Mann the introspection about his own core beliefs published as *Reflections of a Non-Political Man* in 1918. Portraying himself as 'a genuine child of the nineteenth century', both philosophically and artistically a realist, with a 'truthful, blunt and unfeeling submission to the real and factual', Mann recognises that the twentieth century had rejected the 'basic mood' of its predecessor, especially 'its melancholy lack of belief'.[12] He finds it difficult, however, to accept the easy optimism of the literary left (encapsulated at this time by his brother Heinrich) with its belief in progress and political enlightenment. In fact, he finds it hard to say what he *does* believe. 'True belief', he insists, 'is no doctrine', it is not a matter of 'words and ideas such as freedom, equality, democracy, civilization and progress. It is the belief in God.' This in turn provokes the question, 'But what is God?', a question to which he can only reply with another question: 'Is He not the universal, the forming principle, omniscient justice, encompassing love? The belief in God is the belief in love, in life, and in art'.[13] Mann cannot even muster the confidence to say that he believes in this God. What he can admit is what he labels 'religiosity', by which he means

> the freedom that is a path, not a goal; that means openness, tenderness, openness for life, humility; a searching, probing, doubting and erring; a path, as I have said to God, or, as far as I am concerned, to the devil as well— but for heaven's sake not the hardened certainty and philistinism of belief.[14]

---

9   Donald Prater, *Thomas Mann: A Life* (Oxford: Oxford University Press, 1995), p.13.
10 *Ibid.*, pp.528-9.
11 Kurzke, *Thomas Mann*, pp.89 and 241. See the two sections of his biography entitled 'Church' and 'Faith', pp.241-6, for a discussion of Mann's attitude to religion up to 1918.
12 Mann, *Reflections*, pp.11-14.
13 *Ibid.*, p.371.
14 *Ibid.*, p.394.

As an artist he remains suspicious of concepts, especially theological ones. But he has come to recognise his temperament as fundamentally religious.

Mann's uncertainties and inner conflicts over religion are apparent in *The Magic Mountain* (1924), whose central figure Hans Castorp, similarly rooted in a long but now dying tradition of North German Protestantism, is caught between the progressive platitudes of Settembrini, a believer in 'western' reason and enlightenment, and the religious paradoxes of the Jewish-born but Jesuit-trained Naphta, a believer in 'eastern' mysticism. Settembrini, who believes with the eighteenth-century view that 'man was originally good, happy, and without sin, that social errors have corrupted and perverted him', upbraids Castorp for 'wantonly trifling with the forces of unreason'.[15] Naphta on the other hand, whose father was a fervent 'student of the *Torah*' and exuded an 'aura of uncanny piety' which provoked persecution and finally death,[16] spends his time attacking 'bourgeois irreligiosity' and philistinism.[17] He condemns the uncritical belief in science as an expression of 'the silliest realism...the sorriest, most spiritless dogma ever imposed upon humanity', as if one could 'supersede the first book of Moses, and oppose the pure light of reason to a stultifying fable'.[18] Mann characteristically makes Naphta overstate the case, leaving Castorp stranded between two extremes. But it is clear in this novel that Mann's interest in religion in general and in the Book of Genesis in particular is growing stronger.

It was in the mid-1920s, Mann records in *A Sketch of My Life* (1930), that he first gained the idea of writing a novel about Joseph after being shown a portfolio of illustrations of the biblical narrative: 'I looked up the story which Goethe called "most charming, only it is too short, and one feels inclined to put in the detail"'.[19] Mann's account of the excitement he felt on reading the story, like Steinbeck's of his encounter with Genesis chapter four, explains not only how the project appealed to him as a novelist but how it fitted into his personal religious development:

> I felt an indescribable fascination of the mind and the senses at this idea of leaving the modern bourgeois sphere so far behind and making my narrative pierce deep, deep into the human...The problem of man,...the search for his essence, his origin, his goal, evokes everywhere a new humane interest and sympathy.

Anthropological researches, he feels, have taken us 'down into the depths of the soul', awaking 'a lively curiosity about what is earliest and oldest in human things, the mythical, the legendary'. Mann does not believe (at this stage at least) that it is possible to return to full belief in myth: 'That can only happen as a result of self-delusion'. But he does believe that it is possible to provide a 'psychology' of it, to 'blend reason and sympathy in a gentle irony— that need not be profane'. The appeal of the whole project lay in creating another layer of 'the human tradition',

---

15   Thomas Mann, *The Magic Mountain*, trans. H.T.Lowe-Porter (London: Vintage, 1999), pp.382 and 356.
16   *Ibid.*, p.441.
17   *Ibid.*, pp.448 and 463.
18   *Ibid.*, p.691.
19   Mann, *Sketch*, p.63.

which, like the other layers of biblical interpretation such as midrash, would bear 'the stamp of its own time and place'.[20] Some of these ideas, of course, would find their way into the 'Prelude' to *Joseph and His Brothers*, but the account Mann gives in the *Sketch* provides the clearest account of his motivation in writing and the place of the novel in his own spiritual journey.

Section three of this chapter will provide a fuller account of Mann's research for the novel, in particular his study of the midrashic tradition. Here I am concerned with his developing beliefs. A letter of 1925 shows him sharing not only Goethe's fascination with the Joseph story but his 'reverence for the idea of Christianity... the nobility and *ethical culture* of Christianity as it glimmers and shines in the gospels'.[21]

Mann's attitude towards Judaism was also changing, ironically at the same time as anti-semitism in Germany was on the increase. Having shown little sympathy towards the Jews in his earlier years he began in the 1920s to display a much deeper interest in the whole tradition. His recommended 'Solution of the Jewish Problem' in a symposium of that title in 1907, for example, had been assimilation but the final section of his 1921 'Essay on the Jewish Question', which contains his first published anti-Nazi reference (to 'the Swastika silliness'), praises the Jewish love of *Geist* and contains no mention of assimilation.[22] Embarking on the *Joseph* project, it has been suggested, marked 'a major turning point in Mann's relationship with the Jewish world'. He prefaced a reading from the novel in 1937 with a lecture 'On the Problem of Anti-Semitism' and from the time of his exile in the United States in 1938 was seen as a public spokesman for the Jewish cause, alerting the English-speaking world to the systematic slaughter of Jews in Germany in a series of radio broadcasts from London beginning in January 1942.[23]

Privately too, Mann's attitudes were changing through the 1930s as he worked on *Joseph*. A diary entry of August 1934 refers to his growing 'consciousness of my cultural Christianity that, I confess, hesitates to become "devout" and submit to revelation'. His recognition of his cultural debt to Christianity, his formation by it, remains detached and impersonal, a matter of intellectual respect for the historical roots of his own identity within Christianity, whose own roots, of course, lie within Judaism: 'Say what you will, Christianity, this flower of Jewry, remains one of the two basic pillars on which Western civilization rests, of which the other is Mediterranean antiquity'.[24] This new-found respect for religion may not have been a living faith but it was a significant step towards one.

After completing the *Joseph* tetralogy Mann wrote a summary of his resultant views "On the Book of Books and Joseph" (1944). 'What is the Bible...', he asks,

---

20 *Ibid.*, pp.64-7.

21 Mann, *Letters*, I 135.

22 Alfred Hoelzel, 'Thomas Mann's Atitude Towards Jews and Judaism: An Investigation of Biography and Culture', in Ezra Mendelsohn and Richard I.Cohen, eds, *Arts and Its Uses: The Visual Image and Modern Jewish Society* (Oxford: Oxford University Press, 1990), pp.229-53.

23 *Ibid.*, pp.239-44.

24 Kurzke, *Thomas Mann*, p.414.

considered rationally? It consists of a multitude of heterogeneous and undeniably also variously significant literary works of Jewry and early Christianity: myths, sagas, stories, hymns, and other literary forms, historical chronicles, essays, collections of proverbs, and codicils of laws, the composition of which, or more correctly, the writing down of which, is spread over a very long period of time, from the fifth century B.C. to the second century A.D. But many portions reach, according to their origin, far into the past beyond that realm of time: they are vestiges and fragments of gray antiquity that lie around in the book like colossal orphans.

Some of these 'orphans', of course, do not even know their origins, which lie so far back into the past that they are now irretrievable. The astonishing thing, however, is that this ancient compilation of heterogeneous texts retains its power to provide comfort and guidance in the modern world:

> Calendar of instructions and comfort, book of prayers, textbook of recurring celebratory occasions whose great, unmistakable tones we hear at all stages of human life, with baptism, wedding, funeral, the powerful Book is marked by meditation, pious confidence, searching devotion, and reverent love of the long processions of generations of human beings, a possession of the heart, unpurloinable, untouchable by any criticism of the intellect.[25]

Mann himself remained sceptical about the 'structure of dogma' and 'popular combination of tradition with religious myth' preached by the church.[26] He confided to an American correspondent in 1947 that his religion was not a matter of 'dogmas and Christian mythology'. Christianity, however, had brought 'a real mutation of the human conscience and of human world-consciousness, a spiritual event which can never be effaced'.[27] He told another American correspondent in 1953 that 'a new humanistic ethical system' was needed 'to unite mankind', a set of beliefs less dogmatic and less credulous in the literal truth of myth than orthodox Christianity. But the word 'Christian', he insisted, 'in spite of Nietzsche' was no longer in his view 'a term of abuse'.[28] He was even gratified to be received by the Pope in May of that year, reporting to a friend that 'the *hominess religiosi* are fundamentally of one mind'.[29]

Such broad generalisations, of course, inevitably sound rather bland, which is one reason why Mann preferred to explore religious questions through the indirections and complexities of art. The novels of his final decade, *Doctor Faustus* (1947) and *The Holy Sinner* (1951), provide a more satisfactory expression of his position, allowing as they do for contradiction, paradox and genuine ambivalence. *The Tables of the Law,* a novella published in 1944, also corrects any impression readers might have garnered from *Joseph* that Mann was a literal believer in the foundational myths of the Judaeo-Christian tradition. Mann's Moses, the product of an illicit liaison, between Pharaoh's daughter and a Hebrew labourer, relies on no

---

25 *Ibid.*, p.406.
26 *Ibid.*, pp.406-7.
27 Mann, *Letters*, I 128.
28 *Ibid.*, II 652.
29 *Ibid.*, II 654.

miracles for his achievements. Even His God 'answered Moses from his own soul' as an immanent rather than a transcendent presence.[30] It is more important for Mann that the commandments 'are written in every man's flesh and blood and deep within himself he knows that the words are all valid' than that their origins are precisely as narrated in the Book of Exodus.[31] In Mann's novella there is always a natural explanation for everything that occurs: for Aaron's magic tricks, for the manna in the desert (edible lichen), for the water from the rock (a filter apparatus), for the plagues, including the killing of the first-born (Joshua and his commandos) and for the exodus itself (a specialist knowledge of the tides of the Red Sea). Moses himself dotes on his Ethiopian concubine with a lecherous obsession which is not designed to appeal to the orthodox. Mann appears in this novella, perhaps in reaction to the reverence of his stance in *Joseph*, to be clarifying the limits of his belief.

Doctor Faustus too, at one of its many levels, can be read as a partly-autobiographical confession of the way an artist can only deal with spiritual questions indirectly. Adrian Leverkühn, some of whose biographical details are clearly derived from Nietzsche, himself (as we shall see in the following section) a model for Mann, composes in the same way as Mann writes, through an intertextual relation to earlier works. His *Gesta Romanorum*, for example, is based upon 'a translation from the Latin of the oldest Christian collection of fairy-tales and legends', whose 'historical uninstructedness, pious Christian didacticism, and moral naivete', according to the narrator, 'were in the highest degree calculated to stimulate Adrian's penchant for parody'.[32] *Joseph and His Brothers*, as I will demonstrate in section three, was based on a similar collection of pious fables (albeit translated from Hebrew rather than Latin). Leverkühn's *Apocalypsis*, inspired by a series of woodcuts of the Apocalypse by Dürer, involves a similar intertextual interweaving of 'an extraordinary old volume: a thirteenth-century French metrical translation of the *Vision of St.Paul*, the Greek text of which dates back to the fourth century'.[33] Finally, Leverkühn's *Lamentation of Dr.Faustus* is seen by the narrator to utter 'a proudly despairing "No!"...to false and flabby middle-class piety' before ending with a sustained note on the cello which hints 'that out of the sheerly irremediable hope might germinate'.[34] Mann's own version of *Doctor Faustus* ends similarly with the narrator holding out the possibility that this 'light of hope' will irradiate even the 'uttermost hopelesslessness of post-war Germany'.[35]

The Holy Sinner has been seen as Mann's final attempt 'to rescue religion from religious fundamentalism'.[36] The story it tells of sin and grace, of the election of the incestuous Pope Gregory to the papacy, is complicated, of course, by being narrated

---

30 Thomas Mann, *Mario and the Magician and Other Stories*, trans. H.T.Lowe-Porter (Harmondsworth: Penguin, 1975), p.251.

31 *Ibid.*, pp.297-8.

32 Thomas Mann, *Doctor Faustus*, trans. H.T.Lowe-Porter (Harmondsworth: Penguin, 1968), pp.304-5.

33 *Ibid.*, pp.341-2.

34 *Ibid.*, p.471.

35 *Ibid.*, p.489.

36 Russell A.Berman, 'Introduction' to Thomas Mann, *The Holy Sinner*, trans. H.T.Lowe-Porter (Berkeley: University of California Press, 1992), p.xx.

through the pious eyes of the Irish Benedictine monk, Clemens, who is convinced that his story 'witnesses ...to God's immeasurable and incalculable loving-kindness', showing as it does that He can 'make love come out of evil'.[37] Clemens himself believes that Nature 'is of the Devil', retaining 'a bottomless...indifference' to man's spiritual aspirations.[38] Readers of his story are required to give at least temporary credence to a host of highly unlikely events, including the seventeen years of penance isolated upon a rock in the sea which Gregorius only survives by being transformed into an animal 'not much bigger than a hedgehog'.[39] Mann himself, of course, does not encourage a literal belief in these miracles but he does display here as in *Joseph* a fascination with the Judaeo-Christian tradition which, while falling short of commitment to Christian doctrine, goes well beyond what one would expect from a disciple of Schopenhauer, Nietzsche and Freud. It is to the impact upon him of these three thinkers, however, that I want now to turn.

Philosophical Intertexts: Schopenhauer, Nietzsche, Freud

Mann writes in the *Reflections* about Schopenhauer, Nietzsche and Wagner as 'a triple constellation of essentially united spirits' whose 'reverent disciple' he remains. It was Schopenhauer, he confesses, who made me into a 'psychologist of decadence', a label he applies also to Nietzsche. Between them they established his own 'basic psychological mood, that mood of "cross, death, and grave"' of which Nietzsche himself wrote.[40] Wagner's construction of epic art from ancient myth would also serve as a model for the *Joseph* project. But more important for the ideas on which I wish to focus, in particular Mann's psychological understanding of religion, is Freud, with whose account of monotheism Mann wrestled while writing his tetralogy. The Bloomian biblical metaphor of wrestling is particularly appropriate for Mann, who recognised in his 1938 essay on 'Schopenhauer' that artists often 'betray' philosophers, as Wagner did Schopenhauer, sucking the 'erotic honey' from it and leaving the wisdom behind'.[41] What Mann made of Schopenhauer, Nietzsche and Freud could certainly be seen as a 'misprision' (in Bloom's terms), ending up much more sympathetic to religion than all three of them. Mann came to his own 'psychology' of myth and religion in reaction to them rather than in passive reflection of them. In order to follow this process, however, I will need to consider each in turn.

The 'shattering impression' of reading Schopenhauer, Mann confesses in the Freud essay, came after his own reading of Nietzsche.[42] But since Nietzsche's philosophy was itself a reaction to Schopenhauer, it makes sense to begin with *The World as Will and Representation*, the book Mann first encountered while writing *Buddenbrooks*, immediately inserting a similar encounter into the novel. Thomas

---

37 Mann, *The Holy Sinner*, pp.55-6 and 145.
38 *Ibid.*, p.206.
39 *Ibid.*, p.294.
40 Mann, *Reflections*, pp.54-5.
41 Mann, *Essays*, pp.396-7.
42 *Ibid.*, p.415.

Buddenbrooks finds in Schopenhauer an escape from the miseries of the world (in particular death) simply through understanding them. Schopenhauer himself, of course, finds no genuine cause for optimism. *Reflections* too cites a lengthy passage from Schopenhauer in which he pours contempt on those who blame 'governments for the misery that is inseparable from human existence itself; for the misery that is, to speak mythically, the curse that Adam received, and with him his whole race'. Such shallow optimists, Schopenhauer continues, have no higher ambition than a 'heaven on earth' in which everyone would, without effort or difficulty, be able to booze and gorge and breed to his heart's content, and then to croak'.[43] For the religious temperament which Mann shared with Schopenhauer this falls well short of the ideal.[44]

The most important concept in Schopenhauer, of course, is that of the Will, that formless, irrational, endlessly creative energy or life-force which strives to realise itself in the world. Human representations, as Michael Minden explains, are seen by Schopenhauer as refractions of this basic reality, which cannot itself be represented (though music comes closest to doing so).[45] Mann himself, in his essay on Schopenhauer, sees the Will as anticipating what Freud would call the *id*, a claim he repeats in his essay on Freud.[46] Myth, for Schopenhauer, is another indirect means by which the Will finds expression:

> Myth is a middle-thing between the world as will and the world as representation. As the pre-ego, unconscious motivation force behind human character and behaviour, it [the Will] is 'the innermost essence, the kernel of every blindly acting force of nature and also in the deliberate conduct of man'...structured into forms and roles and clothed in story.[47]

It is possible, according to Schopenhauer, for exceptional individuals, artists and saints, to rise above the morass in which most of us are plunged and to achieve 'the freedom of self-negation'. In this Hegelian process of sublation, by which the Spirit succeeds in cancelling out and distilling Matter, Schopenhauer sees the possibility of a 'saintliness...brought before our eyes by art',[48] which becomes a medium of at least partial redemption, transforming the misery of the world into something both true and beautiful.[49]

Mann, as he explains in his essay on Schopenhauer, feels that Nietzsche distorted his master's views on this subject. For while Schopenahuer argues 'that the essence of life itself, the will, existence itself, is a constant suffering, partly pathetic, partly

---

43   Mann, *Reflections*, p.272.

44   Erich Heller, *Thomas Mann: The Ironic German* (Cambridge: Cambridge University Press, 1981 [1958]), p.46.

45   Michael Minden, "Introduction", in Minden, ed., *Thomas Mann* (London: Longman, 1995), p.12.

46   Mann, *Essays*, pp.408 and 415.

47   Elaine Murdaugh, '*Joseph and His Brothers:* Myth, Historical Consciousness, and God Energy', in Harold Bloom, ed., *Thomas Mann* (New York: Chelsea House, 1986), pp.241-73 (p.253).

48   Heller, *Thomas Mann*, p.28.

49   *Ibid.*, p.52.

terrible' which can only be made into a 'significant spectacle' through art, Nietzsche attempts to turn this intellectual redemption into an anti-moral way of life, a dionysian 'justification of life'.[50] Mann values the 'icy brilliance' of Schopenhauer's writing precisely for its 'veracity' about the 'utter misery of the world'. There is a 'spiritual rebellion' in Schopenhauer, a revenge of the 'heroic Word' against the miserable world.[51] 'Every expression of the will to live', Mann argues, on the other hand, has 'something of the infernal about it, being itself a metaphysical stupidity, a frightful error, a sin, *the* sin'. Only through the intellect, through philosophy and art, 'knowledge wrenches itself free from Will'.[52] Schopenhauer, therefore, although an atheist, reaches 'a doctrine of compassion and redemption in agreement with Christianity'. Mann quotes Schopenhauer's own claim to have achieved 'the moral result of Christianity...rationally...whereas in Christianity they are based on sheer fables'.[53] The masses may still need these fables, the exoteric metaphysics of the church, but philosophers can distil their esoteric essence. However sympathetic Mann would become to myth, at least in the earlier stages of human history, he would retain a sense derived from Schopenhauer that the truly philosophic mind would see below it to the reality beneath.

Mann's encounter with Nietzsche, as I have said, preceded his reading of Schopenhauer. From 1895 onwards he collected, read and annotated the complete works of Nietzsche, which, according to T.J.Reed, would dominate his own thinking from this point on.[54] Early stories such as 'The Will to Happiness' (*Der Wille zum Glück*) of 1896 and 'Disillusionment' (*Enttäuschung*) of 1898 describe a Nietzschean breakdown of the ordered Christian world.[55] *Buddenbrooks* itself represents even more fully the decadence of Christianity as Nietzsche saw it. Nietzsche grew famously to loathe

> the self-abnegation and self-hatred given excuse and affirmation through Christianity. It remained precisely these priestly cures for the agonies of existence, the impoverishing morality and life-hatred in Christianity, the fantasies of flight to another world, a series of childish whims harbouring a deep self-contempt and vindictive resentment toward life which posed a threat toward the continuance of culture.[56]

Both the extent of Mann's identification with Nietzsche and the distaste he felt for his later, more rabidly anti-Christian writing celebrated by a new generation of

---

50 Mann, *Essays*, p.404. It could be argued that Lowe-Porter's translation here is understandable only with difficulty. For a clearer translation of this passage see Paul Bishop, 'The Intellectual World of Thomas Mann', in Robertson, ed., *Thomas Mann*, pp.27-8.

51 *Ibid.*, p.382.

52 *Ibid.*, pp.303-4.

53 *Ibid.*, p.397.

54 T.J.Reed, *Thomas Mann: The Uses of Tradition* (Oxford: Clarendon Press, 1974), p.18.

55 Herbert Lehnert, 'Mann's Beginnings and *Buddenbrooks*', in Lehnert and Eva Wessell, ed., *A Companion to the Works of Thomas Mann* (Rochester, N.Y.: Camden House, 2004), pp.34-5.

56 John Tuska, 'Thomas Mann and Nietzsche: A Study in Ideas', *Germanic Review* 39 (1964) 281-99 (288).

disciples are evident in the notes Mann made in 1910 for a projected essay on 'Geist und Kunst' (Spirit/Mind and Art):

> We who were born around 1870 are too close to Nietzsche, we participate too directly in his tragedy, his personal fate (perhaps the most terrible, most awe-inspiring fate in intellectual history). Our Nietzsche is Nietzsche militant. Nietzsche triumphant belongs to those born fifteen years after us. We have from him our psychological sensitivity, our lyrical criticism, the experience of Wagner, the experience of Christianity, the experience of 'modernity'— experiences from which we shall never completely break free, any more than Nietzsche himself ever did. They are too precious for that, too profound, too fruitful. But the twenty-year-olds have from him what will remain in the future, his purified after-effect....They have from him the affirmation of the earth, the affirmation of the body, the anti-Christian and anti-intellectual conception of nobility, which comprises health and serenity and beauty.[57]

Reflections (1918) shows Mann continuing to celebrate the positive side of Nietzsche, 'the lyrical philosopher's dithyrambic-conservative concept of life'[58] while expressing reservations about 'the later grotesque Nietzsche, who had become fanatic'. His 'psychology of Christianity', Mann had by now come to feel, was 'a grotesquely distorted, a fanatic's psychology'.[59] By 1930, in *A Sketch of My Life*, Mann would claim to have held himself 'scornfully aloof from the fashionable and popular doctrines of Nietzscheism— the cult of the superman, the easy "Renaissancism," the Caesar Borgia aesthetics, all the blood-and-beauty mouthings then in vogue'. He would also suggest that 'the spectacle of his hatred of Christianity' needed to be understood in the same 'psychological sense' as his battle with Wagner, as a 'war upon what he loved best'.[60]

Mann's ambivalence towards Nietzsche emerges most clearly in his postwar lecture, 'Nietzsche's Philosophy in the Light of Our Experience' (1947), where he admits on the philosopher's part at least some responsibility for what had happened to Germany. Mann looks back with a 'mixture of reverence and pity' at the tragic life of 'an overstrained, overtaxed soul, which was called to knowledge but not born for it and, like Hamlet, was broken by it'. Nietzsche stands as a tragic example of

> a spirituality at first deeply pious, entirely prone to reverence, bound to religious tradition, which was dragged by fate practically by the hair into a wild and intoxicated prophesy of barbaric resplendent force, of stifled conscience, of evil, a state devoid of all piety and raging against its very own nature.[61]

Some of this tragic history, as we have seen, is transferred to Adrian Leverkühn in *Doctor Faustus* (also 1947) to whom the Devil (or a projection in his own mind of

---

57 Reed, *Thomas Mann*, pp. 137-8.
58 Mann, *Reflections*, pp.63 and 104-5.
59 *Ibid.*, pp.224 and 252.
60 Mann, *Sketch*, pp.22-3.
61 Thomas Mann, 'Nietzsche's Philosophy in the Light of Contemporary Events', in Heinrich Tolzmann, ed., *Thomas Mann's Addresses Delivered in the Library of Congress* (Oxford: Peter Lang, [1963] 2003), p.70.

the Devil) explains that the dionysiac excesses of barbarism display 'more grasp of theology than has a culture fallen away from cult, which even in the religious has seen only culture, only the humane, never excess, paradox, the mystic passion, the utterly unbourgeois ordeal'.[62] Mann could see the temptation to follow Nietzsche along the road of excess but also, in hindsight, its dangers. His notes for the novel make the connection with Nietzsche and the recent history of Germany even clearer, discussing the dionysian 'desire to escape from everything bourgeois, moderate, classical, [added: Apolline]…into a world of drunken release'.[63] Fascism, in other words, fed by a Nietzschean scorn for bourgeois morality, had led Germany into an irrationalism from which the later Mann was eager to dissociate himself.

The third major philosophical force with which Mann can be seen to have wrestled is Freud, whom he started to read seriously in the mid-1920s. 'I came to you shamefully late', he wrote to Freud in January 1930.[64] As William McDonald has shown, however, his portrait of Joseph the dreamer is woven together intertextually with Freud's writings not only on dreams and the unconscious but also on the origins of religion. Mann wrote to Ernst Bertram in 1926, clarifying the purpose of his new project and the link between psychoanalysis and Genesis:

> My real and secret text is the Bible, at the end of the story [Gen. 49:25]. It is the blessing that the dying Jacob pronounces upon Joseph: 'The Almighty shall bless you with the blessings of heaven above, blessings of the deep that lie beneath.'[65]

Joseph himself uses this phrase from Genesis when he tells Pharaoh that 'the pattern and the traditional come from the depths which lie beneath'.[66]

As with Schopenhauer and Nietzsche, however, what Mann took from Freud was not exactly what the founder of psychoanalysis said, especially on the origins of religion. This is evident first in his lecture of 1929, 'Freud's Position in the History of Modern Thought', which McDonald describes as 'an essay of containment and artful transformation'.[67] *Totem and Taboo* sees the origins of religion to lie in a primeval act of parricide, in which the 'chief of the horde' was 'murdered and devoured by his sons'. In reaction to the guilt this raised, the primal father was then worshipped in the form of a totem animal, which was regularly sacrificed and eaten in an ambivalent ritual expression of triumph and guilt.[68] All religion, Freud argues, repeats this pattern 'according to the stage of civilization at which they arise'. Mann, while accepting that 'civilization has stages, and that religious figuration is always

---

62 Mann, *Doctor Faustus*, p.236.
63 Reed, *Thomas Mann*, pp.364-5.
64 Mann, *Letters*, I 174.
65 William E.McDonald, *Thomas Mann's 'Joseph and His Brothers': Writing, Performance, and the Politics of Loyalty* (Rochester, N.Y.: Camden House, 1999), 59. See a different translation of the same letter in Mann, *Letters*, I 156-7.
66 Thomas Mann, *Joseph and His Brothers*, trans. H.T.Lowe-Porter (Harmondsworth: Penguin, 1978), p.937.
67 McDonald, *Thomas Mann's 'Joseph'*, p.103.
68 The quotations are taken from the admirable summary of the book given in Hartwich, 'Religion and Culture', p.159.

appropriate to the stage in which it occurs' and adopting Freud's conclusion that 'men, via remorse and totem substitution, in effect convert their fathers into gods', holds a much more positive view of men's theological imagination and of the moral values inculcated by religion.[69]

A similar transformation, as McDonald has shown, takes place in Mann's reading of *Civilization and Its Discontents*, a copy of which Freud sent him in 1930, which he claimed to read 'at one sitting'.[70] Mann takes the positive elements of Freud's argument, that 'all experience is encased in memory, and no memory is permanently lost', that the unconscious acts as 'an infallible storehouse of the personal and cultural past, with each of its memories potentially available to dream-work and, via interpretation, to the considering conscious mind'.[71] But he does not take on board the negative implications of Freud's reading of religion as an expression of collective neurosis. He even transforms the conflicts of Freud's Oedipus Complex, about which he remains silent,[72] into a much more positive account of the role of the father in the construction of moral and religious values.

Mann's lecture on 'Freud and the Future' of 1936 is similarly more positive about religion than about Freud himself. He quotes Jung, that 'able but somewhat ungrateful scion of the Freudian school', on the 'psychological conception of God... one with the soul and bound up with it' in a manner more familiar to the eastern than the western mind. In Genesis too, he claims, we can find similar 'talk of the bond (covenant) between God and man, the psychological basis of which I have attempted to give in the mythological novel *Joseph and His Brothers*'.[73] Supposedly discussing *Totem and Taboo,* Mann writes about the way in which myth can be seen to be 'the foundation of life...the timeless schema, the pious formula into which life flows when it reproduces itself out of the unconscious'.[74] This may be the belief to which Mann comes in response to Freud's arguments but it is certainly not what Freud said. And Freud (mercifully too ill to attend) would surely have disliked what Mann goes on to say about 'life as...sacred repetition' evidenced most powerfully in the life of Jesus, which 'was lived in order that that which was written might be fulfilled', so that his citation of Psalm 22 on the cross is a way of claiming to be the long-awaited Messiah, equivalent to the phrase through which Joseph reveals himself to his brothers, 'Yes, it is I'.[75]

Mann's thinking is in many respects more akin to Jung's on religion than to Freud, though it is a moot point how much he owed to Jung and how much he simply shared similar beliefs in the collective unconscious, in Gnosticism, and in an immanent God within the soul.[76] It is not possible, of course, to make a comprehensive audit of all Mann's intellectual debts. But it should by now be clear that all three of these figures

---

69 McDonald, *Thomas Mann's 'Joseph'*, pp.115-21.
70 *Ibid.*, pp.175-6.
71 *Ibid.*, p.180
72 *Ibid.*, p.226.
73 Mann, *Essays*, pp.418-20
74 *Ibid.*, p.422.
75 *Ibid.*, pp.423-5.
76 For readings of Mann in the light of Jung, see Elaine Murdaugh, *Salvation in the Secular: The Moral Law in Thomas Mann's 'Joseph und seine Brüder'* (Bern: Peter Lang,

contributed significantly to the Joseph-project. It was in reaction to them more than any others that Mann formulated his own position. For the most important intertexts between Genesis and *Joseph,* however, we need to consider some considerably older material, the midrashic stories Mann encountered in the work of Micha bin Gorion.

Midrashic Sources: bin Gorion's 'Joseph-Novel' and *Die Sagen Der Juden*

The pervasiveness of midrashic material in *Joseph and His Brothers* is still a fairly well-kept secret. An article of 1998 claimed that Mann's use of midrash had only received 'thorough analysis' in an isolated doctoral dissertation.[77] If that is so, Bernd-Jürgen Fischer's *Handbuch zu Thomas Mann's 'Josephsromanen'* of 2002 has now doubled that figure, providing in its commentary detailed references to passages from bin Gorion's anthologies of midrash which found their way into the novel.[78] The fact that Mann consulted midrashic sources for the novel had been recognised in reviews of the novel in the 1940s.[79] Käte Hamburger also referred to Mann's study of midrash in her 1945 study of the novel.[80] When Herbert Lehnert in the 1960s provided a summary of all the sources for the Joseph novel surviving in the Thomas Mann Archive in Zurich, he too included discussion of both of bin Gorion's anthologies, which are heavily marked and annotated (Mann made 54 pages of notes on *Die Sagen der Juden*).[81] Later books on Mann's interest in myth by Lehnert

---

1976) and Charlotte Nolte, *Being and Meaning in Thomas Mann's Joseph Novels* (London: T.S.Maney, 1996).

77 Alan Levenson, 'Christian Author, Jewish Book? Methods and Sources in Thomas Mann's *Joseph*', *German Quarterly* 71 (1998) 166-78 (166). The dissertation he refers to is Doris Sommer, 'Mann, Midrash, and Mimesis', Rutgers Ph.D., 1977, which provides considerable analysis of bin Gorion's anthology *Die Sagen der Juden* but seems not to know about his translation of the Joseph part of *Sepher ha Yashar*, which he entitled *Joseph und seine Brüder: Ein altjüdischer Roman*.

78 Bernd-Jürgen Fischer, *Handbuch zu Thomas Mann's 'Josephromanen'* (Tübingen: A.Francke Verlag, 2002), pp. 37-8. See the index under Gorion for the many references to midrashic material incorporated into the novel from these two anthologies.

79 See Ludwig Lewisohn's review in *New Palestine* 34 (15/9/44) 519-20 and Bertha Badt-Strauss, 'Thomas Mann and the Midrash', *The Reconstructionist* (April 1945), 15.

80 Käte Hamburger, *Thomas Mann's Roman 'Joseph und seine Brüder'*, (Stockholm: Bermann-Fischer, 1945), pp.153-7. Another early recognition of Mann's debt to midrash came in Julius Bab, 'Joseph and His Brothers', in Charles Neider, ed., *The Stature of Thomas Mann* (New York: New Directions, 1947), p.197.

81 Herbert Lehnert, 'Thomas Manns Vorstudien zur Josephstetralogie', *Schillerjahrbuch* 7 (1963), 458-520. The bin Gorion anthologies are items 5 and 6, discussed on pp.471-4.

himself, by Manfred Dierks and by Willy Berger also include brief discussion of his interest in midrash.[82] But the subject remains relatively neglected.[83]

Mann himself, in a 1942 lecture on 'The Theme of the Joseph Novels', acknowledged that his work 'often reads like an exegesis and amplification of the Torah, like a rabbinical midrash'.[84] It has been well known, ever since his notes became available for analysis, that Mann employed a 'highly economical montage technique' which at times comes perilously close to what in other circumstances might be termed plagiarism. Among the more famous examples of his cannibalisation of sources are the biographical material on Goethe in *Lotte in Weimar* and theories of music in *Doctor Faustus*.[85] But nearly all Mann's novels employ this kind of montage, self-consciously advertising their 'intertextual weave'.[86]

Joseph and His Brothers is no exception in this respect, repeatedly advertising the way it draws upon 'tradition', upon earlier 'learned Hebrew commentators'. In this section I will first outline what the Jewish tradition about Joseph involved: a wide range of apocryphal, literary and midrashic material, overlapping at times with Islam (both in the Koran and in later Persian poetry). Mann had encountered this material not only in bin Gorion's two anthologies *Joseph und seine Brüder* (Joseph and His Brothers) and *Die Sagen der Juden* (The Legends of the Jews) but also in scholars such as Rabbi Jakob Horovitz, whose study of *Die Josephserzählung* (The Joseph Narrative) is the third of the three main sources for Jewish legends about Joseph listed in Fischer's *Handbuch*.[87] Horovitz regarded the midrashic tradition as in many ways preferable to Higher Criticism in coming to an understanding of the character of Joseph since it preserved the unity of the text. I will consider some of the material Mann gleaned from him but my main focus will be on the passages from the two anthologies of midrash compiled and translated into German by bin Gorion which found their way (usually with significant mutations) into the text of *Joseph and His Brothers*. This will involve citing both bin Gorion and Mann in German since the precise textual details are all-important.[88] English quotations from the novel are all taken from Lowe-Porter's translation.

The earliest layer of the Joseph tradition comprises apocryphal material of the first two centuries of the Common Era, books such as *Jubilees* and *The Testaments of the Twelve Patriarchs*, which are normally dated around 100CE and 200CE

---

82 Herbert Lehnert, *Thomas Mann: Fiktion, Mythos, Religion* (Stuttgart: Kohlhammer, 1965); Willy Berger, *Die mythologischen Motive in Thomas Manns Roman Joseph und seine Brüder* (Köln: Böhlau, 1971); Manfred Dierks, *Studien zu Mythos und Psychologie bei Thomas Mann* (München: Francke, 19272.

83 Golka's two-volume study of Thomas Mann's biblical exegesis, while making occasional references to his knowledge of midrash, concerns itself more with his reading of the biblical text in the light of Higher Criticism. See Friedemann W.Golka, *Jakob: Biblische Gestalt und Literarische Figur* (Stuttgart: Calwer Verlag, 1999) and *Joseph: Biblische Gestalt und Literarische Figur* (Stuttgart: Calwer Verlag, 2002).

84 Tolzmann, ed., *Thomas Mann's Addresses*, p.12.
85 Reed, 'Thomas Mann and Tradition', pp.226-8.
86 McDonald, *Thomas Mann's 'Joseph'*, p.51.
87 Fischer, *Handbuch*, p.38.
88 I provide my own English translations of bin Gorion here.

respectively. Both, as Mann would have read in Horovitz,[89] stress how 'handsome and very good-looking' Joseph was.[90] *Jubilees* has Potiphar's wife plead with Joseph for two years to lie with her,[91] while the Testament of Joseph complains vociferously of the attentions of 'the Egyptian woman'.[92] Some of the details expanded in later collections of midrash can be found in this testament: her telling Joseph that she really wanted a son, flattering him as 'a holy man', asking for religious instruction, pestering him with gifts and even baring parts of her body before him before threatening to kill first her husband and then herself.[93] The story of 'Joseph and Aseneth', also probably from the second century, draws on the many 'legends about Aseneth circulating in Jewish circles in the first centuries of the Christian era' to construct a Hellenistic romance about Joseph's wooing of his wife. It also claims that upper-class Egyptian women 'used to solicit him to lie with him...because he was so handsome'.[94] More literary versions of Joseph's story were composed by Philo of Alexandria and Josephus, both writing towards the end of the first century CE. Philo, writing in Greek for a gentile audience, idealises Joseph as a statesman, playing down the erotic element to be found in the biblical narrative.[95] Josephus acknowledges Joseph's 'beauty of person' but is more interested in his exceptional mind (*phronesis*), praising Joseph's stoic resistance to the charms of Potiphar's wife.[96] It is in the midrash, however, accumulating over the first four centuries of the rabbinic period and first collected in *Genesis Rabbah* that this part of the Joseph narrative (Gen. 39: 7-19) assumes enormous importance.[97]

Collections of midrash, as Niehoff acknowledges, lack the narrative coherence of the apocryphal and literary material summarised above. They are composed of heterogeneous questions and answers about particular biblical verses rather than 'presented as part of an overall story'.[98] There are nevertheless identifiable themes that can be traced through the pages of a collection such as *Genesis Rabbah*. The rabbis are much more critical of Joseph himself, linking his 'punishments' quite clearly to his 'flaws' (otherwise it would have been unjust of God to make him suffer so much). The stories Joseph tells against his brothers, for example, are reflected in his sufferings: his accusation that they ate the limbs of living animals leads to their

---

[89] Fischer (p.318) reports a range of references in Horovitz to apocryphal and pseudoepigraphic accounts of Joseph's beauty.

[90] H.F.D.Sparks, ed., *The Apocryphal Old Testament* (Oxford: Clarendon Press, 1984) p.116.

[91] *Ibid.*, p.117.

[92] *Ibid.*, p.582.

[93] *Ibid.*, pp.582-7.

[94] *Ibid.*, p.470 (for the dating) and p.479 (for the quotation).

[95] Maren Niehoff, *The Figure of Joseph in Post-Biblical Jewish Literature* (Leiden: E.J.Brill, 1992), p.79.

[96] *Ibid.*, pp.84 and 102.

[97] Niehoff also discusses 'The Figure of Joseph in the Targums' in an appendix to her book, pp.146-64. See James L.Kugel, *In Potiphar's House: The Interpretive Life of Biblical Texts* (Cambridge, Mass.: Harvard University Press, 1990) for a fascinating account of the whole midrashic process with reference to this particular tradition.

[98] Niehoff, *The Figure of Joseph*, p.110.

own attempt to kill him, the report that the sons of Jacob's wives called the sons of the maids slaves leads to his own selling into slavery while the tale that the brothers cast eyes at gentile girls leads to Potiphar's wife casting eyes upon him. Joseph's troubles, in other words, are 'Divine punishment for each of his slanders'.[99]

Genesis Rabbah is altogether critical of the youthful Joseph, who, at the age of 17, displays clear narcissistic tendencies, 'decorating his eyes, curling his hair and prancing along on his heels'.[100] It is by reading Genesis chapter 39 though the prooftext of Proverbs chapter 7 (the account of the young man accosted by a married woman 'dressed as a harlot') that *Genesis Rabbah* manages to expand upon the scene of seduction in the biblical narrative. It also suggests that Potiphar, who 'bought Joseph only for sexual purposes', was castrated for this as a form of punishment, hence his being described as a 'eunuch of Pharaoh'.[101] Always interested in the sexual details of the story, *Genesis Rabbah* has Joseph fail sexually to meet the demands of Potiphar's wife. One rabbi argues that 'he actually tried [to penetrate her] but found that he was not a man... His "bow" grew taut but then became flaccid'. A second suggests that he ejaculated prematurely: 'His semen was diffused and emerged from his fingernails'. A third comes up with the notion that would find its way into Mann's novel: 'He saw his father's face before him and his blood cooled off'.[102] It is in *Genesis Rabbah* too that Joseph's brothers are discovered 'in the red light district',[103] presuming, because of his beauty, that he might have been set to work as a male prostitute.

Mann, whose sources for this midrashic material were mainly bin Gorion's anthologies, would probably not have known the provenance of these details from *Genesis Rabbah*, the earliest of the anthologies of midrash. Bin Gorion's volume *Joseph und seine Brüder*, as it acknowledges in its 'Nachwort',[104] was actually an edited version of a very late collection of midrash, *Sepher ha Yashar*, which is usually dated to the eleventh or twelfth centuries although it may have been compiled as late as the sixteenth.[105] Between *Genesis Rabbah* and the *Sepher ha Yashar*, of course, there were not only many other collections of midrash but a whole Islamic tradition, probably (though not undisputedly) indebted to Jewish folklore, in which the story of Joseph was further expanded. The best known of these, of course, is the Koran itself, the twelfth Surah of which recounts the passion of Potiphar's wife for Joseph, including such details as the shirt torn at the back (thereby supporting Joseph's claim that he was attempting to escape her attention) and the banquet arranged for the

---

99 *Ibid.*, pp.114-7.
100 *Genesis Rabbah*, trans. Jacob Neusner (Atlanta, GA: Scholar's Press, 1985) 3 vols., III 188.
101 *Ibid.*, III 222-7.
102 *Ibid.*, III 235.
103 *Ibid.*, III 272.
104 Micha Josef bin Gorion, ed., *Joseph und seine Brüder: Ein altjüdischer Roman* (Berlin: Schocken Verlag, 1933 [1917]), p.80.
105 H.L.Strack and Günter Stemberger, trans. Marcus Bockmuehl, *Introduction to the Talmud and Midrash* (Minneapolis: Fortress Press, 1992), p.339. Fischer's *Handbuch* (p.247) ascribes it 'probably' to the fourteenth century.

ladies of the city, who are so distracted by his beauty that they cut their own hands.[106] This in turn provoked a range of Persian poetry about the attempted seduction of Joseph, of which the best known (to Mann at least) were by Firdausi and Jami. The narrator of *Joseph and His Brothers* dismisses the way 'these poetasters' developed the story, making it into 'a sugary romance with a proper happy ending'. 'All that', sniffs the narrator, 'is just Persian musk and attar of roses'.[107] Mann also displays familiarity with the Egyptian 'Story of the Two Brothers', one of whom is seduced by the wife of the other, which Joseph claims often to have read 'aloud to my master' Potiphar,[108] and with Ishtar's advances upon Gilgamesh in that Babylonian epic.[109] Fischer's *Handbuch* takes the story of the continued retelling of Joseph's narrative through the baroque period (of which Grimmelshausen provides the prime example) to Mann's own time. My own concern, however, is with the earlier part of this tradition; what follows here will highlight his employment and development of midrash in the *Joseph* novels.

It is possible to differentiate between Mann's use of bin Gorion's two anthologies of midrash: *Joseph und seine Brüder* appears to have provided him with details for the plot while *Die Sagen der Juden* supplied legendary Jewish material not so much *about* Joseph as exemplifying the traditional beliefs he is taught by Eliezer and his father and which he in turn passes on to Benjamin and to various Egyptians with whom he talks, most notably Pharaoh. The scenes in the novel involving the mysterious being he encounters in the field on the way to meet his brothers, as we shall see, also derive much of their detail from the *Sagen*.

Micha Josef bin Gorion, (originally Berdyczewski), the editor and translator of these two anthologies from Hebrew into German, is himself an interesting figure, whose religious and philosophical development was not dissimilar to Mann's. Born in Russia to a long line of Hasidic rabbis, he rebelled early against their traditional teaching. Leaving Russia for Germany in 1890, he fell under the influence of both Schopenhauer and Nietzsche, calling for a 'transvaluation' of Judaism.[110] As well as writing novels and short stories, he produced a number of anthologies of midrash, including the two Mann used for *Joseph*. The first volume of *Die Sagen der Juden* was published in 1913, followed by two more volumes in 1919. Bin Gorion's *Joseph und seine Brüder* first appeared in 1917 with the suggestive subtitle, *Ein altjüdischer Roman*. Material from both books appears in the 'Prelude' and in other early chapters of Mann's novel but, since they are marked for acquisition in a volume in Mann's library which was not published until 1924,[111] we can assume that he acquired and worked on them in the mid-1920s.

---

106 *The Glorious Quran*, trans. Abdullah Yusuf Ali (Leicester: Islamic Foundation, 1975), pp.559-61.

107 Mann, *Joseph*, p.987.

108 *Ibid.*, p.866.

109 John D.Yohannan, *Joseph and Potiphar's Wife in World Literature* (New York: New Directions, 1968), pp.295-8.

110 *Encyclopedia Judaica,* CD Rom Edition (Judaica Multimedia, 1997).

111 Lehnert, 'Thomas Mann's Vorstudien', p.468.

Bin Gorion's *Joseph und seine Brüder*, as explained in the 'Nachwort' at the end of the book, is basically a translation of 'a Hebrew folkbook from the Middle Ages' entitled (in German) *Sefer Hajaschar*, which bin Gorion calls 'an extended/ embellished re-telling of the biblical legends'. Its division into chapters in this German edition, bin Gorion explains, 'stem from the editor', who also acknowledges considerable revision of the Hebrew original. Bin Gorion explains that 'the author of the *Sepher ha Yashar* (as it is known in English) did not just work on Talmudic and Midrashic legends but also used Philo, the Book of Jubilees, and the Testaments of the Twelve Patriarchs'. He also draws attention to the links with the Koran and later Persian poetry and to the fact that 'the Christian Joseph stories find in Joseph's fate traits from the life of Jesus'.[112] So Mann would have known what he was reading in bin Gorion, where it had come from and what kind of writing it was.

Bin Gorion's version of this late midrashic anthology begins with Joseph's dreams and the envy of his brothers, about whom he brings 'evil reports' to their father (chapter 46 of the *Sepher ha Yashar* in its English translation).[113] It's in the second of bin Gorion's chapters that Joseph loses his way and encounters 'an angel of the Lord' (not just the 'man...in the field' of Genesis 37:15). Bin Gorion (translating this medieval compilation of ancient Jewish legends about Joseph) follows the biblical narrative fairly closely after this, adding occasional episodes such as a visit by Joseph to his mother's grave, which Mann will also relate (with significant modifications). In bin Gorion's sentimental and unashamedly supernatural narrative Joseph weeps over his mother's grave, imploring her to awake (*'Erwache, liebe Mutter'*), before being comforted by her voice 'speaking to him from beneath the ground', telling him that she has heard his cries and seen his tears. 'Do not fear', she continues, 'for the Lord is with thee' (*'Fürchte nicht, denn der Herr ist mit dir'*).[114] In Mann's much more realistic version of this visit Joseph murmurs similar 'formulas of veneration' at his mother's shrine but receives a rather different response:

> Nothing answered from the depths. The past kept silence, folded in forgetfulness, unable to feel...Why could the maternal spirit, residing still in his own flesh and blood, not have warned him against his fate? Alas, it could not speak, being held in bonds by childish folly and self indulgence.[115]

Mann's narrator has no belief in dead women speaking; instead, he blames Joseph for not being mature or self-aware enough to have an intuitive sense of what his mother would have warned him against. Supernatural fable mutates into psychological realism.

---

112 Bin Gorion, *Joseph und seine Brüder*, pp.81-2, my trans.

113 Mordecai Manuel Noah, trans., *The Book of Yashar* (New York: Hermon Press, 1972 [1840]).

114 Bin Gorion, *Joseph*, pp.14-15; Noah, *Book of Yashar*, pp.130-1.

115 Mann, *Joseph*, p.357. Future references to this Penguin edition of Lowe-Porter's translation will be in brackets in the text, followed in italics by a reference to the German paperback edition of *Joseph und seine Brüder* (Frankfurt: Fischer Taschenbuch Verlag, 1994), 4 vols. For this passage the reference in this edition is II 145.

There are two even more unlikely episodes in bin Gorion, when firstly the wolf blamed by the brothers for Joseph's death and secondly Potiphar's eleven-month baby burst into speech. The wolf makes quite a lengthy speech while the baby confines itself to a straightforward rebuttal: 'My mother speaketh falsely'. In both cases, not surprisingly, their auditors are 'greatly astonished'.[116] Even Ginzberg appears somewhat embarrassed about these stories, claiming that the legend about the wolf 'seems to be of Arabic origin, since in genuinely Jewish legends animals do not talk'. 'The speaking of babies', he acknowledges, 'is a favourite subject in Jewish and Christian legends'.[117] Not, however, for Mann, whose realistic account of the story abjures such tales, which are passed over in silence.

Bin Gorion devotes separate chapters to the courtship of Joseph by Suleika (the name bestowed upon her by the Islamic tradition) and to 'Das Orangenmahl' (the meal of oranges) at which she confesses her love to her friends. In the first of these chapters Suleika praises in turn Joseph's eyes, his words and his hair, for the proper care of which she gives him a golden comb. We are told that she 'enticed him daily with her discourse to lie with her' but that when this failed, she resorted to threats, including that of death.[118] At the banquet she arranges to make Joseph known to her friends, they too find themselves unable to 'take their eyes off him', cutting their hands to pieces with their orange-knives.[119] Mann, who has other accounts of this banquet at his disposal, greatly expands bin Gorion's two short chapters (each of which occupies only a page and a half in German) to fill his own very much longer chapters, '*Die Berührte*' (The Smitten One) and '*Die Grube*' (The Pit), which between them occupying over 170 pages of the English translation. Some of the details from bin Gorion survive although Mann finds his own name for Potiphar's wife (Mut), who dwells on the beauty of Joseph's eyes while complaining somewhat unconvincingly that 'his lips are too thick' (708; *III 397*).

Bin Gorion at this point has a chapter entitled '*Josephs Standhaftigkeit*' (Joseph's Steadfastness), which corresponds to the (again much longer) chapter in the novel, '*Von Josephs Keuschheit*' (Of Joseph's Chastity). Both versions have everyone apart from Suleika and Joseph going down to the river to celebrate the Nile Festival, leaving the house empty for her final assault on Joseph's virtue. Bin Gorion has Joseph come to the house to do his master's work only for Suleika, having 'decked herself in princely garments' and jewels and 'beautified her face and skin with all sorts of women's purifying liquids' and perfumes, to entice him to sit next to her:

> And she hastened and caught hold of Joseph and his garments, and she said unto him, as the king liveth if thou wilt not perform my request thou shalt die this day, and...she drew a sword from beneath her garments, and she placed it upon Joseph's neck, and she said, rise and perform my request, and if not thou diest this day.[120]

---

116 Bin Gorion *Joseph*, pp.21 and 30; Noah, *Book of Yashar*, pp.135 and 141
117 Ginzberg, *Legends of the Jews*, V 332 and 341.
118 Bin Gorion, *Joseph*, pp.24-5; Noah, *Book of Yashar*, pp.137-8.
119 *Ibid.*, pp.26-7 and 138 respectively.
120 *Ibid.*, pp.30 and 140 respectively.

Mann goes into even greater detail on Mut's attempts to make herself more desirable, devotes a whole chapter to 'The Threat' to kill him, although in his version of the story it is entirely verbal, and considerably expands what she does with his clothing after he flees, focusing on her fetishistic distraction, having her do 'frightful things with...the precious hated object ...still warm with his body': she 'covered it with kisses, drenched it with tears, tore it with her teeth, trod it underfoot' (830, *III 585*). The midrash translated by bin Gorion, in other words, provides a mediating narrative framework between the terse verses of Genesis 39 and Mann's elaborate novel.

Other details in the development of the narrative which Mann clearly takes from bin Gorion include the flies in the wine and chalk in the bread which consign the butler and baker respectively to the same prison as Joseph.[121] Bin Gorion devotes a whole chapter to the false interpretations of Pharaoh's dreams made by 'the wise men and magicians', who see the seven thin cattle as warring princes or nations of Canaan rising against him or queens that will die or children that will be slain.[122] Mann includes all these in his chapter on 'Pharaoh's Dream' (922-3; *IV 126*-7). He does not, however, make the young Pharaoh order all his magicians to be slaughtered for their failure to interpret correctly (as in bin Gorion). Mann also omits bin Gorion's supernatural account of Joseph's facility in languages (the Lord sending an angel to teach him 'all the languages of man' overnight).[123] He returns to bin Gorion's account, however, for the measures Joseph employs to ensure that the entry of his brothers into Egypt is recorded. Bin Gorion has him command the border-guards to make sure that everyone who comes to buy corn must enter 'his name, and the name of his father, and the name of his father's father'.[124] In Mann's novel too the guards are instructed to 'record all immigrants not only according to their names, trades, and places of origin but also by their fathers' and grandfathers' names' (*auch nach ihres Vaters und dessen Vaters Namen*, 1048; *IV 309*). In following his midrashic source for details such as this it would seem that Mann wants to place himself faithfully in the long interpretive tradition to which he makes so many explicit references. He feels free, on the other hand, to omit details that do not fit into his own impression of the characters and their dignity, so the brothers are not apprehended as they are in bin Gorion in the red light district ('*in den Hurengassen*', literally 'in the alleys of the harlots').[125]

Another detail which Mann takes from bin Gorion is the 'cup...of silver beautifully inlaid with onyx stones and bdellium' by which he claims to know the ages of the brothers and their exact parentage. Mann devotes a whole chapter to 'The Silver Cup' and has Joseph tell Benjamin that he can see things from the past and future in it. He also asks Benjamin, as in bin Gorion,[126] 'about his life at home, his father's, wives and children' (1098; *IV 381*). In both accounts too he impresses

---

121 Bin Gorion, Joseph, p.35; Noah, Book of Yashar, p.145 although Noah translates *Kreidestücke* as 'nitre'.
122 *Ibid.*, pp.38-9 and 150 respectively.
123 *Ibid.*, pp. 43 and 154 respectively.
124 *Ibid.*, pp.51 and 159 respectively.
125 *Ibid.*, pp.53 and 160 respectively.
126 *Ibid.*, pp. 65 and 168 respectively.

his younger brother with his 'map of the stars' or zodiac. More importantly, Mann follows bin Gorion in making the brothers worry about how to break the good news to their father. Bin Gorion has them ask, *'Wie stellen wir es mit unserem Vater an? Erscheinen wir unverhofft und bringen ihm die Kunde, so wird er ob unserer Worte erschrecken'* (what shall we do in this matter before our father, for if we come suddenly to him and tell him the matter, he will be greatly alarmed at our words).[127] Mann devotes a whole chapter to the brothers' question 'How Shall We Tell Him?' (*Wie fangen wir's an?*) and their fears that 'he might quite simply "die of joy," in other words of shock' (*von Schockes wegen*, 1123; *IV 419*). Their solution in his novel also follows bin Gorion, making Serach report the news in the form of a song accompanied by the harp.

This important scene in *Joseph and His Brothers* follows the midrashic account translated by bin Gorion quite closely. The *Sepher ha Yashar* (in the English translation) has the brothers encounter 'Serah, the daughter of Asher, going forth to meet them'. Knowing how well she can play the harp, they ask her to go to their father, sit before him and sing:

> And she took the harp and hastened before them, and she came and sat near Jacob. And she played well and sang, and uttered in the sweetness of her words, Joseph my uncle is living, and he ruleth throughout the land of Egypt, and is not dead. And she continued to repeat and utter these words, and Jacob heard her words and they were agreeable to him.[128]

This is bin Gorion's translation of the Hebrew:

> *Da nahm das Mägdlein die Laute aus der Hand der Brüder, lief ihnen voran und betrat das Zelt Jakobs. Sie setzte sich vor den Patriarchen, begann zu spielen und sang mit lieblicher Stimme dabei: Joseph, mein Oheim, der lebt noch und ist nicht tot; über das Land Ägypten ist er Regent! Und sie spielte weiter, sang und wiederholte...Das hörte Jakob, und es klang ihm süss.*[129]

Mann's chapter 'Telling the News' expands greatly on this but incorporates some of the same language: 'When you get to where Jacob, your grandfather is, sit down at his feet and sing as sweetly as you know how: "Joseph is not dead, he is alive."' (*'Und wenn du zu Jaakob komst, deinem Grossväterchen, so sitzest du nieder zu seinen Füssen und singst so süss du nur kannst, "Joseph ist nicht tot, sondern lebet"'*, 1128, *IV 426*). Mann expands greatly upon Serah's song, incorporating elements from the Psalms and from Goethe into Serah's trochaic tetrameters.[130] He also complicates Jacob's response, having him initially praise her music but question the wisdom of trying to comfort him with lies. What she claims appears to him not mere 'poetic licence' but 'disrespectful and cheating make-believe'. It takes the repeated insistence

---

127 *Ibid.*, pp.75 and 176 respectively.
128 Noah, *Book of Yashar*, pp.176-7.
129 Bin Gorion, *Joseph*, p.75.
130 Fischer, *Handbuch*, pp.753-4; Kenneth Hughes, 'The Sources and Function of Serach's Song in Thomas Mann's *Joseph, Der Ernährer*', *Germanic Review* 45 (1970), 126-33.

of the brothers themselves to convince him that Joseph is indeed still alive (1134-7: *IV 434-8*). Mann returns to bin Gorion's account of Jacob blessing Serah and praying, '*Tochter, möge der Tod nie über dich Gewalt haben*' (may death never prevail over thee).[131] Mann refers likewise to 'the blessing which Jacob had gratefully conferred on her, she should not taste death but go up living into heaven' (1143, '*dass sie den Tod nicht schmecke und lebend ins Himmelreich eingehen sollte*', *IV 447*). Again, it is clear that bin Gorion provides Mann with a source for many of the details of his own expansion of the biblical narrative, particularly in terms of plot. Mann develops these details in the midrash into a much fuller and more subtle psychological portrait but the debt to bin Gorion is unmistakable.

Mann employs bin Gorion's other anthology of midrash, *Die Sagen der Juden*, not so much for plot details relating to Joseph (although there are, as we shall see, some examples of this) as for Jewish theological material which he puts into the mouths of the characters. Those who employ midrashic ideas in this way include not only Joseph himself but his father Jacob and his mentor Eliezer, whom Doris Sommer calls his 'fictional master of the Midrash', handing down to Joseph the legendary material of his people. Sommer also notes that the *Sagen* served not only as a source of midrash but a model, encouraging Mann to develop similar midrashic techniques, for instance the use of prooftexts. Like the rabbis, in other words, Mann turns to other biblical texts to supplement and interpret Genesis. Lines from the Song of Solomon appear in the songs sung at Jacob's wedding while the Psalms, as we have seen, feed into Serah's song.[132] Bin Gorion can also be seen to have provided such important elements as the title of the fourth volume, *Joseph, der Ernährer*,[133] and the 'discovery' of God by Abraham. For it is against a marked passage in Mann's copy of the *Sagen,* as Lehnert notes, that Mann wrote '*Entdeckung Gottes*' in the margin, a notion that would be highlighted by a chapter title in the novel, '*Wie Abraham Gott entdeckte*' (How Abraham Found God).[134] Other themes Mann took from the *Sagen* include the image of Joseph as a calf employed by the providence of God to bring Israel (the mother cow) to Egypt and the rivalry between the angels and mankind. This, as we shall see, surfaces at several points in the novel, especially in the two Preludes (to volumes one and four) and in the arguments between Joseph and his angelic guide. As well as providing these major themes, the *Sagen* can be shown to have furnished Mann with a significant amount of textual detail. Mann has been shown to have incorporated whole paragraphs from the *Sagen* almost verbatim, though he also tends to add phrases of his own which contribute to the unique combination of reverence and irony towards the Jewish tradition to be found in the novel.[135]

---

131 Bin Gorion, *Joseph*, p.76; Noah, *Book of Yashar*, p.177.

132 Sommer, 'Mann, Midrash, and Mimesis', pp.168 and 121.

133 Bin Gorion, *Die Sagen der Juden* (Frankfurt: Rütten und Loening, 1913-19) 3 vols, III 70.

134 Lehnert, 'Thomas Mann's Vorstudien', p.473.

135 *Ibid.*, 472. The fullest identification of passages from bin Gorion which can be found in variously modified form in the novel comes in Fischer's *Handbuch*. What follows here is my own attempt to assess the evidence identified (but not analysed) by Fischer.

Mann's selection of material from the *Sagen* corresponds in many respects with his treatment of bin Gorion's other anthology of midrash. He either omits or explicitly rejects the most extravagantly supernatural elements. One of the stories that he dismisses, for example, is the claim that Asenath, Joseph's wife, was in fact the daughter of Dinah and Sechem (and therefore Jewish). Bin Gorion mentions three different versions of the legend, that the baby was transported to Egypt by the Angel Michael, by a merchant and by an eagle.[136] Mann is outspoken in his rejection of all these suggestions and their racial motivation (obviously a sensitive issue in the 1930s and 40s):

> Our teachers and expounders have many of them taken exception to this marriage of Joseph's and even sought to deny the fact. In the interests of purity they have put it about that Asenath was not the child of Potipherah and his wife but a foundling and no other than the offspring of Jacob's own unhappy daughter Dinah, exposed and found floating in a basket. According to this theory, Joseph took his own niece to wife; which, even if it were true would not greatly improve matters, because half of Dinah's child was flesh and blood of the fidgety Sichem, a Baal-worshipping Canaanite. Anyhow our reverence for our teachers must not prevent us from pronouncing the story of the child in the basket to be what it is, an interpolation and pious fraud (1003; *IV 244*).

Mann's own account of Dinah's infant picks up on another suggestion in the *Sagen* that the sons of Israel wanted to kill the child,[137] although in the novel their wishes are actually carried out: 'the infant was exposed, by the stern command of her menfolk', leaving the poor mother to pine and wither, so that at fifteen 'her poor little face looked like an old woman's' (120; *I 180*). The realistic details are Mann's own but the suggestion can be found in bin Gorion.

The *Sagen*, like any other collection of midrash, has a number of stories about angels which Mann cannot take literally. What is surprising in *Joseph and His Brothers*, however, is how much of the rivalry between men and angels to be found in bin Gorion remains in the novel, suitably ironised and demythologised. In the 'Prelude', for example, Eliezer passes on to Joseph some traditional teaching about creation,

> speaking of them just as we read them to-day in the Hebrew commentaries upon early history. Had not God, they say, held His tongue and wisely kept silence upon the fact that not only righteous but also evil things would proceed from man, the creation of man would certainly not have been permitted by the 'kingdom of the stern' [*dass nicht nur Gerechte, sondern auch Böse vom Menschen herkommen würden, so wäre vom Reich der Strenge die Erschaffung des Menschen gar nicht zugelassen worden*] (28; *I 45*).

The final phrase in the English translation is not even signalled in the original as a quotation. The whole italicised passage, however, is taken from the *Sagen*, as is the story of Shemmael's refusal to bow down before the new creation. Bin Gorion has Satan address God directly, '*Herr der Welt! Du hast uns erschaffen aus dem Glanz deiner Herlichkeit und sagst uns, wir sollen niederfallen vor einem, den du aus dem*

---

136 Bin Gorion, *Sagen*, III 64, 236 and 238. See Fischer, *Handbuch*, p.737.
137 *Ibid.*, III 63.

Staub der Erde gemacht hast'.[138] Mann follows bin Gorion almost verbatim although he makes Eliezer report indirectly how Shemmael complained 'that it was ridiculous for beings created of the effulgence of glory to bow down before those made out of the dust of the earth' (28; '*es sei Unsinn, dass die aus dem Glanz der Herrlichkeit Erschaffenen vor dem aus Staub und Erde gemachten nieder sänken.*' *I 46*). As the story appears in the novel, in other words, it functions as an authentic example of the kind of legend passed down by Eliezer to Joseph, illustrative of the whole tradition in its earliest stages.

Similar material about the angels appears in the prelude to the fourth volume of the novel, which appears to take even its title from a phrase in the *Sagen*, '*Vorspiel in oberen Rängen*'(Prelude in the Upper Circles) being a modification of bin Gorion's '*oberen Regionen*'.[139] This prelude, which reports the angels' response to Joseph's difficulties in preserving his chastity, appears to be written *by* an angel, since it refers to 'two of us' ['*zweien von uns*'] having been nearly made to pay 'an unspeakable city tax' in Sodom (843; *IV 9*). The angel-narrator proceeds to relate with sniggering amusement the reply given by Cain to God after killing his brother as recorded in the *Sagen*: 'Thou sayest that Thou alone bearest the whole world and wilt not bear our sins?' (846; '*Du sagst, dass Du allein trägst die Ganze Welt, und willst unsere Sünde nicht tragen?*' *IV 13*). Lowe-Porter's translation here fails to pick up the contemptuous familiarity Cain shows to God (using the *du* form to the creator of the universe) though she does capture some of the insouciance of the angel's approval of Cain's cheek, '*Gar nicht schlecht*' ('Not so bad'). More important, as Lehnert points out, is the fact that Mann alters Cain's reference to '*meine Sünde*' in bin Gorion to '*unsere Sünde*' in the novel, subtly anticipating Christ's bearing all our sins upon the cross.[140] The levels of irony here, as in so much of Mann's writing, are many and complex: he gives to a sneering and jealous angel reporting the cheeky reply of the murderous Cain a phrase that anticipates the sacrificial atonement at the heart of the Christian faith.

Earlier in the novel Joseph himself is given some of this legendary material from the *Sagen,* for example 'how Shemmael shrieked when the man of earth knew how to name the creation as though he were its master and framer' (55, *I 87*).[141] All the angels appear in the story the narrator employs from bin Gorion (in the context of Joseph's betrothal to Asenath) of the 'first great wedding feast' arranged by God for Adam and Eve. 'Our teachers', the narrator acknowledges, 'have painted this presentation in very fine colours', which he proceeds to repeat in exact detail. After washing Eve, 'for naturally she was a bit sticky', and making her up with rouge, God is depicted curling her hair and adorning her with jewels. He then 'brought her, thus embellished, before Adam, with a choir of thousands of angels singing and playing on their lutes' (999; *IV 237*). This whole description is taken verbatim from bin Gorion, providing another authentic example of the Jewish 'tradition'.[142]

---

138 *Ibid.*, I 254, cited in Fischer, *Handbuch*, p.311.
139 *Ibid.*, I 296.
140 *Ibid.*, I 145. See Lehnert, 'Thomas Mann's Vorstudien', p.472.
141 *Ibid.*, I 256.
142 *Ibid.*, I 98; see Fischer, *Handbuch*, p.736.

More significant, it could be argued, is the way in which one of the angels actually participates in the action of the novel. Mann follows bin Gorion in identifying 'the man' who finds Joseph 'wandering in the field' in Genesis 37:15 with an angel, although it is much more difficult in the novel to work out the identity of the mysterious figure who guides Joseph to his brothers, arguing at length about the relative merits of men and of angels. Josipovici, who notes Mann's reliance upon the midrash for this without apparently being aware of Mann's close study of bin Gorion, cites this as an example of a novelist trying to read too much into an insignificant detail of biblical narrative.[143] But this is the whole point of midrash: nothing in the biblical narrative is insignificant. Mann himself follows the rabbis in making a great deal of this apparently minor element in Genesis. He also incorporates whole speeches of the dialogue between Joseph and the angel direct from bin Gorion. The passage about the necessary dualities of life ('Without life were no death, without riches no poverty...(364; *IV 155*)), for example, comes directly from bin Gorion.[144] Mann's angel, who grows increasingly unfriendly and aggressive as the argument develops, rolling his eyes, puckering his chin and showing other similar signs of impatience with the over-confident young man, gives numerous examples (taken from bin Gorion) of the follies of Cain's descendants, in particular his daughters, who 'went with uncovered shame and mated like cattle....The man with mother and daughter and brother's wife openly and on the streets' ('*Sie gingen mit aufgedeckter Blösse und waren Mann und Weib wie Vieh....Der Mann buhlte mit seiner Mutter und Tochter und seines Bruders Weibe offen auf den Strassen*') (365; *II 156*). All this comes from bin Gorion, as does the question posed by the angel, 'Who is more important, the watcher or the watched?' Mann's angel, of course, proceeds 'not without some bitterness' to answer in favour of the watched, the watchers being employed by God to protect his erring (but free) creation (365-6; *II 157*).[145]

These lengthy theological arguments certainly test the patience of Mann's readers, especially if, ignorant of the midrash, they fail to pick up the clues Mann provides about the identity of the 'man in the field'. Mann is also far from clear, like the biblical narrative itself, about the identity of Jacob's wrestling opponent. Mann has Jacob remember 'a frightful, heavy, highly sensual dream' in which he 'had wrestled for the sake of the name with the strange man who had fallen upon him' ('*mit dem besonderen Manne, der ihn überfallen*'). 'Strange' in English does not fully capture the uncanny nature of Jacob's opponent here, whose angelic identity is revealed by the inquisitive (and painful) grip he takes of Jacob's thigh: 'Perhaps it was meant to find out whether there was a socket there, whether it was movable and not, like the strange man's own, fixed and not adapted to sitting down' (58-9; *I 92*). Mann would have read in bin Gorion that an angel's hip-bone is not flexible, since they never sit down: '*der Engel Hüfte ist nicht beweglich, da sie niemals sitzen*'.[146] Mann is here

---

143 Gabriel Josipovici, *The Book of God* (New Haven: Yale University Press, 1988), pp.276-89.
144 Bin Gorion, *Sagen*, I 29-30, cited in Fischer, *Handbuch*, pp.418-9.
145 *Ibid.*, I 191 and III 25, cited in Fischer, p. 419.
146 *Ibid.*, III 17, cited in Fischer, p.326.

using his knowledge of Jewish legend to play games with his readers, challenging them to identify not only Jacob's mysterious opponent but the 'man' in the field.

Another important motif in the novel which derives from bin Gorion is that of Joseph as the calf employed by God to lure Jacob into Egypt. That Jacob hates this land of monkeys is clear from the title of an early chapter, '*Vom äffischen Ägypterland*' (The Monkey Land of Egypt). There's also a rather obscure passage (even more obscure in Lowe-Porter's translation) in which Joseph smiles to himself about his father's prejudice:

> If the good, worthy, and didactic man had known that his lamb was travelling Egyptwards, to the land of Ham, the bare, as he called it, because it was black on account of the black fruitful soil, which its god gave it! The confusion of thought was right indicative of the pious prejudice of his judgment (461).

This is certainly confusing for a reader, partly because Mann omits the missing link in bin Gorion, which is that Ham had been punished by God for seeing his father naked by having his hair and beard singed.[147] More importantly, Mann develops from bin Gorion the metaphor of God as a farmer luring an unwilling cow into a field to be ploughed. The *Sagen* says quite straightforwardly that God made Jacob follow Joseph into Egypt '*wie einst ein Landmann mit einer störrischen Kuh verfahren war*' (like a farmer once dealt with a refractory cow).[148] Mann follows the details of bin Gorion's extended metaphor to the letter:

> Once there was a man who had a refractory cow, that would not bear the yoke for the plough, but always shook it from her neck. The man took her calf from her and brought it to the field which was to be ploughed. When the cow heard the lowing of her calf she let herself be driven to the field and submitted her neck to the yoke (550; *III 159*).

It is not until well into the following paragraph in Mann that it becomes clear that this story relates to Joseph, who only gradually comes to understand, 'as in a dream', that his transportation to Egypt is 'part of a plan, in which one thing follows upon another', that his personal history is part of a larger story. Mann softens the crude providential agency of the midrash, attributing to Joseph himself an intuitive understanding of the possible consequences for his people of his journey to Egypt.

Mann takes many other details from bin Gorion (Fischer notes about seventy), many of them relating to the stories that Eliezer and Jacob tell Joseph in the first volume of the novel, stories about Abraham and about Jacob. One of the most important stories for Mann's own account of 'How Abraham Found God' involves the patriarch observing the sun, the moon and morning star and deciding that these cannot be gods in themselves but must have an organising principle above them. God is so impressed by Abraham's reasoning that he promises to protect him against all difficulties.[149] Mann reproduces this passage in the *Sagen* almost verbatim (284; *II 42*). He is happy to reproduce the tradition as Eliezer passed it on to Joseph although

---

147 *Ibid.*, I 229, cited in Fischer, p.454.
148 *Ibid.*, III 85, cited in Fischer, p.538.
149 *Ibid.*, II 92-3, cited in Fischer, p.394.

he understands 'God' somewhat differently than the ancient master of midrash, even going so far as to call Abraham 'God's father', since he had not simply 'perceived Him' but 'thought Him into being'. The 'mighty properties of God were indeed something objective, existing outside of Abraham; but at the same time they were also in him and of him' (285; *II 44*).

I will explore Mann's theology more fully in the following section but it is worth noticing here how much of it was prompted by the midrash. Genesis itself, of course, has Abraham barter with God over the fate of Sodom, reducing significantly the numbers of righteous within its wall required for it to be spared (Gen. 18: 23-33). The midrash develops this yet further, having Abraham reprimand God for trying to have it both ways, demanding justice from men but not keeping it Himself, breaking the promise made to Noah never again to destroy the world.[150] Again Mann reproduces these arguments in the novel (286; *II 44-5*). He also makes Abraham wrestle with the balance between God's immanence and His transcendence in a manner anticipated by midrash. The rabbis had asked why the name 'makom' (place) functioned as another name for God (in Ex. 33:21) before answering, '*Weil Gott der Raum der Welt ist, die Welt aber ist nicht sein Raum*' (because God is the place in which the world is but the world is not his place).[151] In the novel it is Abraham who ponders the same question:

> He must be much greater than all his works, and just as necessarily outside of His works. *Makom* he was called, space, because he was the space in which the world existed; but the world was not the space in which He existed (287; *II 47*).

Mann's characterisation of Abraham and his theology, in other words, draws directly from authentic Jewish patterns of thought.

Mann is similarly true to 'the tradition' in reproducing from bin Gorion the midrashic stories relating to Jacob, although he characteristically omits the more absurd supernatural elements. The *Sagen*, for example, describe how Jacob's anxiety about deceiving his father in order to gain the blessing made the sweat run down his joints and his heart melt like wax. But God sent two angels, one on either side, to support his neck and prevent him from falling.[152] Mann gives Jacob some of the same symptoms of anxiety ('the sweat had run down his joints for fear') but omits the two angels (88; *I 133*). The novel also makes Jacob take a rather more realistic time to complete the journey to Laban than the midrash: 'the way was long, and he was not Eliezer, to whom the land "came to meet him" as he went' (142; *I 212*). The inverted commas here acknowledge the rabbinic account of God's miraculous aid to Eliezer while recognising that Jacob has to travel at the normal human speed. Mann also employs a suggestion in bin Gorion to provide an entirely natural explanation for the faster increase of Jacob's speckled and spotted sheep than those of his father-in-law. The *Sagen* explain that many people came to Laban's house to do business and that Jacob took the opportunity to profit on the exchange, trading a

---

150 *Ibid.*, II 234, cited in Fischer, p.395.
151 *Ibid.*, III 4, cited in Fischer, p.395.
152 *Ibid.*, II 385, cited in Fischer, p.340.

sheep for a slave and a donkey for a camel.[153] Mann incorporates these details into a passage complaining that 'the tradition' (*'die Überlieferung'*) is often 'guilty of exaggerations', for instance on the question of the supernatural increase of Jacob's sheep. What 'really' happened was that people

> came from far and wide to trade with him, and if when they got there they discovered that it was after all a question of ordinary and not supernatural sheep, they forced themselves to find them miraculous....It was said that he had traded a sheep for a camel, an ass for a slave, male or female (184; *I 275*).

He acknowledges in the following paragraph that he is not 'a mere inventor of tales' but rests 'upon the traditional facts', a phrase which is in this case particularly appropriate.

Many of the details of Joseph's story also emanate from bin Gorion, for instance the tales he tells his father about his brothers eating the flesh out of living animals (54, *I 87*).[154] Much of the substance of Joseph's 'Dream of Heaven'(*'Der Himmelstraum'*) comes from the *Sagen*, for example when Joseph tells Benjamin that he heard some of the angels complaining about one 'begot of the white drop of semen' daring to join them (311; *II 80*).[155] Mann then transfers to Joseph the promise God makes to Matatron in the midrash to bless him with 365,000 blessings and to make him a throne 'with a tapestry over it woven out of pure brilliance, light, glory and splendour' (311; *II 81*).[156] Joseph describes for his younger brother's benefit how not only his earthly father but his heavenly Father 'threw over me a priceless garment with all sorts of light woven into it' while 'all the sons of heaven bowed themselves and likewise the princes among the angels' (312; *II 81*). These details, as Fischer demonstrates,[157] can be found in the midrash, but by transferring them from Matatron to Joseph Mann is able to develop the motif of the many-coloured coat bestowed by the Father on his favourite while also adding substance (and some justification) to the brothers' hatred of the arrogant dreamer.

The *Sagen* also provide significant details of Joseph's time in Egypt, for instance the way he is idolised by the young ladies (*'die Jungfrauen'*). Mann gives these words verbatim to Mut herself, who explains to her husband that

> when he [Joseph] shows himself in the streets of the city and in the bazaar, it often happens that the maidens mount on the housetops and fling down gold rings upon him from their fingers, that he may look up at them. But he never does (696; *III 381*).[158]

The novel also incorporates the veiling of the idols in one of the temptation scenes directly from bin Gorion.[159] The climax of the whole process of attempted seduction in the novel also draws on the *Sagen*, which record that Joseph was about to commit

---

153 *Ibid.*, III 99, cited in Fischer, pp.371-2.
154 *Ibid.*, III 66, cited in Fischer, p.323.
155 *Ibid.*, I 297, cited in Fischer, p.408.
156 *Ibid.*, I 301, cited in Fischer, pp.409-10.
157 Fischer, p.410.
158 Bin Gorion, *Sagen*, III 70, cited in Fischer, pp.624-5.
159 *Ibid.*, III 70, cited in Fischer, p.647.

the sin when his father's face appeared to him ('*Joseph war schon nahe daran, die Sünde zu begehen; da ward ihn das Antlitz seines Vaters sichtbar*').[160] Mann, who takes this phrase as the title for his chapter, '*Das Antlitz des Vaters*' (The Father's Face), interprets this to mean that Joseph's body unwittingly rebels, revealing the strength of his sexual attraction: 'his flesh stood up against his spirit', discovering 'a manly readiness'. In case his readers fail to grasp the full meaning of these circumlocutions, he gives Mut a line from Apuleius: '*Me'eni nachtef!* I have seen his strength!'[161] But he returns to bin Gorion to explain how it was that Joseph was nevertheless able to preserve his chastity: 'He saw his father's face—all the more detailed versions say so, and we may take it for the truth'. He proceeds to bolster bin Gorion with a psychoanalytic account of the way this may have worked:

> he saw it in his mind and with his mind's eye: an image of memory and admonition, the father's in a broad and general sense. For in it Jacob's features mingled with Potiphar's fatherly traits, there was something of the modest departed, Mont-kaw, and over and above all these were other, mightier traits (830; *III 584*).

What may appear superstitious in the midrash becomes in the novel a symbol of the psychological and religious basis for Joseph's moral strength.

When Joseph repeats some of the traditional Jewish legends to Amenhotep, however, both the Pharaoh and his mother scream with laughter, since they seem so primitive. Joseph explains that he himself 'did not know the child of the cave' (Abraham) though 'the cozened clodpate whom the clever one tricked [Isaac and Jacob respectively] were closer to home'. Amenhotep finds the story of Isaac's deception by Jacob 'grotesque' and 'barbaric', exploding with laughter when Joseph proceeds to Rachel's outwitting of Laban. 'One on top of the other!', he cries, applauding the comic routine of 'this son of jesters' (942-5; *IV 156-60)*. But when Joseph proceeds to tell Pharaoh another midrashic tale from bin Gorion about Adam and Eve having to be comforted by God with the gift of fire on being frightened of their first night,[162] he begins to realise that 'not all your tales are jests' (960; *IV 182*). The German people, conditioned by years of Nazi propaganda, might also have been inclined to treat the midrash as a crude and grotesque set of superstitious tales, the product of a barbaric inferior people. Mann, however, by embedding them in his own humorous and often ironic narrative, demonstrates the profound truths that they embody. He omits, as we have seen, some of the more fanciful fables, providing more realistic psychological explanations for the development of his characters. But what needs wider recognition is the extent of the novel's debt to midrash, the sheer scale of Mann's borrowing from bin Gorion. In the final section of this chapter I will attempt to show how Mann's 'modern' understanding of theology can be said to have added another layer to the midrashic tradition, providing (in the manner of the rabbis) a version of the story which makes sense for his own time.

---

160 *Ibid.*, III 69, cited in Fischer, p.683.
161 Fischer, p.685.
162 Bin Gorion, *Sagen*, I 109, cited in Fischer, p.723.

Mann's Part in the Tradition: Exploring 'the Depths Beneath'

For Mann, as we have seen, the key biblical text for *Joseph and His Brothers*, was the blessing passed on to Joseph by his father at the end of Genesis, 'blessings of heaven above, blessings of the deep that lie beneath' (Gen. 49:25). Variations on this blessing recur throughout the novel, handed down from father to son over so many generations. The 'Prelude', for example, after outlining the Gnostic parable of the 'fall' of the soul into matter and its subsequent redemption, looks towards a 'genuine penetration of the spirit into the world…which should bring about a present humanity blessed with blessing from above and from the depths beneath' (29). In discussing Isaac's 'primordial bleating' on his deathbed, his identification with the 'slain ram' which anticipates the divine Son's sacrifice, the narrator claims that he was intuitively, unconsciously returning to a level of the 'primevally, primordally sacred, which lay beneath all the civilized layers in the most unregarded, forgotten and ultra-personal depths of their souls' (122). Joseph will later tell Pharaoh that 'the typical and the traditional…come from the depths which lie beneath', which need to be understood by 'the I', which 'is from God and is of the spirit' (937). Mann is clearly employing a Freudian model here of the '*Geist*' (Mind/Spirit/Intellect/Ego) coming gradually to an understanding of the *id*, the unconscious levels beneath the surface of the mind. His prophetic interpreter of dreams, Joseph, like Freud, has a level of sympathy and understanding which comes 'from the deepest depth of his nature', a 'double blessing with which he was blessed from the heights above, and the depths which lay beneath' (996). The novel traces the gradual growth of his understanding of the tradition, the blessing, which he has inherited from his ancestors. It is, as has often been noticed, a *Bildungsroman*, a novel about the development not only of its central character but of the whole Judaeo-Christian tradition.

The whole point of the 'Prelude', however, is that this tradition is 'bottomless': 'the earliest foundations of humanity, its history and culture, reveal themselves unfathomable', though there may be 'provisional origins, which…form the first beginnings of the particular tradition held by a given community, folk or communion of faith' (3). Mann sets out accordingly to uncover the origins of the Jewish tradition (and therefore, of Christianity, that 'flower of Jewry') but finds that he can't really get further back than Babylonian tales (such as the *Enuma Elish*), 'preserved in graceful cuneiform characters on greyish-yellow clay…our earliest documented source for the Great Flood' (10). These too, he notes, were 'copied from an original a good thousand years older, from the time, that is, of the Lawgiver and moon-wanderer' (Moses and Abraham). Even this, he realises, in a passage as complex as anything in Derrida on the impossibility of reaching a 'final' origin, is not

> *the* original, when you come to look at it. It was itself a copy of a document out of God knows what distant time; upon which…one might rest, as upon a true original, if it were not itself provided with glosses and additions by the hand of the scribe, who thought thus to make more comprehensible an original text lying again who knows how far back in time (11).

Mann has to settle for 'an arbitrary beginning' (12), attempting to understand the texts which survive from the Jewish tradition, the stories about Joseph and his ancestors collected in the Bible and in the midrashic anthologies.

Joseph and His Brothers, even when not specifically using the material from the midrash cited above, is full of references to this tradition. In describing Joseph by the well in the opening pages of the novel, for example, the narrator notes that 'saga and story have woven a halo of legendary loveliness about his head' (38). And even when not employing actual midrash, Mann adopts the midrashic technique of posing questions of the biblical text. He cites Genesis 29:31, for example, 'And when the Lord saw that Leah was hated, he opened her womb: but Rachel was barren', before commenting, 'The letter of the tradition is all we have, when we seek to explain this melancholy fact'. This 'arbitrary favouritism', this apparent jealousy on God's part of Jacob's love for Rachel, he suggests, can be regarded 'as a relic, spiritually unabsorbed, of earlier and less disciplined stages in the development of the divine essence' (209-10). The narrator feels obliged (like the rabbis themselves) to explain the biblical text in terms that make sense in the world in which the interpreter lives.

Details of Joseph's early life are also, he suggests, matters that call for 'explanation, qualification, and expansion' (263). How is it, for example, that he was found 'wandering in the field' (Genesis 37:15) on his way to meet his brothers: 'what is the meaning of that?' (359). Like the rabbis too, Mann feels the need to defend Joseph against 'a reproach which has often historically been levelled against him...why after the pit, had he not bent all his strength to get in touch with Jacob in his pitiable state' (449). This midrashic questioning of the biblical text continues unabated. When Joseph arrives in Egypt, for example, the narrator asks, 'What part of it did he see first?' (484) and when he becomes part of Potiphar's household, 'how many [years] were spent in Potiphar's house and how many in the grave [the prison?]' (552). There is always something to be added to the story, some detail not fully explored.

Mann clearly feels that it is his duty to fill these gaps in the existing tradition, to explore what 'lies beneath' the biblical text and earlier attempts to make sense of it. He is also careful to draw our attention to any original features in his account, boasting for example that the first conversation between Joseph and Potiphar in the garden 'has not been described in any of the sources; none of the accounts, Oriental or Occidental, in prose or verse, so much as dream of it' (589). He begins the third volume with a pastiche of Genesis 39, employing two of the most common phrases in biblical narrative, 'And it came to pass after these things that his master's wife cast her eyes upon Joseph; and she said—...' (667). But he interrupts the narrative at this point to declare, 'All the world knows what Mut-em-enet, Potiphar's chief wife, is supposed to have said'. He does not deny, either, that she 'did make use of the frightfully direct and frank expression which tradition puts in her mouth'. But he expresses horror, as a fellow-story-teller, 'at the briefness and curtness of the original account, which does so little justice to life's bitter circumstantiality' (667). There is irony here, of course, since Mann knows well enough the impossibility of getting back to what Potiphar's wife 'really' said; he is playing self-consciously with the different generic conventions of ancient folktale and modern novel. But he is quite serious about the need for modern readers to give imaginative substance to the story, to work out how the high-born wife of a prominent Egyptian leader could come to direct so lewd a proposition to a foreign employee of low status.[163]

Mann's answer to this question, based upon midrashic and other sources, is that the process was a much longer one than the biblical text suggests, that Mut must have battled for years against her feelings for Joseph, and that her 'lewd proposal' would thus have been 'the final outcry of her utter agony of spirit and flesh' (667). A few verses in the original text are therefore expanded to a whole volume of the novel, 'Joseph in Egypt'. Mann devotes pages to the inner battles not only of Potiphar's wife but of the object of her affections. He devotes a chapter, for example, to explaining the motivation 'Of Joseph's Chastity', spelling out seven different contributing strands to what 'must strike a modern sense as absurd and even glaring'. The first and foremost, is that he feels 'betrothed to God'. But there are several other contributing factors, including the desire to preserve his racial purity which Mann had criticised in the rabbis. Loyalty to his father, which will reach its climax in the seduction scene itself, is another motive, along with the loyalty Joseph necessarily feels towards Potiphar himself (as in Genesis 39: 9).

It is not just the psychological but the theological gaps in the narrative which Mann feels obliged to fill. Hence the lengthy conversations with Pharaoh in the Cretan Loggia. Mann's starting point again is the biblical narrative, whose 'summary nature' in recording Pharaoh's sudden admiration for Joseph (in Genesis 41:39 he decides, simply on the basis of the interpretation of his dream, 'Nobody is so knowledgeable and wise as you. I will set you over all Egypt') Mann finds, 'however venerable, unconvincing....There is too much abridgment and condensation about this, it is too dry, it is a drawn and salted and embalmed remnant of the truth, not truth's living lineaments' (979). He therefore presents a lengthy theological discussion between the young Pharaoh, himself keen to reform Egyptian religious practice, and the now mature Joseph, inheritor of the Jewish tradition. Mann is able to base Amenhotep's reforming zeal upon history, since this Pharaoh did indeed attempt to introduce the worship of the one god Aton to Egypt. He can legitimately be shown to share Joseph's distaste for idolatry, telling his mother that they should not direct their worship towards 'the image...but rather to him whose image it is' (967). Less convincingly perhaps, he anticipates Jesus in thanking his father for sending to 'his beloved son...a messenger and dream interpreter' in the form of Joseph. He even begins a prayer, "My Father *who art in heaven*" (968-9).

What Mann is attempting, I suggest, in these theological discussions is to present traditional concepts of God in the biblical and midrashic narratives in a way that makes sense for modern (and mostly Christian) readers. 'Tradition has it', he writes in the 'Prelude' that 'his god [necessarily a capital G in the German, of course, since it is a noun]— that god upon whom his spirit laboured...for whom he sought a name and

---

163 This, incidentally, is a question also posed by Horovitz, 'wieso es kommen konnte, dass eine Frau, die eineso hohe Stellung einnahm, schlieslich so tief sinken sich so sehr vergessen konnte'. See Jakob Horovitz, *Die Josephserzählung* (Frankfurt: Kauffmann, 1921), p.80, quoted in Sommer, 'Mann, Midrash, and Mimesis', p.155. Sommer also argues that Mann's method is 'midrashic' in the manner that it poses questions of the biblical text, even when he is not using actual midrashic sources.

found none sufficient,…had made him promises' (5-6). Mann signals here that both the 'name' and the concept are necessarily inadequate. Abraham is 'blessed' (and Mann uses scare quotes for this word too to indicate both its traditional character and, in Derridean fashion, its problematic status) by a 'personal experience of God' (the capital G now restored by Lowe-Porter) which may cause him 'unrest' but leads to 'a novel conception of the deity' which 'is destined to make its mark upon the future' (6). Joseph too suffers from a similar 'spiritual unrest', the necessary accompaniment of any testing and development of the inherited tradition, as does his father: 'Disquiet, questioning, hearkening and seeking, wrestling for God…found expression in Jacob's look, in his lofty brow and the peering gaze of his brown eyes' (30). For all three patriarchs the God with whom they wrestle is 'not repose and abiding comfort' but 'a God of designs for the future, in whose will inscrutable, great, far-reaching things were in process of becoming', a God of 'brooding will' and 'world-planning', a God who was 'Himself only in process of becoming' (31). Judaism has always, of course, had a sense of God being dependent on man for the full realisation of His will but this traditional Jewish idea is amplified in Mann's case partly by a Hegelian notion of *Geist* realising itself through history and partly by a psychological notion of a collective unconscious that has to be brought to the surface.

Mann makes it clear that the ancient Jewish concept of God was very much in need of development. The God of Abraham and Jacob's 'tribe', he tells us, was one of 'intemperateness' and 'majestic caprice' (51), first worshipped in the wilderness, 'a fire-breathing and storm-breeding warrior named Yahu, a troublesome sort of hobgoblin, with more demonic than godlike traits, spiteful, tyrannical and incalculable', who had to be propitiated 'by means of spells and blood rites' (83). This 'sinister deity', the narrator continues, enjoyed 'an extraordinary theological career' (*Laufbahn*), coming to contribute at least some elements to 'the conception of the divine essence which was struggling towards realization through the spirit of mankind' and its 'experiments in the inexpressible' (84, *I 127*). The Hegelian elements in Mann's understanding of God are once again all too apparent in this passage, along with a Kantian awareness of the impossibility of our conceptions ever reaching 'the thing in itself' (Mann's essay on Schopenhauer makes clear his shared inheritance with the pessimistic philosopher of this phenomenological tradition).

The God of Abraham and of Jacob, as the latter is made to recognise, is altogether different from other gods worshipped in the form of idols and temples. Their God 'possessed no house at all upon earth' and claimed to be the only true God (165). He may retain some qualities of the original Yahu, the jealousy, for example, which is offended by Jacob's love for Rachel, but the narrator encourages us to see this as 'a relic…of earlier and less disciplined stages in the development of the divine essence'. The narrator also insists that the bond of this God 'with the human spirit active in Abram' was one in which 'human and divine necessity were so mingled that one can scarcely say from which side, human or divine, the original impulse went out' (210). This is the point of the chapter 'How Abraham Found God' (*Wie Abraham Gott endeckte*), already discussed above in terms of its employment of midrashic material. God, Mann suggests, may only be known through the human heart but He remains independent, a 'Thou' to Abraham's 'I', independent of him and 'independent of the world' (287).

Jacob learns of God's independence from his own wishes when he thinks that he has lost Joseph for good, coming like Job to see that what the Lord gives he can also take away (429). Mann brings the Book of Job to Genesis as a midrashic prooftext, having Jacob cry out like the man of Ur , 'He hath milked me like milk and let me curdle like cheese' and 'He gnasheth with his teeth against me' (431; cp. Job 10:10 and 16:9). Eliezer meanwhile plays the role of God in their dialogue, reminding Jacob that he should not 'sit in judgment upon Him who made not only the behemoth...and leviathan' but the whole of creation (432). Joseph too has to develop his own understanding of God, puzzling over the primitive attempts to appease a wrathful God apparent both in Laban's sacrificing of his first-born and in Huia and Tuia castrating their son: 'one must emerge and escape from the stage of the traditionally sacred and come over into the light' (587-8). Even the theatrical metaphor here indicates the limitations of any language employed about God.

As a result of all this meditation upon his own religious tradition, Joseph is able to grow into the man who teaches Potiphar about 'the father and creator of the world' (599), tells Pharaoh about the way in which Abraham 'discovered God and made a pact with Him that they should be holy the one in the other' (958), and instructs Mai on 'the purposes of God in history...how it depends on us, it is our affair to give it a fine form...putting all our wits at the service of God' (1052). After Joseph has been re-united with his brothers, telling them as Jesus tells Thomas after the resurrection, 'Put your hands on me, take hold of me, feel and see that I am...alive' (1116), he insists that they failed to play their part in the covenant that is history, that they 'missed the meaning of the whole story we are in'. The narrator too, in the final words of the novel, announces (not without an element of relief), 'so endeth the beautiful story and God-invention [*Gotteserfindung*] of *Joseph and His Brothers*' (1207; *IV 539*).

God, in other words, has to be 'found' or 'discovered' (Lowe-Porter is surely wrong to translate 'invented'). He is within us but also independent of us. In many respects, of course, Mann's theology here is entirely orthodox. He makes it clear throughout the novel that all our conceptions of God are necessarily inadequate, historically contingent, and couched in the form of stories and legends, which should not be taken literally but probed for 'the depths that lie beneath'. His massive 'pyramidlike piece of work', to quote his own 'Foreword' to the novel (v), layer upon layer of building with ancient materials, is the most impressive of all the novels considered in this book, I would argue, because it grapples seriously with the fundamental questions raised by the biblical stories it relates. It is also profoundly midrashic, not only incorporating much material directly from rabbinic midrash but following its method, probing and probing at the details of the text until some answers begin to emerge. Not all Mann's answers will elicit agreement from his readers but his questions, I would argue, nearly always go to the heart of the biblical story.

Conclusion

There can, of course, be no straightforward 'conclusion' to a study such as this. It is to be expected, however, that I should at least attempt to draw some conclusions from this detailed analysis of six very different novelists. The primary aim of the project, as spelt out in the preface, was to illustrate the ways in which these novelists had reworked stories from the Book of Genesis, probing their underlying significance. I wanted also to explore how familiar these writers were with midrash and to what extent their writing could be labeled 'midrashic'. All of them, it transpires appear at least to have been aware of midrash. More surprisingly perhaps, three of them were found to have incorporated substantial amounts of rabbinic material into their novels, displaying a significant continuity between their writing and that of the ancient rabbis.

What the analysis of these novels also reveals, I think, is the extent to which these authors succeed in shedding new light on some aspects of the biblical text, grappling with genuine problems 'in' the Book of Genesis. I need to place scare quotes around the preposition here because new questions, as we have seen, are themselves responsible for highlighting aspects of the text to which over-familiarity may have blinded more conventional biblical critics. We have seen, for example, how Twain became scandalised by the sheer unfairness of blaming Adam and Eve for the supposed 'Fall', given their complete ignorance even of the concept of death (God's threatened consequence of their disobedience), and how Steinbeck unpacked the basis of moral choice and responsibility embedded in the Hebrew verb *timshol* (you may conquer [sin]) in Genesis 4:7. *East of Eden* also explored the psychological processes which would have been necessary for Cain to overcome his resentment at the rejection of his gifts. Winterson brought out some of the absurdities in the biblical story of the Flood (in particular the rashness of God's decision to destroy all but a remnant of his creation), while Diski explored the traumatic 'residue' of the Akedah not only for Isaac, the most obvious 'victim', but also for his wife Rebekah and even their son Jacob. Diamant foregrounded further questions about the wives of the patriarchs while Mann not only dramatised one of the most notorious attempted seductions ever recorded but also investigated the subtleties of Joseph's understanding of religion and morality. All of the writers, in other words, have been shown to have added further layers of interpretation to the midrashic process simply by asking new questions of the biblical text, exploring the powerful stories in the Book of Genesis with all the imaginative insight at their disposal.

Such creative modes of interpreting the Bible, as I hope to have shown, are in many ways more appropriate than those narrower, more limited methods practised by many religious institutions. How properly (or at least appropriately) to read the Bible, of course, is a question which concerns not only members of faith communities within the Judaeo-Christian tradition but anyone interested in this foundational text of western civilization. One aim of my book is to highlight the complexity and power of the stories to be found in the Book of Genesis. Such a realisation should also serve to counteract the increasing fundamentalism which limits much current reading of the Bible. It may also persuade non-believers that this is at least a book worth reading.

All six of these writers, it will have been noted, have some difficulty in giving imaginative substance to the 'character' of God, a difficulty which is probably shared by most of their readers. Twain, as we saw, rejected altogether 'the God of the Bible', whom he found arbitrary and capricious. Steinbeck ignores Him altogether while Winterson and Diski poke fun at Him. Diamant is more interested in the goddesses He supposedly replaced. Mann is the only one of these six writers to have made a serious attempt to redefine our understanding of God in the light of our 'modern' world view. As he said in his lecture of 1942 on 'The Theme of the Joseph Novels',

> God, too, is subject to development, He, too, changes and advances: from the desert-like and demoniacal to the spiritual and holy; and He can do so without the help of the human spirit as little, as the human spirit can without Him.[1]

This, of course, is a notion of God with a profound history in rabbinic and kabbalistic thought. Harold Bloom too writes of the Lurianic concept of *Tikkun*, the contribution man makes to God's work of restitution or restoration after the 'breaking-apart-of the vessels' in the catastrophic moment of creation.[2] Mann adds to this a Hegelian understanding of the 'world spirit' in history and a psychoanalytic view of the collective unconscious. These are merely his attempts to make the concept of God' comprehensible to a 'modern' mind.

I would suggest that any believing community has to attempt this, combining a reverence for the sacred texts with an openness to ways in which its interpretation must necessarily adapt to coincide with the modes of thought of its interpreters. That was always the guiding principle of midrash and remains the case in respect to these writers. As the rabbis themselves knew, we can never completely 'grasp' the mysterious reality at the heart of all life (certainly not in the sense of scientific modernity's attempted reduction of everything to the status of an 'object' of knowledge). Even in the Bible, God introduces himself to Moses as a verb (Exodus 3:14). All our theology is bound therefore to be inadequate (and these writers display just how inadequate even biblical theology can be). Like the authors of the Book of Genesis, all these writers can do is to continue to tell (and to rework) stories which at least reveal some aspects of the mystery indicated by the word 'God'.

Above all, however, these writers approach the stories in the Book of Genesis *as stories*. This may sound obvious (in some respects it is) but, as Emerson (cited by Bloom) complained, once a book is wrapped in black covers only to be opened on special occasions, it is astonishing how readers, who would normally spot an absurdity of plot or characterization without any difficulty, find themselves cowed into unquestioning blindness. Members of faith communities are thus frightened into numbness while others refuse even to open the Bible's pages, assuming (wrongly)

---

[1] Heinrich Tolzmann, ed., Thomas Mann's Addresses Delivered at the Library of Congress (Oxford: Peter Lang, [1963] 2003), p.15.
[2] Harold Bloom, A Map of Misreading (Oxford: Oxford University Press, 1975), p.5.

that there cannot be anything worth reading in a book so long employed as a vehicle for repression, for keeping people (especially women) in order. These writers have had the courage to open the Book of Genesis and to read its stories without any such preconceptions (all readers have some preconceptions, of course, but the point of all reading is to allow them to be challenged). Having re-read the biblical narratives afresh, as Steinbeck so memorably recorded, they have been drawn so far into the new imaginative world thus opened up that they have begun to think at least partly in its terms, exploring what remains unclear in the original. The resultant stories, a combination of readerly response and creative rewriting, develop the original text in ways which are often unpredictable, nearly always interesting and sometimes, as I hope to have shown, full of genuinely novel insight.

Select Bibliography

Since each chapter of this book has employed very different material relevant to the specific subject-matter with which it is concerned, I have divided this bibliography into sections. For ease of reference, I have numbered these sections in correspondence with the chapters to which they refer. Numbers in square brackets indicate the date of the first edition.

1. The Book of Genesis

a) Biblical Criticism

Alter, Robert, *The Art of Biblical Narrative*. London: Allen and Unwin, 1981.
———, *Genesis: Translation and Commentary*. New York: Norton, 1996.
Alter, Robert and Kermode, Frank, editors, *The Literary Guide to the Bible*. London: Collins, 1987.
Amos, Clare, *The Book of Genesis*. Peterborough: Epworth, 2004.
Auerbach, Erich, *Mimesis: The Representation of Reality in Western Literature*, trans. Willard Trask. Garden City, N.Y.: Doubleday Anchor, 1957.
Bloom, Harold, *The Book of J*, trans. David Rosenberg. London: Faber and Faber, 1991.
Clements, R.E., *A Century of Old Testament Study*, revised edition. Guildford: Lutterworth Press, 1983.
Clines, David, *The Theme of the Pentateuch*. Sheffield: JSOT Press, 1978.
Fishbane, Michael, *Biblical Interpretation in Ancient Israel*. Oxford: Oxford University Press, 1985.
———, *The Garments of Torah: Essays in Biblical Hermeneutics*. Bloomington and Indianapolis: Indiana University Press, 1989.
Frye, Northrop, *The Great Code: The Bible and Literature*. London: Routledge and Kegan Paul, 1982.
Gunkel, Hermann, *The Stories of Genesis*, trans. John Scullion, ed. William Scott. Vallejo, CA: Bibal Press, 1994.
Jacobson, Dan, *Biblical Narratives and Novelists' Narratives*. London: University of London, 1989.
———, *The Rape of Tamar*. London: Weidenfeld and Nicolson, 1970.
———, *The Story of the Stories: The Chosen People and Its God*. New York: Harper and Row, 1982.
Josipovici, Gabriel, *The Book of God*. New Haven: Yale University Press, 1982.
Kessler, Martin and Deurloo, Karel, *A Comentary on Genesis*. New York: Paulist Press, 2004.
Rad, Gerhard von, *Genesis*, revised edition, trans. John H.Marks. Philadelphia: Westminster Press, 1973.

Rogerson, John. *Genesis 1-11*. Sheffield: JSOT Press, 1991.
Darna, Nahum M., *Understanding Genesis*. New York: Schocken Books, 1970 [1966].
Sparks, H.D., ed., *The Apocryphal Old Testament*. Oxford. Clarendon Press, 1984.
Sternberg, Meir, *The Poetics of Biblical Narrative*. Bloomington: Indiana University Press, 1987.
Westermann, Claus. *Genesis: An Introduction*, trans. John Scullion. Minneapolis: Fortress Press, 1992.
Zornberg, Avivah Gottlieb, *The Beginnings of Desire: Reflections on Genesis*. Philadelphia: Jewish Publication Society, 1995.

b) *Midrash*

Curzon, David, ed., *Modern Poems on the Bible: An Anthology*. Philadelphia and Jerusalem: Jewish Publication Society, 1994.
Friedlander, Gerald, trans., *Pirkei de Rabbi Eliezer*. New York: Hermon Press, 1970 [1916].
Ginzberg, Louis, *The Legends of the Jews*. Translated by Henrietta Szold, 7 vols, Philadelphia: Jewish Publication Society, 1909-25.
Gorion, Micha Josef bin, ed., *Joseph und seine Brüder: Ein altjüdische Roman* (Berlin: Schocken Verlag, 1933 [1917].
———, *Die Sagen der Juden*. Frankfurt: Rütten und Loening, 1913-19, 3 vols.
Horovitz, Jakob, *Die Josephserzählung*. Frankfurt: Kauffmann, 1921.
Hartman, Geoffrey H., and Budick, Sanford, editors, *Midrash and Literature*. New Haven and London: Yale University Press, 1986
Kraemer, David, *Reading the Rabbis: The Talmud as Literature*. Oxford: Oxford University Press, 1996.
Kugel, James L. *In Potiphar's House: The Interpretive Life of Biblical Texts*. Cambridge, Mass.: Harvard University Press, 1994.
Neusner, Jacob, ed., *Genesis and Judaism: The Perspective of Genesis Rabbah: An Analytical Anthology*. Atlanta,Georgia: Scholar's Press, 1985.
———, trans., *Genesis Rabbah: The Judaic Commentary to the Book of Genesis*. Atlanta, Georgia: Scholar's Press, 1985, 3 vols.
———, *The Midrash: An Introduction*. Northvale, New Jersey: Jason Aronson Inc., 1990.
———, *Midrash in Context: Exegesis in Formative Judaism*. Philadelphia: Fortress Press, 1983.
———, *What is Midrash?* Philadelphia: Fortress Press, 1987.
Niehoff, Maren, *The Figure of Joseph in Post-Biblical Jewish Literature*. Leiden: E.J.Brill, 1992.
Noah, Mordecai Manuel, trans., *The Book of Yashar*. New York: Hermon Press, 1972 [1840].
Porton, Gary, 'Defining Midrash', in *The Study of Ancient Judaism*, ed. Jacob Neusner New York: Ktav, 1981.
Schwartz, Howard, *Reimagining the Bible: The Storytelling of the Rabbis*. Oxford: Oxford University Press, 1998.

Spiegel, Shalom *The Last Trial,* trans. Judah Goldin. Woodstock, Vermont: Jewish Lights, 1993 [1950].
Stern, David, *Midrash and Theory.* Evanston, Illinois: Northwestern University Press, 1996.
Strack, H.L. and Stemberger, Günter, *Introduction to the Talmud and Midrash*, trans. Marcus Bockmuehl. Minneapolis: Fortress Press, 1992.
Townsend, John, trans., *Midrash Tanhuma.* Hoboken, NJ: Ktav Publishing House, 1989.
Wills, Lawrence M., ed. and trans., *Ancient Jewish Novels: An Anthology.* Oxford: Oxford University Press, 2002.
Yohannan, John D., *Joseph and Potiphar's Wife in World Literature.* New York: New Directions, 1968.

c) Intertextuality

Allen, Graham. *Intertextuality.* London: Routledge, 2000.
Bakhtin, Mikhail M., *The Dialogic Imagination: Four Essays*, ed. Michael Holquist, trans. Caryl Emerson and Michael Holquist. Austin: University of Texas Press, 1981.
———, *Problems of Dostoevsky's Poetics*, ed. and trans. Caryl Emerson. Manchester: Manchester University Press, 1984.
———, *Speech Genres and Other Late Essays.* Trans. Vern W. McGee. Austin: University of Texas Press, 1986.
Bloom, Harold, *The Anxiety of Influence.* Oxford: Oxford University Press, 1973.
———, *The Breaking of the Vessels.* Chicago: Chicago University Press, 1982.
———, *Kabbalah and Criticism.* New York: Seabury Press, 1975.
———, *A Map of Misreading.* Oxford: Oxford University Press, 1975.
———, *Ruin the Sacred Truths: Poetry and Belief from the Bible to the Present.* Cambridge, Mass.: Harvard University Press, 1989.
Boyarin, Daniel, *Intertextuality and the Reading of Midrash.* Bloomington and Indianapolis: Indiana University Press, 1990.
Dentith, Simon, *Bakhtinian Thought: An Introductory Reader.* London: Routledge, 1995.
Derrida, Jacques, 'Circumfession', in Geoffrey Bennington and Jacques Derrida, *Jacques Derrida.* Chicago: Chicago University Press, 1993.
———, *Dissemination*, trans. Barbara Johnson. Chicago: University of Chicago Press, 1981.
———, *The Gift of Death*, trans. David Wills. Chicago: Chicago University Press, 1995.
———, *Glas*, trans. J.P. Leavey, Jr., and Richard Rand. Lincoln: University of Nebraska Press, 1986.
———, 'Living On/ Border Lines', in *Deconstruction and Criticism*, ed. Harold Bloom *et al.* New York: Continuum, 1979.
———, *Of Grammatology*, trans. Gayatri Spivak. Baltimore and London: Johns Hopkins University Press, 1976.

Fewell, Danna, ed., *Reading Between Texts: Intertextuality and the Hebrew Bible*. Louisville, Kentucky: Westminster/ John Knox Press, 1992.
Handelman, Susan A., *The Slayers of Moses: The Emergence of Rabbinic Interpretation in Modern Literary Theory*. Albany: State University of New York Press, 1982.
Leitch, Vincent B., *Deconstructive Criticism: An Advanced Introduction*. London: Hutchinson, 1983.
Moi, Toril, ed., *The Kristeva Reader*. Oxford: Blackwell, 1986.
Ostriker, Alicia, *Feminist Revision and the Bible*. Oxford: Blackwell, 1993.
———, *The Nakedness of the Fathers: Biblical Visions and Revisions*. New Brunswick, N.J.: Rutgers University Press, 1997.
Still, Judith and Worton, Michael, ed., *Intertextuality: Theories and Practice*. Manchester: Manchester University Press, 1990.

2. Mark Twain

a) Primary Texts

The Bible According to Mark Twain: Writings on Heaven, Eden, and the Flood, eds Howard G. Baetzhold and Joseph B. McCullough. Athens, GA: University of Georgia Press, 1995.
The Complete Essays of Mark Twain, ed. Charles Neider. Garden City, NY: Doubleday, 1963.
The Diaries of Adam and Eve, ed. Shelley Fisher Fishkin. Oxford: Oxford University Press, 1996.
The Diary of Adam and Eve and other Adamic Stories. London: Hesperus Press, 2002.
The Love Letters of Mark Twain, ed. Dixon Wecter, New York: Harper, 1949.
Mark Twain's Fables of Man, ed. John S. Tuckey. Berkeley: University of California Press, 1972.
Mark Twain's Letters, eds Edgar M. Branch, Michael B. Frank and Kenneth M. Sanderson. Berkeley: University of California Press, 1988-2002, 6 vols.
Mark Twain's Mysterious Stranger Manuscripts, ed. William M. Gibson. Berkeley: University of California Press, 1969.
Mark Twain's Notebooks and Journals, eds Frederick Anderson, Michael B. Frank, and Kenneth M. Sanderson, Berkeley, LA: University of California Press, 1975, 3 vols.
Mark Twain's Quarrel with Heaven, ed. Ray Browne, New Haven: College and University Press, 1970.
Mark Twain's Speeches, ed. A.B.Paine. New York: Harper and Brothers, 1923.
Pudd'nhead Wilson, ed. Malcolm Bradbury, Harmondsworth: Penguin, 1969.
'Reflections on Religion', ed. Charles Neider, *Hudson Review* 16 (1963-4) 332-52.
Travelling with the Innocents Abroad: Mark Twain's Original Reports from Europe and the Holy Land, ed. Daniel M. Mckeithan. Norman, Oklahoma, 1958.

What is Man? And Other Philosophical Writings, ed. Paul Baender, Berkeley: University of California Press, 1973.

b) *Secondary Sources*

Andrews, Kenneth R., *Nook Farm: Mark Twain's Hartford Circle*. Seattle: University of Washington Press, 1969.

Baetzhold, Howard G., McCullough, Joseph B. and Malcolm, Donald, 'Mark Twain's Eden/Flood Parable: "The Autobiography of Eve"', *American Literary Realism* 24 (1991) 23-38.

Brodwin, Stanley, 'The Humour of the Absurd: Mark Twain's Adamic Diaries', *Criticism* 14 (1972) 49-64.

———, 'Mark Twain's Masks of Satan: The Final Phase', *American Literature* 45 (1973-4) 206-27.

———, 'The Theology of Mark Twain: Banished Adam and the Bible', in Louis J.Budd, ed., *Critical Essays on Mark Twain, 1910-1980* (Boston: G.K.Hall, 1983), pp.176-93.

Carter, Paul, *The Spiritual Crisis of the Gilded Age*. DeKalb: Northern Illinois University Press, 1971.

Ensor, Alison. *Mark Twain and the Bible*. Lexington: University of Kentucky Press, 1969.

Fishkin, Shelley Fisher, ed., *A Historical Guide to Mark Twain*. Oxford: Oxford University Press, 2002.

Gribben, Alan, ed., *Mark Twain's Library: A Reconstruction*. Boston: G.K.Hall, 1980, 2 vols.

Hays, John Q., *Mark Twain and Religion: A Mirror of American Eclecticism*. New York: Peter Lang, 1989.

Hill, Hamlin, *Mark Twain: God's Fool*. New York: Harper, 1973.

Kahn, Sholom J., *Mark Twain's Mysterious Stranger: A Study of the Manuscript Texts*. Columbia: University of Missouri Press, 1978.

Kaplan, Justin, *Mr.Clemens and Mark Twain*. New York: Simon and Schuster, 1966.

LeMaster, J.R. and Wilson, James D., eds, *The Mark Twain Encyclopedia*. New York: Garland, 1993.

Macnaughton, William, *Mark Twain's Last Years as a Writer*. Columbia: University of Missouri Press, 1979.

McCullough, Joseph B., 'Mark Twain's First Chestnut: Revisions in "Extracts from Adam's Diary"', *Essays in Arts and Sciences* 23 (1994) 49-58.

Paine, Albert Bigelow, *Mark Twain: A Biography*. New York: Harper, 1912, 4 vols.

Rasmussen, R.Kent, *Mark Twain A to Z*. Oxford: Oxford University Press, 1996.

Szasz, Ferenc Morton, *The Divided Mind of Protestant America, 1880-1930*. Alabama: University of Alabama Press, 1982.

3. John Steinbeck

a) Primary Texts

America and Americans and Selected Nonfiction, ed. Susan Shillinglaw and Jackson J.Benson (New York: Viking, 2002).
East of Eden, London: Mandarin, [1952] 1990.
Journal of a Novel, London: Heinemann, 1970.
The Log from the Sea of Cortez, London: Mandarin, [1951] 1990.

b) Secondary Sources

Benson, Jackson J., *The True Adventures of John Steinbeck, Writer.* New York: Viking, 1984.
Campbell, Joseph, *The Hero with a Thousand Faces.* Princeton: Princeton University Press, [1949] 1972.
Ditsky, John, *Essays on East of Eden.* Munci, Ind.: John Steinbeck Society of America, 1977.
Fromm, Erich, *Psychoanalysis and Religion.* London: Victor Gollancz, 1951.
Gladstein, Mimi R.,'The Strong Female Principle of Good— or Evil: The Women of *East of Eden*', *Steinbeck Quarterly* 24 (1991) 30-40.
Givoni, Mark M., 'Symbols for the Wordlessness: The Original Manuscript of *East of Eden*', *Steinbeck Quarterly* 14 (1987) 14-23
Heavelin, Barbara A., 'Steinbeck's Exploration of Good and Evil: Structural and Thematic Unity in *East of Eden*', *Steinbeck Quarterly* 26 (1993) 90-100
Larsen, Stephen and Robin, *A Fire in the Mind: The Life of Joseph Campbell.* New York: Doubleday, 1991.
Marks, Lester, *Thematic Design in the Novels of John Steinbeck.* The Hague: Mouton, 1971.
Murray, Isobel and Merrilees, Jim,'*East of Eden*', *New Blackfriars* 53 (1972) 130-5.
Parini, Jay, *John Steinbeck: A Biography.* London: Heinemann, 1994.
Quinones, Ricardo J., *The Changes of Cain: Violence and the Lost Brother in Cain and Abel Literature*, Princeton: Princeton University Press, 1991.
Timmerman, John H., 'Steinbeck as a Literary Artist', in his *John Steinbeck's Fiction.* 1986, pp.15-41.
——, 'John Steinbeck's Use of the Bible', *Steinbeck Quarterly* 21 (1988) 24-39.

4. Jeanette Winterson

a) Primary Texts

Art and Lies. London: Vintage. 1995 [1994].
Art Objects: Essays on Ecstasy and Effrontery. London: Vintage, 1996 [1995].
Boating for Beginners. London: Minerva, 1990 [1985].
Gut Symmetries. London: Granta Books, 1998.

Lighthousekeeping. London: Harper Perennial, 2005 [2004].
Oranges Are Not the Only Fruit. London: Vintage, 1996 [1985].
The Powerbook. London: Vintage, 2001 [2000].
Sexing the Cherry. London: Vintage, 2001 [1989].
The World and Other Places. London: Vintage, 1999[1998].

b) Secondary Sources

Barr, Helen, 'Face to Face: A Conversation Between Jeanette Winterson and Helen Barr', *English Review* 2:1 (1991), pp.30-33.
Bengston, Helene, Borch, Marianne and Maagaard, Cindie eds, *Sponsored by Demons: The Art of Jeanette Winterson.* Odense, Denmark: Scholar's Press, 1999.
Bilger, Audrey, 'Jeanette Winterson: The Art of Fiction', interview in *Paris Review* 39 (Winter 1997/8) 68-112.
Cosslett, Tess, 'Intertextuality in *Oranges Are Not the Only* Fruit: The Bible, Malory, and *Jane* Eyre', in Grice and Woods, *'I'm Telling You Stories*', pp.15-28.
Eide, Marian, 'Passionate Gods and Desiring Women: Jeanette Winterson, Faith, and Sexuality', *International Journal of Sexual and Gender Studies* 6 (2001) 279-91.
Grice, Helena and Woods, Tim , *'I'm Telling You Stories': Jeanette Winterson and the Politics of Reading.* Amsterdam: Rodopi, 1998.
Maagard, Cindie Aaen, 'Jeanette Winterson: Postmodern Prophet of the Word', in Erik Borgman, Bart Philipsen and Lea Verstricht, eds., *Literary Canons and Religious Identity.* Aldershot: Ashgate, 2004, pp.151-61.
Reynolds, Margaret and Noakes, Jonathan, *Jeanette Winterson: The Essential Guide.* London: Vintage, 2003.
Wachtel, Eleanor with Jeanette Winterson, 'Interview', *Malahat Review* 118 (Spring 1997), 61-73.

5. Jenny Diski

a) Primary Texts

After These Things: A Novel. London: Little Brown, 2004.
Don't. London: Granta Books, 1998.
The Dream Mistress. London: Granta Books, 1999 [1996].
Happily Ever After. Harmondsworth: Penguin, 1992 [1991].
Like Mother. London: Granta Books, 1998 [1988].
Monkey's Uncle. London: Phoenix, 1994.
Only Human. London: Virago, 2000.
On Trying to Keep Still. London: Little, Brown, 2006.
Rainforest. Harmondsworth: Penguin, 1988 [1987].
Skating to Antarctica. London: Granta Books, 1997.
Stranger on a Train. London: Virago, 2002.
Then Again. London: Vintage, 1991 [1990].

The Vanishing Princess. London: Phoenix, 1996 [1995].
A View from the Bed. London: Virago, 2003.

b) Secondary Sources

Rorty, Richard, *Contingency, Irony, Solidarity.* Cambridge: Cambridge University Press, 1989.
Tuten, Frederic, 'Jenny Diski', *Bomb* 66 (Winter 1999) pp.42-7.

6. Anita Diamant

a) Primary Texts

Choosing a Jewish Life. New York: Schocken Books, 1997.
Good Harbor. London: Pan Books, 2003 [2001].
Living a Jewish Life (with Howard Cooper). New York: HarperCollins, 1991.
The New Jewish Wedding. New York: Fireside, 2001.
Pitching My Tent. New York: Macmillan, 2005.
The Red Tent. London: Pan Books, 2002 [1997].

b) Secondary Sources

Braun, Rabbi Laurie Katz, *'The Red Tent': A Study Guide*, http://urj.org/Articles/index.cfm
Broner, E.M., *Bringing Home the Light.* San Francisco: Council Oak Books, 1999.
———, *Her Mothers.* New York: Holt, Rinehart, and Winston, 1975.
———, *A Weave of Women.* New York: Holt Rinehart, and Winston, 1978.
Frymer-Kensky, Tikva, *In the Wake of the Goddesses: Women, Culture, and the Biblical Transformation of Pagan Myth.* New York: Free Press, 1992.
Heschel, Susannah, ed., *On Being a Jewish Feminist.* New York: Schocken Books, 1983.
Justice, Faith L., 'An Interview with Anita Diamant',www.copperfieldreview.com/interviews/diamant.html
Kushner, Lawrence, *Honey from the Rock.* San Francisco: Harper and Row, 1977.
———, *The River of Light: Spirituality, Judaism, Consciousness.* Woodstock, Vermont: Jewish Lights, 1995 [1981].
———, *God was in this Place and I, i did not know.* Woodstock, Vermont: Jewish Lights, 1991.
Schneider, Susan Weidman, *Jewish and Female.* New York: Simon and Schuster, 1984.
Sjoo, Monica and Mor, Barbara, *The Great Cosmic Mother: Rediscovering the Religion of the Earth.* San Francisco: Harper and Row, 1975.

7. Thomas Mann

a) Primary Texts

Doctor Faustus, trans.H.T.Lowe-Porter. Harmondsworth: Penguin, 1968.
Essays of Three Decades, trans. H.T.Lowe-Porter. London: Secker and Warburg, n.d.
The Holy Sinner, trans. H.T.Lowe-Porter. Berkeley: University of California Press, 1992.
Joseph and His Brothers, trans. H.T.Lowe-Porter. Harmondsworth: Penguin, 1978.
Joseph und seine Brüder. Frankfurt: Fischer Taschenbuch Verlag, 1994 [1933-44], 4 vols.
Letters of Thomas Mann, 1889-1955, ed. and trans. Richard and Clara Winston. London: Secker and Warburg, 1970, 2 vols.
The Magic Mountain, trans. H.T.Lowe-Porter. London: Vintage, 1999.
Mario and the Magician and Other Stories, trans. H.T. Lowe-Porter. Harmondsworth: Penguin, 1975.
Reflections of a Non-Political Man, trans. Walter D.Morris. New York: Frederick Ungar, 1983.
Thomas Mann's Addresses Delivered in the Library of Congress, ed. Heinrich Tolzmann. Oxford: Peter Lang, [1963] 2003.

b) Secondary Sources

Berger, Willy, *Die mythologischen Motive in Thomas Manns Roman Joseph und seine Brüder*. Köln: Böhlau, 1971.
Bloom, Harold, ed., *Thomas Mann*. New York: Chelsea House, 1986.
Dierks, Manfred, *Studien zu Mythos und Psychologie bei Thomas Mann*. München: Francke, 1972.
Ezergalis, Inta M., ed., *Critical Essays on Thomas Mann*. Boston: G.K.Hall, 1988.
Fischer, Bernd-Jürgen, *Handbuch zu Thomas Mann's 'Josephromanen'* . Tübingen: A.Francke Verlag, 2002.
Golka, Friedemann W., *Jakob: Biblische Gestalt und Literarische Figur.* Stuttgart: Calwer Verlag, 1999.
———, *Joseph: Biblische Gestalt und Literarische Figur*. Stuttgart: Calwer Verlag, 2002.
Heller, Erich, *Thomas Mann:The Ironic German*. Cambridge: Cambridge University Press, 1981 [1958].
Hoelzel, Alfred, 'Thomas Mann's Attitude Towards Jews and Judaism: An Investigation of Biography and Culture', in Ezra Mendelsohn and Richard I.Cohen, eds., *Arts and Its Uses: The Visual Image and Modern Jewish Society.* Oxford: Oxford University Press, 1990.
Hughes, Kenneth, 'The Sources and Function of Serach's Song in Thomas Mann's *Joseph, Der Ernährer*', *Germanic Review* 45 (1970) 126-33.
Koopman, Helmut, ed., *Thomas-Mann-Handbuch.* Stuttgart: Alfred Kröner, 1990.
Kurzke, Hermann, *Thomas Mann: A Biography*, trans. Leslie Willson. London: Allen Lane, 2002.

Lehnert, Herbert and Wessell, Eva, eds., *A Companion to the Works of Thomas Mann*. Rochester, N.Y.: Camden House, 2004.

Lehnert, Herbert, *Thomas Mann: Fiktion, Mythos, Religion*. Stuttgart: Kohlhamer, 1965.

———, 'Thomas Manns Vorstudien zur Josephstetralogie', *Schillerjahrbuch* 7 (1963) 458-520.

Levenson, Alan. 'Christian Author, Jewish Book? Methods and Sources in Thomas Mann's *Joseph*', *German Quarterly* 71 (1998) 166-78.

McDonald, William E., *Thomas Mann's 'Joseph and His Brothers': Writing, Performance, and the Politics of Loyalty*. Rochester, N.Y.: Camden House, 1999.

Minden, Michael, ed., *Thomas Mann*. London: Longman, 1995.

Murdaugh, Elaine, *Salvation in the Secular: The Moral Law in Thomas Mann's 'Joseph und seine Brüder'*. Bern: Peter Lang, 1976.

Nolte, Charlotte, *Being and Meaning in Thomas Mann's Joseph Novels*. London: T.S.Maney, 1996.

Prater, Donald, *Thomas Mann: A Life*. Oxford: Oxford University Press, 1995.

Reed, T.J., *Thomas Mann: The Uses of Tradition*. Oxford: Clarendon Press, 1974.

Robertson, Richie, ed., *The Cambridge Companion to Thomas Mann*. Cambridge: Cambridge University Press, 2002.

Scaff, Susan von Ruhr 'The Religious Base of Thomas Mann's World View: Mythic Theology and the Problem of the Demonic', *Christianity and Literature* 43 (1993) 75-93.

Sommer, Doris, 'Mann, Midrash, and Mimesis', Rutgers Ph.D., 1977.

Tuska, John , 'Thomas Mann and Nietzsche: A Study in Ideas', *Germanic Review* 39 (1964) 281-99.

Index

Abel
   in Diski 114
   in Genesis 5, 52, 53
   in midrash 12, 53, 54, 65
   in Steinbeck 54, 63, 67
   in Twain 43, 49
Abraham
   in Diski xii, 87-8, 97, 103-8, 110-2
   in Genesis 5, 6, 7, 58, 94, 100, 102, 119, 160
   in Kierkegaard 24
   in Mann 155, 159-60, 162, 163, 166, 167
   in midrash 12, 92, 93, 94, 96
Adam
   in Diski 89, 90
   in Genesis 28
   in midrash 12
   in Mann 141, 157, 162
   in Steinbeck 59, 62, 66
   in Twain xi, 27, 29-30, 32, 34-50, 52-4, 169
   in Winterson 83
Adler, Rachel 120
Agnon, S.Y. 16
Akedah, The
   in Diski xii, 13, 85, 87, 91, 102, 107-8, 111-2, 169
   in midrash 93-8
Alter, Robert
   on biblical narrative 2, 3-4, 91
   translation of Genesis 1, 91, 99-101, 106
Amos, Clare 9
Asenath 126, 127, 156, 157
Asherah 124-5, 129
atheism 88, 89, 142
Auerbach, Erich 2-3, 16, 108
Augustine of Hippo, St. 35

Babel, Tower of
   in Diski 106
   in Genesis 5
   in Winterson 20, 72, 74, 76, 83, 84
Bakhtin, Mikhail Mikhailovich 19-10
Barnes, Julian 69
Barthes, Roland 9
Beecher, Henry Ward, 30, 35
Bellow, Saul 15
Benjamin 25, 150, 153, 161
Bilhah 99, 112, 113, 126, 127, 130
Blake, William 22
Bloom, Harold x, 1-2, 15, 20-2, 25, 69, 73, 75, 84, 120, 170
Braun, Rabbi Laurie Katz 114, 115
Broner, E.M. 114, 121-2, 129
Bruns, Gerald 18
Buber, Martin 22
Budick, Sanford 13, 14

Cain
   in Diamant 114
   in Diski 103
   in Genesis 5-6, 51-2
   in midrash 12, 53-4
   in Mann 157, 158
   in Steinbeck xi, 59-67, 169
   in Twain 41, 45
Calvinism 27, 31
Campbell, Joseph 51, 56-7, 62, 63, 67
Christ, Jesus 24, 55, 57, 157
Christianity
   Mann's attitude to 134-5, 137, 138, 140, 142-3
   Steinbeck's relation to 55
   Twain's satire of 27, 31, 33-6, 47
   Winterson's attitude to 75
   see also Calvinism; Congregationalism; Presbyterianism; Protestantism; Roman Catholicism
Clines, David 9
Congregationalism 31
Conservative Judaism 104
Covici, Pascal 51, 60, 61, 64

Cupitt, Don 88
Curzon, David 13

Darwin, Charles 82, 84, 90
Dawkins, Richard 88, 104
deconstruction 22, 119
Derrida, Jacques 11, 14, 15, 22-5, 82, 163
Deuteronomy, Book of 76, 80, 24
Diamant, Anita vii, xi, xii, 169-70
  discussion of midrash 114, 117
  interest in feminism 116, 120-5
  relation to Judaism 115-7, 122
  study of midrash x, 26, 125, 126
  Works
  Good Harbor, The 113, 115-6
  Red Tent, The 25, 26, 113, 127-33
Dinah
  in Diamant 113, 121, 123, 127-31
  in Genesis 12, 101
  in Mann 156
  in midrash 13, 94, 99, 118, 125-7
Diski, Jenny 13, 169
  early life and work 85-8
  interest in Catholicism 88
  relation to Judaism 87-8
  study of midrash 26, 91-102
  Works
  After These Things 85, 91, 102, 107, 108-112
  Only Human 85, 102-8
documentary hypothesis x, 1, 4, 9, 31
Dumuzi 124, 129

Eliot, T.S. 21, 75
Elohist, The 1
Emerson, Ralph Waldo 21, 170
Enoch, Book of 128
Enuma Elish 78, 80, 124, 163
Esau
  in Diamant 127
  in Diski 110, 111
  in Genesis 5, 6, 52, 98, 99
  in midrash 93-4, 99, 126
Eve
  in Diski 89, 90, 103
  in Genesis 2, 11, 52, 58
  in Mann 162
  in midrash 11, 12, 52-3, 126, 157, 162
  in Steinbeck 66
  in Twain 19, 25, 27, 29, 36-50, 169
Exodus, Book of 48, 76, 83, 139, 170

Fall, The
  in Diski 90
  in Judaism 9, 20, 73
  in Mann 163
  in Steinbeck 57
  in Twain xii, 19, 27, 28, 30, 32, 34-52, 169
  in Winterson 77
fascism xi, 144; *see also* Nazis, The
Fielding, Henry 3, 16
Findley, Timothy 69
Firdausi, Hakim Abol Qasem 150
Fisch, Harold x, 15-6
Fischer, Bernd-Jurgen 146, 147, 148, 149, 150, 155, 159, 161
Fishbane, Michael 17-8
Flood, The
  in Diski 106
  in Genesis ix, 58
  in Mann 163
  in Twain 32, 43, 45, 48
  in Winterson xi, xii, 69-70, 76-8, 81-4, 169
Freud, Sigmund 57, 64, 90, 133, 140-1, 144-5, 163
Fromm, Erich 51, 56, 57-8, 61, 62, 64, 67
Frye, Northrop 69, 78-9, 80, 82
Frymer-Kensky, Tikva 114, 124-5, 129, 131
fundamentalism 29, 72, 76, 78, 88, 90, 139, 170

Gabriel (angel) 27, 47, 92
Garnett, David 69
Genesis Rabbah 11-2, 13, 53, 54, 56, 98, 99, 119, 125-6, 148-9
Gilgamesh, Epic of 71, 124, 150
Ginzberg, Rabbi Louis
  in relation to Diamant 125, 126, 152
  in relation to Diski 85, 91-4
  in relation to Steinbeck x, 26, 51, 52-4
Goethe, Johann Wolfgang 136, 137, 147, 154
Gorion, Micha Josef bin vii, 133, 146-7, 149-62
Gottlieb, Rabbi Lynn 123
Gould, Stephen Jay 89

Index

Graf, Karl Heinrich 4
Graves, Robert 80
Greene, Graham 91
Grimmelshausen, Hans Jakob, Christoffel
    von 150
Gunkel, Hermann 4-7, 8

Hagar, 6, 7, 106
Haggadah 10, 92, 94, 117, 123
Ham 159
Haran 92, 104
Hartman, Geoffrey x-xi, 13, 14
Hasidism 23, 58, 88, 120, 150
Hegel, Georg Wilhelm Friedrich 23, 141,
    166, 170
Heschel, Susannah 114, 117, 120-2
Hesse, Hermann xii
Higher Criticism 1, 31, 147
Horovitz, Rabbi Jakob 147-8, 165

Inanna 124-5, 128-9
intertextuality 14, 15, 17-24, 70
Isaac
    in Diski 107-12
    in Genesis 2, 5-6, 12, 16, 24, 52, 65,
        100, 101
    in Mann 162, 163, 169
    in midrash 12-3, 26, 92-9
Isaiah, Book of 83
Ishmael 6, 52, 106, 110, 128
Islam 2, 85, 147, 149, 152; *see also* Koran,
    The

Jacob
    in Diamant 113, 118, 127-8, 129, 130,
        131
    in Diski 110-2, 169
    in Genesis 3, 6, 21, 22, 25, 52, 65, 98-9,
        101, 119, 124, 144
    in Mann 144, 149, 154-5, 158-9, 160-2,
        164, 166-7
    in midrash 13, 92, 93-4, 95, 98-9, 126,
        154-5, 160-2
Jacobson, Dan 17
Jami, Nur ad-Din Abd ar-Rahman 150
Job, Book of 34, 36, 49, 87, 93, 167
Joseph
    in Diamant 113, 127, 130
    in Diski 112

in Genesis ix, 2, 3, 7, 16, 25, 52
in Mann 17, 56, 133-4, 136-7, 139, 140,
    144-67, 169, 170
in midrash 147-62
Joseph and Aseneth 126
Josephus, Flavius 16
Joshua, Book of 76
Josipovici, Gabriel ix, 158
Joyce, James 3
Jubilees, Book of 92, 126, 147, 148, 151
Judaism xii, 1, 9, 10, 25, 35, 74, 150, 166
    Diamant's relation to 85, 87, 90, 91, 104
    Diski's relation to 85, 87, 90, 91, 104
    feminism in 120-2
    Mann's relation to 137
    see also Conservative Judaism,
        Orthodox Judaism,
        Reconstructionsit Judaism,
        Reform Judaism
Judges, Book of 83
Jung, Carl Gustav 57, 64, 145

Kabbalah 20-1, 22, 49, 73, 74
Kafka, Franz 2
Kant, Immanuel 166
Kazan, Elia 63
Kermode, Frank ix, 18, 91-2
Kierkegaard, Soren 17, 21, 24, 107
Koran, The 147, 149, 151
Kristeva, Julia 19
Kugel, James L. 11, 148
Kushner, Rabbi Lawrence 114, 118-20

Laban
    in Diamant 128, 129
    in Genesis 6, 95, 122, 128
    in Mann 160, 162, 167
    in midrash 94, 99, 126
Lawrence, D.H. xi, 72, 128
Leah
    in Diamant 113, 126-31
    in Diski 111, 112
    in Genesis 6, 25, 26, 101, 121, 125, 164
    in Mann 164
    in midrash 94, 123, 126
Lecky, W.E.H. 35
Lessing, Doris 86
Levinas, Emmanuel 22
Leviticus, Book of 76, 80

Life of Adam, The 53
Lilith 115, 120
Lot 5, 6
Luria, Rabbi Isaac 20, 170
Lutheranism 134, 135

McCaughrean, Geraldine 69
Maitland, Sara 69
Maine, David 69
Malamud, Bernard 16
Maimonides (Rabbi Moshe ben Maimon, also known as Rambam) 96
Mann, Luiz Heinrich 135
Mann, Paul Thomas ix, 56
   and Freud 140, 144-5
   and Nietzsche 140, 141, 142-4
   and Schopenhauer 140-2
   attitude to religion 133-40
   opposition to fascism xi, xii
   relation to Judaism 137
   relation to Christianity 138, 142
   understanding of God x, 11, 165-7, 170
   use of midrash x, 15, 17, 26, 146-62
   Works
   Buddenbrooks 134, 140-1
   Doctor Faustus 134, 138-9, 143, 147
   Holy Sinner, The 134, 138, 139-40
   Joseph and His Brothers x, xi, xii, 17, 56, 133, 134, 137, 139, 145, 146-67
   Magic Mountain, The 134, 136
   Reflections of a Non-Political Man 133, 135, 140, 141, 143
   Sketch of My Life, A 136, 143
   Tables of The Law, The 134, 138
Mark, Gospel of St. ix
Melville, Herman 89
Merton, Thomas 88
Midrash Rabbah 17, 98
Midrash Tanhuma 13, 24, 97, 98
Mikveh 116, 118, 123
Milton, John 14, 22, 44, 46
Miriam 86, 115, 117
Mishnah 16, 20
Modernism 21, 25, 75, 76
modernity 79, 90, 116, 143, 170
Montaigne, Michel Eyqueme de 89
Moses 2, 63, 74, 134, 136, 138-9, 163

Mut-em-enet (Mann's name for Potiphar's Wife) 152-3, 161, 162, 164-5

Nahmanides (Rabbi Moshe ben Nahman, also known as Ramban) 96, 97
Nazis, The xi, xii, 137, 162
Neusner, Jacob 10-1, 53
Nietzsche, Friedrich Wilhelm ix, 21, 50, 133, 138, 139, 140-4, 150
Nimrod 74, 92
Noah
   in Diski 103
   in Genesis 4-5, 6, 12
   in midrash 12
   in Twain 27, 47, 48
   in Winterson 69, 77-81, 84
Numbers, Book of 76, 80

Oort, H. 31-2
original sin 31 35, 52, 59, 62, 66
Orthodox Judaism 1, 2, 25, 58
Ostriker, Alicia Suskin 25-6, 80
Ozick, Cynthia 122

Paine, Thomas 29, 30, 35
patriarchy xii, 88
Pentateuch, The 1, 22, 73, 80
Philo (of Alexandria) 14, 148, 151
Pirkei de Rabbi Eliezer 97, 119, 126
postmodernism 14, 15, 16, 25, 88, 107, 123
Potiphar
   in Mann 150, 162, 164, 165, 167
   in midrash 149
Potiphar's wife
   in Genesis 2, 16, 25
   in midrash 148-9; *see also* Mut-em-enet, Suleika
Presbyterianism 29, 30, 61, 115
Priestly Writer ix, 1, 73, 79, 81, 84, 103, 111, 112
Protestantism 29, 30, 33, 134, 135, 136
Proverbs, Book of 149
Psalms, Book of 36, 72, 94, 154, 155

Rachel
   in Diamant 113, 125, 126-31
   in Diski 110, 111, 112
   in Genesis 2, 7, 25, 26, 100, 101, 121, 122
   in Mann 162, 164, 166

in midrash 11-2, 13, 94, 99
Rad, Gerhard von 4, 7-8
Rambam, *see* Maimonides
Ramban, *see* Nahmanides
Rashi (Rabbi Shlomo Yitzaqi) 97, 98-9, 103, 106, 119
Rebecca (also transliterated Rebekah)
   in Diamant 128-9, 131
   in Diski 95, 108, 109-10, 169
   in Genesis 2, 6, 25, 26, 100-1, 125
   in midrash 93, 94, 98
Reconstructionist Judaism 113, 116
Reform Judaism 31, 113, 115, 116, 120
Reuben 99, 101, 112, 130
Revelation, Book of 21, 72
Ricketts, Edward Flanders Robb 55
Roberts, Michele 69, 71
Rorty, Richard McKay 107
Rosh Hodesh 116, 122, 123
Ruth, Book of 76

Sagen der Juden, Die 146-7, 150, 155-62
Samson 82-3
Samuel, Book of 17, 62
Sarah (also Sarai)
   in Diamant 128
   in Diski 102, 103-7, 109
   in Genesis 2, 6, 7, 11, 24, 26, 100, 104, 121
   in midrash 92, 93, 94, 95, 97, 109
Satan
   in Diski 87
   in midrash 13, 24, 52, 93, 96, 97, 156-7
   in Twain 27, 37, 39, 43, 46-50
Schopenhauer, Arthur 133, 135, 140-2, 144, 150, 166
Schneider, Susan Weidman 114, 120, 122-3, 129
Sepher ha Yashar 146, 149, 151-4
Shechem 13, 94, 112, 126
Shem 27, 94
Solomon, Song of 155
Spiegel, Shalom 85, 91, 92, 94-6
Stanton, Elizabeth Cady 25, 37-8
Steinbeck, John x, xi, xii, 26, 51-67, 92, 136, 169, 170-1
   Works
      East of Eden 51, 54, 56, 57, 59, 60, 61-7, 92, 169

Grapes of Wrath, The 55
Journal of a Novel 52, 56-61
Sea of Cortez, The 55-6
Stephenson, Robert Louis 82
Stern, David 11
Sternberg, Meier 3
Suleika (Potiphar's wife's Persian name) 152

Talmud, The 16, 21, 28, 58, 96, 119, 123, 151
Tamar xii, 2, 25, 125, 131
Testament of Joseph, The 148
Torah, The 21, 23, 26, 88, 94, 104, 115, 117, 122, 126, 136
Tsena Urena 122
Twain, Mark xi, xii, 19, 22, 25, 26, 170
   critique of Bible 31-5
   knowledge of midrash x, 28
   subversion of orthodox doctrine 36-9
   Works
      Diaries of Adam and Eve 39-46
      Letters from the Earth 46-8
      Mysterious Stranger, The 49-50
      What is Man? 33, 36, 37, 39, 42

Va-yikra Rabbah 97
Voltaire, Francois-Marie Arouet

Wagner, Wilhelm Richard 82, 140, 143
Wandor, Michelene 69
Wellhausen, Julius 4
Wells, H.G. 69
Westermann, Claus 4, 8-9
Wiesel, Elie 53
Winterson, Jeanette x, xi, xii, 26, 169, 170
   indoctrination in childhood 71-2
   interest in Judaism 74
   on intertextuality 69-70
   review of Bloom 73
   Works
      Boating for Beginners 77-82
      Lighthousekeeping 82-4
      Oranges Are Not the Only Fruit 76-7
Woolf, Virginia 71

Yahwist, The 1, 7, 8, 20, 21, 73, 81, 103
Yehoshua, A.B. 16

Zilpah 113, 127, 128, 130

Zohar, The 21, 119

Zornberg, Avivah Gottlieb 85, 91, 92, 95-9, 103, 108, 109, 110, 111